THE
MASS KILLER

SIX CASE HISTORIES
THAT TELL US WHY

GERALD SCHOENEWOLF PH.D.

DEFIANCE PRESS
& PUBLISHING

THE MASS KILLER

DEFIANCE PRESS
& PUBLISHING

ISBN-13: 978-1-959677-10-9 (Paperback)
ISBN-13: 978-1-959677-09-3 (eBook)

Published by Defiance Press & Publishing, LLC

Bulk orders of this book may be obtained by contacting Defiance Press & Publishing, LLC. www.defiancepress.com.

Public Relations Dept. – Defiance Press & Publishing, LLC
281-581-9300
pr@defiancepress.com

Defiance Press & Publishing, LLC
281-581-9300
info@defiancepress.com

Also by Gerald Schoenewolf

Nonfiction:

101 Common Therapeutic Blunders (with R. Robertello)

101 Therapeutic Successes

Sexual Animosity Between Men and Women

Turning Points in Analytic Therapy: The Classic Cases

Turning Points in Analytic Therapy: From Winnicott to Kernberg

The Art of Hating

Jennifer and Her Selves

Counterresistance: The Therapist's Interference in the Therapeutic Process

Erotic Games: Bringing Intimacy Back to Relationships

The Couple Who Fell in Hate

The Dictionary of Dream Interpretation

Psychotherapy with People in the Arts

111 Common Therapeutic Blunders

Psychoanalytic Centrism: Collected Papers of a Neo-Classical Psychoanalyst

76 Typical Therapy Mistakes

The Rise of Feminism: A Psychoanalyst Probes the Meaning of a Movement

Forbidden Psychology: A Book for Dark Minds

Fiction and Poetry:

A Way You'll Never Be (novel)

Flugelhorn's Flight, or Kidnapped by Babes from Outer Space (novel)

An Ordinary Lunacy (novel)

Scenes from a Man's Life (novel)

The Way According to Lao Tzu, Chuang Tzu and Seng Tsan (illustrated translation; poetry)

The Adventures of Dolly Lahma: Licensed Private Investigator (novel)

Robodoll (novel)

Reality (novel)

Freud in Love: A Biographical Novel

Holding On and Letting Go (poems and drawings)

Poems from the Heart: Collected Words of Truth and Beauty (Edited by G.Schoenewolf)

The Dhammapada: Teachings of Buddha (illustrated translation) (poetry)

The Way to Be (poetry and philosophy)

Lizzie, a biographical novel.

PREFACE

America has become the mass killing capital of the world. Twice as many mass killings happen in the United states than in any other country. It seems like almost every week we have another mass killing somewhere within the 50 states, each more violent and more shocking than the next. After each killing, we look for reasons why they are happening. We decide on what the reasons are, and we take actions and pass laws that are designed to stop the mass killings. But the mass killings continue to multiply.

There is perhaps no problem in America that is more urgent than the problem of mass killings, and perhaps no problem that is more difficult to solve. Unfortunately, we have been looking for a quick fix for the problem, such as gun control, rather than recognizing the complexity of the problem and the many possible causes for it. It is very easy to figure out that the availability of guns is not the cause of mass killings. Guns have always been available in the United States from its birth as a nation, and particularly since the 2nd Amendment was passed in 1791, which gives U.S. citizens the legal right to bear arms. For almost 200 years of American history, despite the availability of guns, mass killings were rare. But from the 1970s to the present, mass killings

5

started occurring more frequently. They were not happening because guns were available; guns were always available. They were happening because our culture was deteriorating.

This book explores two broad factors in America's cultural deterioration. First it looks at family dysfunction. Families in America became more dysfunctional as politics in America became more important than parenting. From the 1970s on, as radical movements began to view families as oppressive to women, the family's importance became degraded. It seemed that an individual's identity came to be based more on their political affiliation than on their family background. At the same time, the psychiatric establishment also made the family less important by downplaying the role of parenting with respect to the formation of mental disturbances. By the end of the 20th Century, psychiatrists had decided that chemical imbalances, genetics and biology were the chief determinants of emotional disturbances, rather than parenting, and therefore treated such disturbances with medicines first and psychotherapy second. Parenting was put on the back burner, and as a result, parents no longer needed to take responsibility for their children's disturbances. In the public's mind, mass killers were born that way. Therefore, studying the family backgrounds of mass killers was a fascinating hobby for some, but no longer that relevant. It wasn't dysfunctional families that caused mass killers, but defective biology. Many experts disagree with the psychiatric establishment, and I am one of them.

A second, and related factor, alongside of family dysfunction, is cultural dysfunction. After the end of World War II, American culture began to go off the rails and as it did so, it became more dysfunctional. America flourished and reached a peak of power and influence during World War II, when it was hailed for helping to contain Germany and Japan and ending World War II. During the 1950s and 1960s America continued to attain world influence. However, beginning in the late

1960s, it began to lose its way and began to take itself too seriously as the "defender of freedom." It seemed to become more interested in fighting foreign wars (often putting itself above the United Nations), than in safeguarding the quality of life of American citizens. At the same time, political and religious groups became radical and reactionary. These movements accomplished many things on behalf of their followers, but they may also have been harmful to American culture as they became more extreme. For a long time, social critics have been discouraged from being objective about these political and religious movements, but a healthy culture needs objective social criticism.

Mass killings are symptoms of family and cultural dysfunction. The United States has twice as many mass killers because of the family and cultural dysfunction in our society. This book explores that dysfunction and shows how it relates to the rise of mass killings. It begins with an introduction to the deterioration of the American family and of American culture and its relation to mass killing, and then it proceeds to six case histories of mass killers. Each of the mass killers represents a different approach to mass killing and a different plot, but the outcome in each case is similar. From these studies, I hope to illuminate the path through which mass killers develop in their families and in culture, what they have in common and the source of their extreme urge to kill.

The book ends with a chapter on how to prevent mass killings. Since mass killings are caused by deep and complicated social issues related to poor parenting and defective cultural design, preventing them will be a complicated and difficult task.

A WORD TO THE WISE

This book is controversial. It considers topics that many people may prefer to keep hidden—the benefits and harms of families and the benefits and harms of political and religious movements. We will be studying both, not in order to blame or rebuke parents and social movements, but in order to understand them. We know that no parents want to raise a mass killer, nor do families not become dysfunctional because they choose to. Disturbances occur in families over generations, and every parent has been raised by another parent. None of us chooses to become who we are: it is our family background, our upbringing and our genes that determine who we are. Mass killers are not demons who pop out of the ground to menace innocent people. They are tragic figures who have been soul-murdered by broken families and forgotten by a lost culture.

This book may be seen as the literary practice of tough love. It may offend some people and hurt their feelings, but it is a necessary offense.

CONTENTS

"The child who is not embraced by the village will burn it down to feel its warmth."

African Proverb

CHAPTER 1

INTRODUCTION

Some say mass killers kill because they can get guns. Some say they kill because they have played too many violent video games. Some say they kill because they want attention. Some say they kill because they are born that way. After spending many years studying the problem of mass killings, I have come to a different conclusion. There is no single reason why people go on killing sprees, but instead a confluence of complex psychological and sociological factors.

Mass killers grow up in dysfunctional families. From the time they are born, they are tossed and turned by out-of-touch parenting—a kind of parenting that has multiplied over the years. It can include physical, sexual and emotional abuse and sometimes spoiling and sometimes neglect. Bad parenting has grown over the years, while good parenting has declined, and that decline is directly related to mass killings. This book looks at the kinds of dysfunctional parenting that cultivate mass killers, focusing particularly on the years from birth until two—the period of development when the deepest traumas occur. That early period is the time in which a child either learns to be attached or not attached to other human beings; to love or not love other human beings; to know how to navigate life or to know nothing about navigating life. If children do not learn how to live in the beginning of life, they will probably never learn to live at all.

Mass killers also grow up in American culture, and whatever is going on in that culture will affect them. Cultural stressors such as the schism between the two parties in American politics affect all citizens, just as schisms between mothers and fathers affect all children. In a divided family parents might favor one child over another or ask their children to favor one parent over another. This destroys family unity and integrity. When the media of a country focuses primarily on one side of a conflict over another, it also destroys country unity and integrity. When a government focuses on only one aspect of mass killings, such as the guns they use for the killings over other explanations, it obscures the meaning of mass killings and discourages people from investigating the deeper causes of these killings. Social scientists not only need to study families, they also need to study our culture and the political divide that has caused our society to be conflicted and punitive rather than nurturing and supportive.

The United States fell under the sway of radical and reactionary political movements and religions in the 20th and 21st Centuries. Many people had strong feelings about these movements and affirmed that they were very helpful to disadvantaged individuals. Others found these movements to be disturbing because of the arbitrary communication they used. It appeared that people on the extreme left and right did not want a conversation about their issues, but simply believed their views were so noble or divine that they needed no discussion. They seemed offended if people wanted to discuss these issues and often punished them for not staying in step with the movement.

During the early parts of American history, the United States was primarily a Christian country, and churchgoers followed the teachings of the "good book" by shunning those who did not follow the precepts of the Bible. First Corinthians 5:11 says, "But now I am writing to you not to associate with anyone who bears the name brother if he is guilty of sexual immorality or greed, or is an idolater, reviler, drunkard, or swindler — not even to eat with such a one" (1). Christians managed to get laws passed to have the phrase "one nation under God" added to the Pledge of Allegiance that every child learns in school. Nonbelievers were ostracized.

Later, people on the left began to shun nonbelievers of leftist ideas. For example, from the 1970s on, feminists repeated slogans such as, "Women make 80 cents to a man's dollar." This contention of a wage gap was investigated by many experts and found to be misleading. One organization that studied the wage gap was The Foundation of Economic Education (FEE). After conducting its own investigation, the FEE concluded, "That 80 percent is an aggregate—it is not an apples-to-apples comparison of men and women doing the same work. Thus, the claim that women get paid 80 percent of what men do for the same work is a myth" (2). However, to the extreme left, belief in such slogans seemed a matter of faith; feminists had strong feelings about women having been discouraged from working in former times, and they dismissed critics such as the FEE out of hand.

DYSFUNCTIONAL FAMILIES

Families have always been the bedrock of societies. How children are parented in a society determines how those children turn out and whether they become constructive members of the society and help it to flourish. Healthy, functional families take responsibility for child-rearing and do whatever is necessary to make sure it is successful. When parenting is healthy and functional, children grow up with self-esteem, confidence and the ability to take care of themselves in the world. When parenting is unhealthy and dysfunctional, children grow up with low self-esteem, low confidence and an impaired ability to take care of themselves in the world. We have had a rise of mass killers in America, in part, because of a rise in dysfunctional families.

There were many factors that contributed to the breakdown of the family, including prosperity, which enabled people to come and go from their families to seek a wider range of employment opportunities, a change of values that permitted females to choose to enter the workplace and the expansion of higher education, which produced more men and women who were job ready, and an economic need for both parents in families to work. Another important reason for the breakdown of the family in the 20th Century was the feminist movement's negative view of the family. During the Christian era, women were told by the Bible in Corinthians 11:3 to obey their husbands: "the head of every man is Christ, and the head of the woman is man." Children were commanded by God in Exodus 20:12 to "honor your father and your mother" (3). These strictures sometimes became too rigid, preventing women from fully actualizing themselves or children from speaking up against parents who were abusive. However, Christian values tended to hold families together. When feminists later began to speak out, they saw things much differently.

Feminism was a powerful movement beginning at the end of the 19th Century and continuing into the 20th Century, and it had a decidedly different view of women's role. It did not believe that wives should obey their husbands, nor that children should honor their fathers. On the contrary, feminists saw fathers and men as engaging in sexual caprices outside the family while keeping their wives "domesticated." Late in the 19th Century feminist writers were suggesting that the family was a form of domestic slavery by men. They encouraged women to stand up to that slavery. Simone de Beauvoir, wrote that:

> Man in his sovereignty indulges himself in sexual caprices.
> Among others—he fornicates with slaves or courtesans or
> he practices polygamy. Whenever the local customs make

reciprocity at all possible, the wife takes revenge through infidelity—marriage finds its natural fulfillment in adultery. This is woman's sole defense against the domestic slavery in which she is bound; and it is this economic oppression that gives rise to the social oppression to which she is subjected" (4).

Beauvoir was in the vanguard of women who saw marriage and motherhood as a trap and began to portray men not as friends, but more like enemies. These feminists dismissed Freud's assumption that healthy development for women meant embracing the role of motherhood and instead began an opposing trend which deemphasized motherhood and emphasized that women should have outside careers. There is no doubt that encouraging women to go to work was beneficial to many women, raising their self-esteem and expanding their horizons. But it was not beneficial to men who were being accused of slavery, nor beneficial to the institution of the family, which was being degraded.

The prosperity of the 1920s gave way to the depression of the 1930s. Then, in the 1940s, World War II swept America back to prosperity. Prosperity brought with it a sense of entitlement. In the 1960s, the second wave of feminism emerged and Betty Friedan revived the theme that women needed to move out of their homes to actualize themselves. *The Feminine Mystique*, which came out in 1963, espoused the view that women were under the sway of a mystique, by which she meant the glorification (by men) of women's traditional role of taking care of the home, raising children and watching over their husbands and the workings of the family. She urged women to awake from this mystique and find out who they really were by getting jobs and being independent of men. Friedan called it "a problem that had no name," that is, the yearning she believed every woman felt to free herself from domestic slavery and find her true identity. She wrote, "I think this crisis of women growing up—is a turning point from an immaturity that has been called femininity to full human identity" (5).

Note, Friedan called femininity an "immaturity." It was immature, she seemed to be saying, for women to want to do feminine things such as being homemakers and mothers. Friedan's writing was persuasive and her book and all the thousands of subsequent books by feminists that deemphasized the importance of the home and pitched the prospects of the workplace convinced women to revolt against what they were told was patriarchal oppression. Before long, large numbers of women bought into the idea that being a good wife and mother was immature while being a good manager was mature and they were swept along with the tide.

This movement away from the home had two negative effects that impacted boys. While the old value system encouraged women to be supportive and cooperative in their relationships with their husbands and to make motherhood a priority, the new value system began accusing men of keeping women down and gave women permission to compete rather than cooperate with their husbands, putting motherhood at a lower priority. Competing with men might have been productive at work, but not at home, where it ended up causing friction. Who was in charge of raising the children? Before, men were in charge at work and women were in charge at home; now nobody was designated as the leader. When there is no designated leader, people compete about leadership.

Viewing domesticity as a kind of slavery from which women needed to escape also meant that children no longer received quality parenting. It may have felt liberating to women that they had the chance to actualize themselves outside of the home the same way men did. But the new trend advocated by feminists was never properly researched to see what the effects of the trend would be on children, families and boys. They never really studied whether it would be possible for women to actualize themselves outside the home and still be able to perform well in the home. Some research seemed to validate women's movement to the workplace and to assume that the duel occupation of worker and homemaker was feasible, but this research was not the most empirical kind.

A news article, "Working Moms Feel Better than Stay-at-Home Moms, Study Finds," reported on a 2011 study by the National Institute for Child Health and Human Development. The study concluded that "Mothers with jobs tend to be healthier and happier than moms who stay at home during their children's infancy and pre-school years" (6). The study was published by the American Psychological Association, and yet the research for the study consisted only of reports by mothers. Self-reports are not reliable. Working mothers might, for example, have a need to justify working outside the home, which might cause them to give more positive reports while not being honest about the stresses of juggling homemaking with working. Also, there is no real indication in this study of the quality of their mothering. And the study only interviewed mothers, not their children, particularly not their boy children.

Nevertheless, after Friedan's book came out in 1963, the number of women in the workforce began to grow exponentially. In 1950, 70 percent of workers were male, 30 percent female. By 1970, the split was 60/40. By 2015, the percentages of male and females in the workforce was nearly equal (7). Women seemed to believe Friedan and other feminists, and they went to work in droves, thinking that working outside the home would provide them with a higher self-identity. Again, this may have been good for many women, but was it was good for society and for men?

Once women had left the "slavery" of the home, feminists began speaking about the slavery of work—that is, about how men oppressed women in the workplace. First, it was suggested that there was a "glass ceiling" of male comradery that kept women from being promoted to the top of the corporate world. Second, as previously noted, feminists contended that there was a wage gap between male and female workers in favor of men. Then feminists looked for the equivalent of "domestic slavery" at work, and came up with the term, "sexual harassment." Soon sexual harassment accusations began to accumulate; new laws were passed, and men were being fired from jobs and women were being hired. Women believed this calling out of men was long overdue and justified by years of male misbehavior. Because these women were so angry, few dared to oppose them. In the process, perhaps nobody properly assessed how these accusations might affect the family or men, particularly men who were already in a rage and who might be potential mass killers.

Later, feminists came up with the term, "toxic masculinity." Toxic masculinity is defined in Wikipedia as "adherence to traditional male gender roles that consequently stigmatize and limit the emotions boys and men may comfortably express while elevating other emotions such as anger. It is marked by economic, political, and social expectations that men seek and achieve dominance" (8). The APA came up with new guidelines for how men should be treated in therapy, focusing on their toxic masculinity, homophobia and racism (9). Boys and men were subsequently told by society to tame their masculinity and give up their male privilege. They were lectured, not only by their mothers, but by the culture they were growing up in, that girls deserved to be favored and boys needed to yield to the needs of girls. How would a potential mass killer, witnessing this new double standard and the accusations and degradation of men, feel about it? If a young man was already in a funk from a trauma in his early childhood, wouldn't he be doubly hurt by any perceived insult toward men in the culture or callousness about the needs of men?

A website called The Feminist Parent appeared in the late 2000s and was devoted to teaching mothers how to raise their girl and boy children. It was evident from this website that the new double standard was now regarded as a truism. There was a lot of writing about gender equality on the site, but what it seemed to mean was that girls were more equal than boys. "Ever wonder how to teach your girls about gender bias and sexism without scaring them?" a blurb on the website asks. "Or how to teach your boys about gender inequality without shaming them" (10)? Women were being encouraged on this site to raise their girls to regard themselves, without question, as victims of male bias, and to teach their sons that they were carriers of male bias. How did websites such as these and the hundreds of similar places affect the parenting of boys and girls and the self-esteem of boys—especially the self-esteem of potential mass killers?

The assault on the family was also boosted by a tangent of the black rights movement that emerged in 2013, called "Black Lives Matter." On the Black Lives Matter website, it stated its anti-family mission: "We disrupt the Western-prescribed nuclear family structure requirements by supporting each other as extended families and villages... (11). This new attack on the nuclear family by BLM may have further diminished the importance of families and the breakdown of the family—especially among Blacks—which had by the turn of the 21st Century become a factor that led to one-third of American families being single-parent families.

There was a radical revolution in America, not of guns but of emotional aggression, that in turn also provoked a reactionary movement among conservatives. Many of the mass killers described in various chapters of this book grew up in religious communities, and those religious cultures, often fundamentalist in nature, spawned potential mass killers with holier-than-thou attitudes that clashed with mainstream radical-liberal culture. Mainstream culture largely rejected religion and religious values and equated them with gun ownership and White supremacy. Research on mass killers showed that this conflict between the left and right was upsetting to potential mass killers and made them dig their heels into the ground even more. They felt encouraged by the reactionary right and perceived the radical mainstream as degrading them, which caused them to be resentful with the mainstream's anti-religious and hedonistic practices. Potential mass killers were thus in all probability negatively influenced by what was going on in American culture.

A revolution of radicals and a counterrevolution of Trump conservatives (people inspired by President Trump's blatant anti-liberalism) emerged to contribute to the American cultural divide. The cultural mainstream harped on the accessibility of guns and tried to link gun ownership with White supremacy and mass killings. "The U.S. faces a confluence of dangerous challenges from white supremacists, anti-government militias, and other armed groups and individuals of the extreme right that seek to perpetrate violence, spread conspiracies, traffic in hate speech, and engage in armed intimidation," wrote a radical organization called Everytown in the late 2010s. "Guns and gun rights are central to many extreme-right groups and individuals" (12). On the other hand, a reactionary conservative, James Dobson, stated in his speech before the Taxpayer Party, "This Christmas I want you to do the most loving thing and I want you to buy each of your children an SKS rifle and 500 rounds of ammunition" (13).

By the 2000s, a new generation of students had grown up in radical and reactionary families and the rift had seemingly widened. In reactionary families, children grew up hating liberals, collecting guns, and joining militias whose aim was to bring down a government that they perceived as hostile to them. In radical families, children grew up hating conservatives whom they had been taught to think were dangerous to them. I watched a number of newscasts in those years that showed radical students shouting down a professor whom they contended was engaging in "violent speech," that is, speech that disagreed with the radical-liberal view. This kind of censorship spread to all aspects of society, from education to government to the media and corporations. An example of this was the case of James Damore at Google. Damore was an engineer at this corporation in 2017 who attended a sensitivity training seminar and came away feeling angry and insulted that male employees had to attend events that they saw as biased against them. When he complained by writing a company memo entitled, "Google's Ideological Echo Chamber," he was fired for violating Google's Code of Conduct (14). If you multiply instances such as this by the hundreds of thousands, you will have an idea of what potential mass killers have had to listen to and what they have had to go through for the last century.

Families and child-rearing changed over the 20th and early 21st Centuries. During that time there was a gradual devaluation of fathers, men, and the family, and the family was tagged as a patriarchal institution erected to benefit men and enslave women. Women were encouraged to put families and motherhood on the backburner, leading to a breakdown of the family. While feminism was beneficial to some women, some aspects negatively affected the family and men. I have attempted to shine a light on how and why family values changed over the years, and how those changes may have affected parenting—particularly the parenting of vulnerable White males—in a harmful way.

THE CULTURAL DECLINE

America has the highest number of mass killings of any country in the world. Therefore, one must look at why and how American culture has become a breeding ground of mass killers. Although many, both in America and around the world, think that America's obsession with guns is the cultural factor that breeds mass killers, it is not. As previously stated, guns have always been accessible in America and certain guns, such as assault rifles, have become less accessible over the years. At the same time, mass killings have risen dramatically. Lankford, who defined mass killing as four or more murders in one setting, has done research on the topic that shows how mass killings have mushroomed. In 2000, there was only one mass killing; in 2018, there were 18 mass killings (15). This rise in mass killings is not because of guns. It is because of a culture that is disturbed and no longer has healthy values. Saying that guns are the reason that people go on killing sprees, and if we ban guns the problem will be solved, is like saying cars are the reason people drive into a crowd and kill people. Should cars be banned?

There has been a rise in social problems in America since the end of World War II, and social problems can be seen as symptoms of a cultural disturbance. According to statistics collected by UNICEF, America ranks 46th in literacy compared to other countries, whereas it used to rank number one (16). The literacy rate can be interpreted as an indicator of how educated a culture is and how well socialized its children are; thus, the fall of literacy may represent a drop in effective parenting. On the other hand, America ranks first in a survey by the World Health Organization in illegal drug use among seventeen industrialized countries (17). It also ranks first in a survey of obesity rates in the industrialized world, with 30 percent of American adults reported to be overweight (18). It also ranks first in crime rate among all countries. In fact, it has twice as much crime as the second-ranked country, the United Kingdom (19). America has the third highest divorce rate of all countries, with 50 percent of first marriages ending in divorce (20). America, France and the Netherlands have the highest rates of depression, with 30 percent of the U.S. population reporting at least one episode of major depression in its lifetime (21). And America ranks third in sleep deprivation, with 37 percent of Americans reporting sleep problems (22). Finally, there has been a decline in commitment to family, with single-parent families on the rise; by 2000, more than a third of all families in the U.S. were single-parent families (23). All of these statistics can be interpreted to indicate a culture that is disturbed and is no longer providing the controls that would keep it healthy.

While social problems rose during the second half of the 20th Century and the first quarter of the 21st Century, these problems occurred at the same time that the country became increasingly divided by politics. There has been an ongoing ideological conflict between the left and the right, a conflict that resulted in the left gaining the ideological upper hand. By the start of the 21st Century, radical values had become the prevalent values in American and had made huge changes in the culture, including how men and women related to one another, how Blacks and Whites related, and how children were raised. This mainly came about through a subtle drive to change laws. From the years 1972 to 2017, radicals succeeded in passing 24 new laws or acts, which effectively overhauled American culture (24). The legal changes pushed through the courts included:

1972, Roe v. Wade legalized abortion.

1978, The Pregnancy Discrimination Act banned discrimination against pregnant women.

1981, Kirchberg v. Feenstra ruled that the husband is no longer head of household

1984, Roberts v. U.S. Jaycees banned sex discrimination in organizations.

1984, Hishon v. King and Spaulding, banned law firms from discriminating again women.

1986, Meritor Savings Bank v. Vinsom defined sexual harassment as a hostile work Environment.

1987, Johnson v. Santa Clara County ruled that it was discrimination if a company had more male than females at any position.

1993, Harris v. Forklift Systems, Inc. ruled that women who accused a man of sexual harassment did not have to show physical or psychological injury.

1994, Gender Equity in Education Act promoted math and science learning by girls.

1994, The Violence Against Women Act codified that there is mass violence against women and required funding services for women to counteract it.

1996, United States v. Virginia ruled that Virginia Military Academy had to admit women.

1997, Title IX, college athletics must provide equal funding for women and men.

1998, Mitsubishi Motors offered a $34 million settlement of an EEOC lawsuit contending that hundreds of female employees were sexually harassed.

2000, CBS Broadcasting offered an $8 million settlement of an EEOC lawsuit that 200 female employees were sexually harassed.

2003: Nevada Department of Human Resources v Hibbs rules that states could be in federal court for violations of the Family Leave Medical Act.

2005, Jackson v. Birmingham Board of Education ruled female students cannot be punished for making complaints about sexual discrimination.

2006, Reauthorization of the Violence Against Women Act protected female victims of sexual violence from becoming homeless.

2009, The Lily Ledbetter Fair Pay Restoration Act allows women victims of pay discrimination to file complaints with the federal government.

2010, The Affordable Care act required insurers to provide birth control without charge.

2010, The Hate Crimes Prevention Act called for stiffer punishment if a crime was linked to a person's gender or race, among other things.

2013, The ban against women in military combat roles was removed.

2013, Reauthorization of the Violence Against Women Act protected native American women, lesbians and immigrant
women.

2017, The Canadian government passed Bill C-16 made it illegal
to address a transgender person by a pronoun that do not
approve of, such as "he" or "she."

Over the years, radical groups convinced lawmakers that women and
minorities were victims of White males. Hence, a new double standard
emerged in which girls and women were viewed favorably and men
unfavorably under the law. Most of these new laws benefited women
and minorities, but none of them benefited White males. For example,
the 2010 Hate Crimes Prevention Act called for stiffer punishments if
a woman or a member of a minority group was murdered, but White
males were not on that list of targets of hate crimes, so if one of them
were murdered, their murderer only received scant attention or punishment. This made the murder of a White male way less important than
any other group.

The degradation of White males kept building during these years. In
radical Black culture of America, not only White police officers were
viewed as corrupt, but also whiteness itself was seen as something bad.
In fact, it began to be seen almost as a disease and it was increasingly
depicted in dark terms. An article, "On Whiteness," appeared in the
prestigious *Journal of the American Psychoanalytic Association.*

Whiteness is a condition one first acquires and then one has —
a malignant, parasitic-like condition to which "white" people
have a particular susceptibility. The condition is foundational,
generating characteristic ways of being in one's body, in
one's mind, and in one's world. Parasitic Whiteness renders
its hosts' appetites voracious, insatiable, and perverse. These

deformed appetites particularly target nonwhite peoples. Once established, these appetites are nearly impossible to eliminate. Effective treatment consists of a combination of psychic and social-historical interventions (25).

This author, a San Francisco psychoanalyst, ignored the basic principles of psychoanalysis, such as scientific objectivity. The article was mostly subjective, as the author made statements about the nature of whiteness and its malignant, parasitic quality without presenting evidence to back up his contentions. It was, in effect, a biased put down of white people disguised as analysis.

In 2022, John Blake, of CNN reported on a growing number of White people who had taken offense to the term, "white privilege" and had contended, instead, that there was Black privilege. "In America you can't even talk about whiteness," said Drew Domalick of Green Bay Wisconsin. "If you try to embrace being white, you are portrayed as being a racist. If we had a White History Month, that would be viewed as a racist holiday." Blake alluded to a widely publicized survey in which a majority of White Americans said "they suffer from racial discrimination more than Blacks" (26).

There was evidence in education that White boys and boys in general were affected by this perceived discrimination toward White males. American boys lagged behind in education. According to a report in CNN in 2010, enrollment at U.S. colleges was 60-40 female—the largest gender gap in American history. NYU Professor Scott Galloway said this meant America was producing too many of "the most dangerous persons in the world: a broke and alone male" (27). Males, he contended, were either choosing not to go to college or were dropping out.

Among those who wrote about this topic was Christina Hoff Sommers of the American Enterprise Institute, who described herself as a moderate feminist. She was critical of the radicals who she contended had taken over feminism. "All the rhetoric in the gender equity movement is about how schools shortchange girls," she wrote. "There is almost nothing about how we could reach out to boys." In her book, *The War Against Boys*, she asserts, "In order to advance girls, they exaggerated how vulnerable girls were, and they understated the needs of boys. They depicted boys as…the privileged beneficiaries of a patriarchal society that oppresses women, demeans them and trains young men to be sexists and misogynists." If you repeatedly tell a boy he is a sexist, misogynist, male chauvinistic or toxic, Sommers contends, he will become what you tell him he is (28).

"Girls outperform boys in elementary school, middle school, high school, and college, and graduate school," say Kindlin and Thompson, in their book *Raising Cain*. After researching the topic for several years, they came to the same conclusion as Sommers did: decades of dedicating special attention to girls while neglecting the needs of boys, was a cause of the decline. "Girls are achieving while boys are stagnating," they added (29).

This gender imbalance in schools seemed to be attached to a shift in the way American culture viewed boys—especially White boys. The derogatory view of boys was epitomized by a nurse in Indiana, who posted on twitter: "Every white woman raises a detriment to society when they raise a son. Someone with the *highest* propensity to be a terrorist, rapist, racist and domestic violence all-star. Historically, every son you had should be sacrificed to the wolves B-tch" (30). Brian Epps suggested that inherent male bias was linked to mass killings. In an article entitled, "America's Gun Violence Problem is a Symptom of Toxic Masculinity" (31), he expounded on the thesis that boys are born that way and should be kept under a watchful eye.

As previously mentioned, the United States had twice as much crime as any other industrialized country during the 20th and 21st Centuries. Kids grew up watching violent movies and television shows and playing violent video games. A 2018 study of violence in television movies found that "91% of movies on television contain violence, including extreme violence" (32). Often violence was portrayed as having a positive outcome, as in numerous movies that depicted superheroes committing violence against bad guys or mothers taking revenge on bad husbands or wives getting revenge on sex traffickers who kidnaped theirs or their daughters. The victimizers in these movies, so it seemed, were most often White males. Such movies were cheered by radicals, but how did they affect potential mass killers?

According to my research, all of these situations had an impact on men and particularly on mass killers. The combination of all these things, including the fact that angry White men may have perceived that nobody was listening to them, probably led to a kind of isolation and hopelessness among potential mass killers. They had grown up in a culture that was sympathetic to the plight of Blacks, women, gays or transgender people, but turned a deaf ear and blind eye to the plight of men, particularly White males. When people perceive unfairness and experience frustration everywhere, they are forced to hold in that frustration until they find another outlet.

THE END-OF-THE-WORLD SYNDROME

World culture can also have an impact on people, including young people who may end up being mass killers. In a previous book, *Forbidden Psychology* (33), I devoted a chapter to a new syndrome, which I called the end-of-the-world syndrome. This syndrome is spreading among younger people today, who grow up believing that the world is going to end soon. This syndrome may help us understand how not only American culture, but also the world situation creates a hopelessness that assists in breeding disgruntled deviates like mass killers.

"This is all wrong," sixteen-year-old Greta Thunberg said, addressing a UN meeting on climate change in 2019 (34). "I shouldn't be up here. I should be back in school on the other side of the ocean. Yet you all come to us young people for hope. How dare you! You have stolen my dreams and my childhood with your empty words. And yet I'm one of the lucky ones. People are suffering. People are dying. Entire eco-systems are collapsing. We are in the beginning of a mass extinction, and all you can talk about is money and fairy tales of eternal economic growth. How dare you!"

Thunberg speaks for a generation born at a time when the end of the world seems to be just around the corner. Humans have been walking the earth for millions of years, and for nearly all of those years they grew up thinking that their planetary home would live forever. Now, in the last century, they have been learning about climate change, hearing predictions that the earth will be too hot in 50 years to support life, and reading that there are nuclear bombs all over the world and madmen who are crazed enough to drop them. They learn that the rainforests are being cut down by land developers and the oceans are being polluted with plastic and chemicals that are slowly killing sea life and perhaps earth life as well. They learn that there is a hole in the ozone layer that is letting in increased UV radiation that harms human health. But most of all, what they learn is that the generations that came before them did not seem to know what they were doing and have left them with a mess. The unrest in American culture is exacerbated by the unrest in the world.

Young people today are showing up for their therapy sessions with the usual conditions related to social phobias or performance anxiety or abandonment depression or fear of intimacy, but in addition to these staples, they are suffering from another malady, which I am labeling, "end-of-the-world syndrome." It is an anxiety-based syndrome that causes young people to feel they no longer have a future, to lose faith in their parents, in nearly all adults, and especially in our leaders. They feel outraged—as Gretta Thunberg obviously did when making her speech—and lose their motivation to succeed in life and in some cases to even go on with life.

Mostly, the loss of motivation is associated with a disinterest in getting ahead in life, since they do not think there is much to live for. Nor are they interested in getting a job and working hard for a promotion. Indeed, they are not at all enthused about working at all, but rather in finding ways of not working, such as living on unemployment or on social security disability. And, in particular, young people today are not interested in getting married and having children. "Why have children," one of them asked me recently, "When the world is falling apart."

This syndrome cropped up toward the end of the 20th Century as humans became aware that they were destroying the world they live on. To the younger generation, born in those years, the gradual sense that our world was going to end must have felt like one slap in the face following another. First, they learned—as all humans must—that they personally had to die, but in this first instance, they could console themselves with the thought that at least their children and the human species would live on. But then, later, they learned that the world would also die—much sooner than anyone thought—and that neither they nor any other animals nor our planet itself will live on. Upon pondering this situation, some came to the grim conclusion that adults did not know what they were doing and, along with Gretta Thunberg, they may have become outraged by the predicament the older generation had gotten them into. They may have decided that there was no longer any hope for them or for humankind, and they may have withdrawn from the world.

It seemed that this situation of becoming aware, at a young age, that the world would end soon, resulted in the development of a psychological disturbance. And it also seemed that it added another level of stress to the lives of certain young White males who were potential mass killers.

There are many aspects of the world situation that can be oppressive to young people in general and to young White males in particular, and the world-wide conflict over global warming is one of them. It is not surprising that a young girl, Greta Thunberg, became the spokesman for young people, but it is noteworthy that a young woman, not a young man became the spokesperson for this generation. Young White males not only grow up believing that the world is against them, but also that the world is going to end, which may compound their depression and anxiety. This holds particularly for angry White males who are potential mass killers.

PROFILE OF THE MASS KILLER

Peterson and Densley published, in 2021, a wide-scale study of mass killers called *The Violence Project* (35). Funded by the National Institute of Justice, their research came up with a database of every mass shooter since 1966 who shot and killed four or more people in a public place—including shooting incidents at schools, workplaces and places of worship since 1999. As a result of the study, they constructed a profile of a mass killer that pretty much coincides with the one I am offering in this book; however, like many studies, the focus is too narrow, in that the authors only consider how child-rearing is related to the problem, but not wider sociological and cultural factors.

In an interview in *Politico,* Peterson summarized what he described as the pathway to becoming a mass killer: Early childhood trauma, consisting of violence in the home, sexual assault, parental suicides, extreme bullying are, according to Peterson, early signs. Then you see the trend toward hopelessness, despair, isolation, self-loathing, and oftentimes rejection from peers. That turns into a really identifiable crisis point where they're acting differently. Sometimes they have previous suicide attempts. From there, mass shooters develop self-hate that at first turns against themselves in terms of low confidence and low self-worth, and later turns against a group. "They start asking themselves, 'Whose fault is this?' Is it the fault of a racial group or women or a religious group, or is it my classmates? The hate turns outward. There's also this quest for fame and notoriety." The interviewer in this article, Melanie Warner, wondered whether politicians would pay attention to an article like this, focusing on the psychology of mass killers, and be willing to actually engage in finding and funding solutions. Probably not, Peterson replies.

In my own research I have found these features of mass killers:

- They are usually White males.

- They often come from broken homes.

- They are usually traumatized in early childhood.

- They internalize their feelings, particularly their anger, until it builds to a breaking point.

- They are loners who are awkward socially and unable to successfully navigate the vicissitudes of life.

- They are usually in their teens or early twenties.

- They are bullied, often beginning in their own homes and then in school and at work.

- They are antisocial, unpopular and do not get along with peers or engage in extracurricular activities.

- They often have above-average intelligence or talent but do not have the emotional maturity to activate them.

- They tend to let people know beforehand of their plans to kill people.

- They displace and generalize their anger from its original source, usually their parents, onto some segment of the public at large.

- If they have children, they often transfer their anger from their parents to their children.

It is a generational thing. Mass killers usually have parents who are themselves disturbed and angry, who in turn also have parents who were disturbed. One generation of parents takes out its anger on its children, and the next generation does likewise. Such parents are not normal parents; they are likely to be sadistic, antisocial, paranoid and sometimes paranoid schizophrenic. They may also have borderline or narcissistic personalities. They are likely to provide only the most bizarre kinds of child-rearing, and yet they have no idea that there is anything wrong with it. They can be the type of parent who cruelly beats their child if the child looks at them in the wrong way. They can be the type of parent who completely neglects their child from birth on and then later brings him to doctors full of concern about why he won't talk. Their son may grow up hearing his parents put down Blacks or Asians or Whites or rich people or religious people and are hence conditioned from early childhood to hate such groups or to want to kill them. Such parents cannot at all see what their bizarre parenting has done to their child or reflect on whether they had anything to do with how their child developed. If their child wins an acting award or a spelling bee or a hundred-yard dash, they had everything to do with it; but if their child shoots 20 people in high school, they have no idea how he got that way.

Mass murderers almost always telegraph their intentions before committing the crime, either directly or indirectly. They repeatedly post strange messages on social media or they may scribble such messages in their school notebooks. They may brag to people about their collection of guns and joke about someday coming to class and shooting everybody. They may call up crisis lines and use a pseudonym to vent to the listener on the other end. They may leave cryptic messages on social media, hoping that somebody can decipher them. They may even confide to close acquaintances about their intensions. But despite giving off all these signs, most of the time people miss them, because the mass killer is usually a person who has always been such a quiet person, such a nerd, that nobody takes him seriously. Of course, there are other mass killers that do not leave any traces of what they intend to do. They are deeply disturbed loners who collect guns and bullets in their rooms or basement and silently gloat each night as they load their guns and imagine what they will do with them.

Mass murderers are usually individuals who internalize their anger. When a person holds in anger over a period of time, that anger sometimes builds up until it explodes. It can explode in a temper tantrum, a brawl or a killing. Or it can implode in a suicide. In other words, the anger can be taken out on others or on one's self—or both. Anger is a feeling that becomes painful as it becomes stronger. The more it builds inside a person, the more it causes internal pain. Anger makes breathing shallow and anxiety deepen; anger causes the veins to narrow, which leads to heart problems; anger causes the chest to tighten, which results in chest pain. If one has back pain, that pain will become much worse as anger builds up. Indeed, any chronic pain will increase as anger expands. Chronic anger also harms the immune system and leads to more illness. Finally, continual anger affects a person's point of view and brings about a doom and gloom mentality, which in turn causes more anger. After years of holding onto anger, a potential mass killer can no longer tolerate the constant pain. Even through their moral system tells them not to kill, the pain inside has built up to such an extent that the person no longer has a choice but to kill. They kill to pass their misery on to others.

One might think that if they are in such pain, they would seek help in the form of psychotherapy. Unfortunately, the people who are most disturbed—and cultures that are most disturbed—are the last to seek help. They prefer to think that it is society or the world that has a problem.

Even when potential mass murderers do seek help, many experts do not know how to help them. It takes a special kind of training to work with someone who is in a rage and has been conditioned not to trust people.

Finally, mass killers tend to be copycats, and when they witness one mass killing after another and see mass killers achieve a dark vengeance and notoriety, the idea grows in their brains that killing lots of people is a great way to express their pent-up rage and end it all with a bang. If you cannot achieve anything worthwhile in life because you are weighed down by feelings of low self-worth, depression and anger, then walking into a church or school or government building and shooting people down and killing them and then offing yourself at least brings about a final feeling of power and satisfaction. It is a dramatic final act of twisted self-affirmation.

THE PSYCHOLOGY OF RAGE

Rage is the result of the buildup of anger. Psychologically healthy individuals verbalize anger as it is felt. If healthy people are angered by something somebody does or says to them, they deal with the situation immediately and then move on. Unhealthy people are to various degrees unable, due to personality factors, to respond when they are angered. They may be caught up in a major depression or deep fears or feelings of inferiority. They repress or suppress their anger and internalize it, and through the years, from childhood on, they collect more and more anger from more and more external forces. Hence, over time, anger builds up and becomes rage. There are three stages of rage.

There is a classical theory about the relationship between frustration and aggression that helps to explain this process. The frustration–aggression hypothesis, also known as the frustration–aggression–displacement theory, is a theory of aggression first proposed by John Dollard, Neal Miller, Leonard Doob, Orval Mowrer, and Robert Sears in 1939 (36). The theory says that aggression is the result of blocking, or frustrating, a person's efforts to attain a goal. As originally stated, the hypothesis explains that frustration always precedes aggression, and aggression is the sure consequence of frustration. Potential mass killers are individuals who become frustrated from the time they are born, because their human needs for self-mastery are squashed and they never learn how to get those needs met. Hence, their entire lives are spent experiencing one frustration after another. The buildup of rage is directly correlated to the build-up of aggression. When the frustration results in a feeling of powerlessness, the rage becomes intolerable.

The buildup of rage happens in three stages, each of which has some distinguishing characteristics.

Stage 1. During stage 1 rage, individuals are still able to function fairly normally. They have pushed down the anger that comes from the original traumas in their childhoods, which left behind unconscious hurt that they could not resolve or release. This first trauma in which they had to repress and internalize their anger, becomes the prototype. If they were sexually abused as a young child and then gaslighted by parents who tell them they are imagining things, this kind of thing will become a repeating pattern for the rest of their lives. From then on, they continue to collect and hold on to anger rather than properly dealing with it. For a time, often for years, they may be able to compartmentalize the anger and keep it repressed (unconscious) or suppressed (consciously pushed down). They go to school, to college, to their jobs, and to their families without excessive acting out, and if they do express anger they express it in the wrong way, such as smoking too much or drinking too much or being overly aggressive at home or work. However, holding in their anger does not take care of their deepest rage, and there is some craving for more release. Despite the underlying rage, they manage to maintain their moral systems and, as stated previously, remain functional. Many people live their whole lives in stage 1 rage, and although they can function, the degree of rage nevertheless affects the extent to which they can function or can actualize themselves.

Stage 2. In stage 2 rage, the repressed and suppressed anger accumulates to such an extent that it begins to fester. It causes a higher degree of anxiety and depression, more tightness in the body and the chest, more constriction of the veins, higher amounts of stress hormones in the body, and other physical symptoms that cause a continual pain. Individuals in this stage begin to suffer from poor health (i.e., back pain, ulcers, heart disease, respiratory disease) and find ways to discharge their anger and its related stress, but in all the wrong ways. There is more smoking, more drinking, more overeating, and more drugs. There is shoplifting and other petty thievery, and road rage or home rage. There can be obsessive-compulsive tyranny, complaining, cheating; loss of temper at those whom they experience as obstructing them in a hundred and one other ways. Some people live their whole lives in this stage, functioning at only a fraction of their native ability and managing to release just enough of the rage for them to go on day to day. For potential mass killers, the rage accumulates until it reaches stage 3.

Stage 3. Only a small segment of a society reaches stage 3. The more out of control a culture is, the more people in it will reach stage 3 rage. Those who are least able to handle their anger in a healthy way will be the ones who will be catapulted to this stage. Serial killers often reach stage 3 rage early in life and go into it again and again throughout their lives, discharging their rage in an ongoing basis each time they kill somebody. Mass killers reach this point and discharge their rage in one setting. They are people who have no clue about how to take care of themselves and express their anger in a constructive way. If you say "You're stupid!" to a healthy person, he will perhaps answer sarcastically, "Thanks a lot!" thus expressing his anger. If you say "You're stupid!" to someone in stage 3 rage, he will perhaps say nothing, but will quietly rage about it for days. If many such incidents, some more frustrating than others, build up, they may propel him to a killing spree. When individuals get to this stage, the anger that they have collected over the years can no longer be repressed or suppressed. The internalized pain and stress can no longer be tolerated, and the moral system by which individuals have been operating breaks down. They have become numb, almost walking zombies (which may explain the popularity of movies like, *The Walking Dead.)* An indication of how many people are in stages of rage is how many people are attracted to zombie movies. Zombies can be seen as symbolic of individuals who are walking in a rage.

Those in stage 3 are so overwhelmed by anxiety, depression and psychological pain that they are compelled to act. As they have accumulated anger, their thinking becomes twisted and they often begin to view other individuals or groups in dark terms—as evil people, perverts, stalkers and enemies. They have harbored resentment about being victimized, misunderstood and abused for many years and have been unable to properly redress their frustration, and therefore they have reached the point in which they are ready to erupt in an act of mad self-assertion. Any final nudge can trigger their final act. Because they feel they have been destroyed, psychologically or physically, they need to destroy others by taking their lives, taking their own life, or both. They will kill off as many people as they need to kill in order to feel better. And then they stop as they begin to feel something for their victims.

Kill Point: There seems to be a kill point for each individual who becomes a serial or mass killer. It is that point at which they have killed enough people to satisfy their craving for revenge. Obviously, the more frustration they have accumulated, the more aggression they will have to discharge in order to reach an equilibrium. For a serial killer, it may come after they have killed 10 people or 20 people or 30 people, one at a time. For a mass killer, the kill point will come after they have killed

10 or 20 or 30 people in one setting. The pent-up rage is discharged with each killing until there is no more rage inside, like a balloon that has no more hot air to release. At that point the urge to kill has been dissipated and the killer begins to experience remorse and caring for the people he has murdered.

It may well be that rage underlies all mental illness. Whether we are talking about schizophrenia, depression, obsessive-compulsion or paranoia, avoidant or self-defeating personality disorder, the original source—at least one source—of the ailment may be the rage that has built up inside the individual due to the frustration of their basic needs.

THE CASES

It was easy to find case histories for this book. I have pulled them right out of the tragic headlines that have unfortunately plagued our culture for a long time. The headlines and the stories have by now almost become routine. "Virginia man shoots 17 and injures 28 in a church in Royal Front." "Classmate kills 11 fellow students with three assault rifles and then shoots himself." "Man shoots at crowd at music festival and kills 62 people." After years of hearing news stories like these, we have become used to them. Each time they happen, there are police and government officials making speeches about the sadness of the occasion and vowing to find a way to end "gun violence." There are the interviews with tearful parents or other relatives of the victim. There are the funerals of confused friends and relatives watching the coffins being lowered into the ground. There are the bouquets of flowers at the scene of the crime. There are panels of experts that come up with plans that may or may not materialize.

I have tried to write these cases so that they will take readers up close and personal to the mass killer, providing them with intimate looks into their lives, detailing their families, neighborhoods and the cultures they grew up in. They are based primarily on the information I was able to find online; but in the case of very early childhood, where scant information is available, they also make use of my clinical experience and my knowledge of similar cases, in order to fill in the gaps. What kinds of childhoods did these mass killers have? How were they treated by their parents? What were their earliest traumas? What were their experiences in school? How did they live their lives? What were the immediate events that led to their killing sprees?

In writing these case histories in a narrative style, I decided to deviate from the standard style of citing references in the text itself. Instead, I have listed sources of each case at the end, because I wanted the text to move as smoothly and poignantly as possible in order to give the reader not just an intellectual but also an emotional understanding of just what it is like to be a mass killer.

It is hoped that these dramatic glimpses into the lives of mass killers will provide a deeper understanding of how mass killers develop and what they mean when they go on their killing sprees. The book concludes with a chapter on how to prevent mass killings, which will be a difficult and complex task.

REFERENCES:

1. Piper, J., "Avoid the Unrepentant—But What if they're Family?" In *Desiring God*. Retrieved from: https://www.desiringgod.org/interviews/avoid-the-unrepentant-but-what-if-theyre-family

2. Family Bible Verses. In *Bible Study Tools*. Retrieved from: https://www.biblestudytools.com/topical-verses/family-bible-verses/

3. Horowitz, S., "Truth and Myth on the Gender Pay Gap." In Foundation for Economic Education, 03/30/2017. Retrieved from: https://fee.org/articles/truth-and-myth-on-the-gender-pay-gap/

4. "Simone de Beauvoir." In Wikipedia. Retrieved from: https://en.wikipedia.org/wiki/Simone_de_Beauvoir.

5. Friedan, B. (1984). *The Feminine Mystique*. New York: Dell/Laurel Paperback.

6. "Labor Force by Sex." Civilian Labor Force by Sex, U.S. Department of Labor. Retrieved from: https://www.dol.gov/wb/stats/NEWSTATS/facts/women_lf.htm#0.

7. Public Affairs (2011). "Working Moms Feel Better than Stay-at-Home Moms, Study Finds." In APA Bulletin. Retrieved from: https://www.apa.org/news/press/releases/2011/12/working-moms#:~:text=WASHINGTON%E2%80%94Mothers%20with%20jobs%20tend,by%20the%20American%20Psychological%20Association.

8. Toxic Masculinity. In *Wikipedia*. Retrieved from: https://en.wikipedia.org/wiki/Toxic_masculinity

9. Pappas, S. (2019). "APA issues first-ever guidelines for practice with men and boys." In *APA Monitor*. Retrieved from: https://www.apa.org/monitor/2019/01/ce-corner

10. The Feminist Parent. "Raising Children with Values and Behaviors that Support Gender Equality." Retrieved from: https://www.thefeministparent.com/.

11. "What We Believe." In BlackLivesMatter.com. Retrieved from: https://blacklivesmatter.com

12. Armed Extremism. In. *Everytown*. Retrieved from: https://www.everytown.org/issues/armed-extremism/

13. Blumenthal, M. (2017). "18 Outrageous Conservative Quotes." In *Daily Beast*. Retrieved from: https://www.thedailybeast.com/18-outrageous-conservative-quotes

14. Google's Ideological Echo Chamber. In *Wikipedia*. Retrieved from: https://en.wikipedia.org/wiki/Google%27s_Ideological_Echo_Chamber

15. Lankford, A., "Mass Shooters in the USA, 1966-2010: Differences between Attackers Who Live and Die." *Justice Quarterly*, 32(2(360-79).

16. "Countries by Literacy Rate." In *Wikipedia*. Retrieved from: https://en.wikipedia.org/wiki/List_of_countries_by_literacy_rate

17. WebMD, "U.S. Leads the World in Drug Use." In *CBS News*. Retrieved from: https://www.cbsnews.com/news/us-leads-the-world-in-illegal-drug-use.

18. Locklear, C., "Obesity: Countries Compared." In *Nation Master*. Retrieved from: http://www.nationmaster.com/country-info/stats/Healgth/Obesity.

19. Murray. 5., "Total Crimes: Countries Compared." In *Nation Master*. Retrieved from: http://www.nationmaster.com/country-info/stats/Crime/Total:crimes.

20. Graham, I., "Divorce Rates Compared." In *Guinness World Records*. Retrieved from: http://www.guinnessworldrecords.com/world-records/highest-divorce-rate.

21. McPhillips, D., "U.S. among Most Depressed Countries in the World," Sept. 17, 2016. In *U.S. News*. Retrieved from: http://www.usnews.com/news/best-countries/articles/2016-09-14/the-10-most-depressed-countries.

22. McInick, M., "Why Americans Are Among the Most Sleepless People in the World," Nov. 11, 2010, in *Time*. Retrieved from: http://healthland.time.com/2020/11/11/wuy-americans-are-among-the-most-sleepless-people-in-the-world.

23. Vespa, J., et al., "America's Families and Living Arrangement, 2013." *U.S. Census Bureau*. Retrieved from: https://www.census.gov/prod/2013pubs/p20-5780.pdf.

24. National Women's History Project, "Timeline of Legal History of Women in the United States." Retrieved from: http://www.nwhp.org/resources/womens-rights-movement/details-timelne/

25. Moss, D. "On Having Whiteness." *Journal of the American Psychoanalytic Association*, 2021 Apr;69 (2):355-371.

26. Blake, J., "It's Time to Talk about 'Black Privilege.'" In CNN. Retrieved from: https://www.cnn.com/2016/03/30/us/black-privilege/index.html

27. "College Women Outnumber Men 60-40." In *CNN*. Retrieved from: https://www.cnn.com/videos/tv/2021/09/25/college-gender-cap-women-outnumber-men-60-40.cnn.

28. Sommers, C. H., (2001). The War Against Boys: How Misguided Feminism is Harming our Young Men. New York: Simon and Schuster.

29. Kindlin, D. and Thompson, M., (2000). *Raising Cain: Protecting the Emotional Lives of Boys*. New York: Ballantine Books.

30. Miller, J. R. "Nurse Fired for Post Suggesting that Sons of White Women be Sacrificed." In *New York Post*. Retrieved from: https://nypost.com/2017/11/27/nurse-loses-job-over-post-suggesting-sons-of-white-women-be-sacrificed/.

31. Epps, B. "America's Gun Violence Problem is a Symptom of Toxic Masculinity. In *Them*. Retrieved from: https://www.them.us/story/beyond-gun-control-we-need-to-end-toxic-masculinity.

32. Position Paper, "Violence in the Media and Entertainment." In *AAFP*. Retrieved from: https://www.aafp.org/about/policies/all/violence-media-entertainment.html.

33. Schoenewolf, G. (2021). *Forbidden Psychology: A Book for Dark Minds*. Bushkill, PA: Living Center Press

34. Transcript: Greta Thunberg's Speech at The U.N. Climate Action Summit. *In NPR*. Retrieved from: https://www.npr.org/2019/09/23/763452863/transcript-greta-thunbergs-speech-at-the-u-n-climate-action-summit

35. Warner, M., "Two Professors Found What Creates a Mass Shooter. Will Politicians Pay Attention?" In Politico, *May* 27, 2022. Retrieved from: https://www.politico.com/news/magazine/2022/05/27/stopping-mass-shooters-q-a-00035762?utm_source=pocket-newtab

36. Dollard, J., et al. (1939). *Frustration and Aggression: Revised Edition*. New York: Praeger (1980).

CHAPTER 2
ADAM LANZA

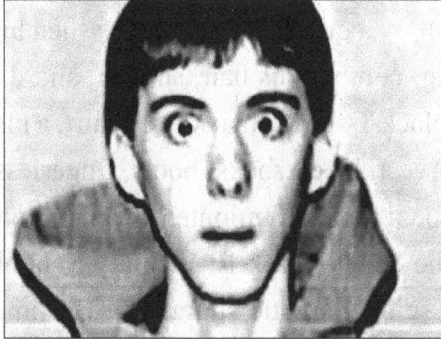

THE SHOOTING

On December 14, 2012, in Newtown, Connecticut, Adam Lanza woke up early. He was a 20-year-old man who had never grown up. He was about six feet tall but only 112 pounds and was known for the odd expression on his face, which sometimes looked like the screamer in Edvard Munch's famous painting. For three months, he had not been out of his bedroom and communicated with his mother only via email, though she was in the same house. His bedroom windows were covered by black plastic garbage bags and the room was like a dark cocoon. He spent most of his time in his bedroom playing video games and thinking about violent actions against others and against himself. In particular, he had long been planning to kill his mother and as many children as he could at the Sandy Hook Elementary School, not too far from his home.

Indeed, a man had reported to the Newtown police four years earlier that Adam had told him that he planned on killing his mother and some elementary school children in Sandy Hook Elementary School, but the police did not take the man's complaint seriously. They pointed out that all the guns in the house were registered to Nancy, Adam's mother. They thought the kid was simply being dramatic, as kids are prone to do.

He had been planning it for years and warning people about it, but nobody had tried to stop him. Now the day had come. After he awoke, at around 6:30, he took a quick shower and washed his face thoroughly with a hot washrag, combed his hair, shaved, and dressed. He put on his black jeans, a black T-shirt, a black Polo shirt, a black beanie hat, an olive-green utility vest, black socks, boots, fingerless gloves and sunglasses. He then spent about 30 minutes checking out the guns he was going to take to the Sandy Hook Elementary School. These included a Saiga 12-gauge semiautomatic shotgun, a Bushmaster .223-caliber semiautomatic rifle, a Glock 20 10mm semiautomatic handgun, and a Sig Sauer 9mm semiautomatic handgun. He also had ten magazines that each held 30 rounds as well as ample ammunition for the shotgun and handguns.

There were probably no thoughts about the future or of the past, no thoughts about the meaning of life or of the consequences of what he was about to do. His thoughts were most likely only about what he would do in the next moment and what he would do in the moment after that. Nor did he have any feelings about what he was going to do; he was completely numb and without feelings and had lived that way for years.

After loading his arsenal, he set it all on the table and then picked up a Savage Mark II .22 caliber rifle, unlocked his bedroom door, and walked down the hall into his mother's bedroom. He found her sleeping in her pajamas on her side, with her face turned toward the door as he walked in. He stood there bedside and aimed the rifle at her eyes, pulling the trigger four times, completely obliterating his mother's face. After those four shots, he looked at his mother's face for a moment, saw that it was a bloody pulp, and hurried back out the door into the hallway. If he felt anything at all, it was a probably only a degree of release and some satisfaction of revenge.

In his bedroom, he put the two pistols in the pockets of his jackets and he grabbed the shotgun and semiautomatic rifle in his two hands and headed out the door to his mother's car. He drove her car to the Sandy Hook Elementary School, which he had attended 14 years earlier. It was five miles away and as he drove, he probably envisioned in his mind what he was going to do when he got there. He was ready. He had been ready for a long time.

Shortly after 9:35 a.m., Adam took his mother's Bushmaster rifle and shot his way through the locked front entrance doors of the school. Students heard the initial shots on the school intercom system, which was being used for morning announcements, and students probably froze in their seats and looked around at one another and at their teachers. Adam kicked open the doors and entered the school with the semiautomatic in one arm and the shotgun in the other. He eyed the doors of the classrooms as he headed down the hall in his all black garb and his sunglasses.

Principal Dawn Hochsprung and school psychologist Mary Sherlach were in a meeting in an office near the front door when they heard the shots. They did not recognize that they were gunshots. Hochsprung, Sherlach, and teacher Natalie Hammond went into the hall to determine the source of the sounds and encountered Lanza. He peered at them through his shades.

"Shooter! Stay put!" Sherlach yelled out.

"Shooter! Shooter! Lock your doors!" the other two women repeated.

Adam lifted the semiautomatic and fired at the three women and killed two of them. He most likely did not did care when they fell to the floor. He simply walked on. He did not care how they felt or what they thought or who they loved. He was too deeply weighed down and dumbed up with rage to care about anything at all. He was angry as a human being can be. He was in stage 3 rage.

Hochsprung and Sherlach were dead. Hammond had superficial wounds and pretended to be dead. She lay still in the hallway and waited until Adam had walked down the hall before crawling back to the conference room and pressing her body against the door to keep it closed.

The school janitor, Rick Thorne, came out of his room, saw Adam, and yelled, "Put the gun down!"

"I don't think so," Adam said.

The janitor ran back into his room and locked the door.

The whole school was now listening on the intercom, which was left on. People could hear Adam walking and all his shots. Teachers were locking their classroom doors from the inside and hiding their students in bathrooms, closets, and cabinets.

As he walked down the hall, people heard Adam say "Put your hands up!" and someone else say "Don't shoot!"

Diane Day, a substitute kindergarten teacher, was closing her door further down the hallway, when Adam came around the corner and shot her in the foot. She ran back into her classroom and Adam kept walking toward the main office.

He entered the main office but did not see the people hiding inside. School nurse Sarah Cox, was hiding under a desk. She later described seeing the door opening and Adam's boots and legs facing her desk. He remained standing for a few seconds before pivoting and going back into the hallway. She and the school secretary, Barbara Halstead, called the police and hid in a first aid supply closet for the next four hours.

When Adam disappeared down the hallway, Janitor Rick Thorne came back out of his office and ran through hallways, yelling, "School Shooter! Shooter in the hallways!"

Then Adam began to enter one classroom after another. He entered

Room 8 first. It was a first grade classroom where Lauren Rousseau, a substitute teacher, had herded her first grade students to the back of the room and was trying to hide them in a bathroom. As soon as Lanza entered the classroom, he began shooting without warning. He shot Rousseau, Rachel D'Avino (a behavioral therapist who had been employed for a week to work with special-needs students), and fifteen regular students, all six and seven years old. The children looked up at the man shooting and some called out, "Please," and "Wait!" and "I have to go to the bathroom."

One of the little boys said to Adam, "Help me! I don't want to be here!"

"Well, you're here," Adam replied, and shot him.

The children were rushing into the bathroom, looking around with their frightened eyes, not understanding what or why this was happening. In a moment, fourteen of them were dead and one, in the back corner, was playing dead. Afterward the student who played dead was found by the police and she ran to her mother.

"Mommy, I'm OK," she said, "But all my friends are dead."

Lanza then went to Room 10, another first grade classroom and opened the door. The teacher, Victoria Soto, had concealed some of the students in a closet and some in a bathroom, and had told other students to hide under desks. Soto was walking back to the classroom door to lock it when Adam entered. "Stop!" she yelled at Adam.

"Sorry, no," he said.

"You're a monster," she said.

"I know," he said.

Soto ran back and stood in front of some students in the back corner and Adam shot her and the students. He saw the children under the desks, and began shooting them. A boy named Jesse Lewis shouted at his classmates.

"Run, everybody, run." He was the leader of the class.

His friends ran but he did not.

He gazed for a moment at Adam and then tried to run for safety while Adam was putting a new magazine in his gun. Before he could get to the door, Adan fatally shot him. Adam then stared at the remaining children on the floor, pointed the gun at a boy seated there, but did not fire. He stared at the boy and slowly blinked his eyes. The boy ran out of the classroom. It appeared he had killed enough. One of the boys who got away later described Adam as "A very angry man. I was so scared of him. I've never been so scared in my life!"

In all, six of the children who escaped from Soto's classroom did so when Lanza stopped shooting, either because his weapon jammed or he was having trouble reloading it. Anne Marie Murphy, the special education teacher who worked with special-needs students in Soto's classroom, was later found covering another student, six-year-old Dylan Hockley, who had been shot and later died. Soto and four children were found dead in the classroom. One child was taken to the hospital, but was later pronounced dead. Six surviving children from the class and a school bus driver took refuge at a nearby home. Nine children ran from Soto's classroom, and police found two hiding in a bathroom.

The whole scene took about five minutes. The police arrived by then, and when they arrived, they heard a final shot. This was at 9:41 a.m. They believed that it was Adam shooting himself, but they were not sure.

Adam had stopped shooting after he finished the second magazine. At that time, he let the rest of the children go, and he went back out to the hallway, turned into Classroom 10, which was empty, and pulled out the Glock 20SF. From the time he had gotten to the school, he had probably felt nothing and thought only about what he was going to do in the next moment. Only at the very end, when he had shot enough children to feed his rage, did he begin to care about the children he had killed to the slightest degree. That is when he stopped shooting.

He had by then reached the kill point and had done as much murdering as he needed in order to assuage and discharge his pent-up rage, to feel human again and to care about his victims.

A lifetime of neglect, abuse and scorn had caused Adam to develop feelings of low self-esteem and worthlessness, and the accumulated pain caused him to go into stage 3 rage. Now, afterwards, he was most likely left with feelings of alienation and despair about what he had done—not to mention fear of reprisal. This took him to the deepest agony a human can experience: suicide. His decision had already been made beforehand and killing himself ended his agony and deprived society of a means to punish him for his deed. It was his grand finale, as though he were crying out, "You did this to me and you have gotten what you deserve."

Adam shot himself in the lower rear portion of his head and sank to the floor. His body was found lying face down in a pool of blood. The sunglasses and beanie were lying a few feet away. The Glock was found, apparently jammed, near the body, and the rifle and shotgun were nearby. Another handgun had not fired during the incident and was found in his pocket.

ADAM LANZA'S FAMILY AND LIFE

Adam Lanza became a mass killer because of the unfortunate way he was raised, and because of the disturbed culture that he was born into.

Voltaire, the French author, once said, "Man is not born wicked; he becomes so as he becomes sick." The psychiatric establishment of 20th Century America disagreed with Voltaire and for the most part insisted that people with mental disturbances were born that way. While most of the reports about Adam Lanza following the mass shooting focused on his mental disturbances, they generally assumed, in line with the psychiatric establishment, that those disturbances were genetic or bio-logical.

Adam Lanza was born in Newtown, Connecticut on April 22, 1992 to Nancy and Peter Lanza. His father was an accountant who worked as a Tax Director for GE Energy Financial Services in New York. His mother was briefly a stock broker at a firm in Boston. His older brother, Ryan, was four years older and was doing well in college. Adam displayed symptoms of developmental arrests before the age of three, which included communication and sensory processing difficulties, socialization delays, and repetitive behavior, such as repeating the same phrase over and over. He was also late to start speaking, which skill did not happen until he was three, and he was reported to dislike physical contact of any kind, particularly hugs. All of these symptoms might have been indicative of autism—and years later he was diagnosed with Asperger syndrome, a mild degree of autism. Before the age of three, he participated in the New Hampshire Birth-to-Three Intervention Program where he received preschool special education services.

The cause of autism has been heavily debated over the years. Mainstream child psychologists and pediatrists have theorized about an array of causes—vaccines, childhood diseases, genetics, certain antidepressants—but they have never seriously considered disturbed parenting. Anyone who tries to say that disturbed parenting is a causal factor of autism is quickly attacked as a quack; neither mainstream professionals nor the public in general want hear that the behavior of depressed mothers may be a cause of autism, and this defensive element of society is quick to protect mothers from anything that smacks of criticism.

However, much recent research centers on the connection between maternal depression—specifically postpartum depression—and autism. I have cited a sampling of this research in a recent book, *Forbidden Psychology: A Book for Dark Minds*. For example, a study in *European*

Psychiatry in 2010 is one of numerous studies that found a link between postnatal depression and autism. The study gave 291 women a battery of surveys, including the Edinburg Postnatal Depression Scale at 6 and 12 months after giving birth, and the Modified Checklist for Autism in Toddlers at around 18 months after giving birth. Self-reported postpartum depression in the mother at 12 months was highly linked with the presence of autism in children at 18 months. Numerous studies like this now exist, but are kept hidden from the public eye by a media intent on protecting mothers and parents, but not babies.

Did Nancy Lanza have postpartum depression? We can only deduce that she did suffer from it, from what we learn from later descriptions of her personality. We know that she was depressed throughout her marriage and afterwards. We know that Peter Lanza was a workaholic who practically lived at his job and only came home for weekends; hence he did not provide much support in taking care of his wife or baby Adam. Nancy probably felt unsupported during pregnancy and angry with her husband during and after birth—and she may have had traumas related to her own birth, which would make her more prone to postpartum depression. From reports of witnesses, Peter seemed to favor his older son Ryan, who he spent more time with and who grew up to be somewhat healthy. By the time Adam was born, the father had become a workaholic and his marriage had deteriorated.

The marriage was troubled from the time Adam was born, and Peter and Nancy divorced in 1992, when Adam was six years old. Adam was deeply affected by the divorce, and a few years later, he abruptly stopped speaking to both his father and his brother. After the mass killing, Peter remarked that he was sure Adam "would have killed me in a minute." He was aware that Adam hated him. The question is why? The possible answer is that Adam may have experienced his father as rejecting. Nancy was embroiled in this toxic marriage at the time Adam was born, and this likely was distracting and depressing to her. From what we know of her life after the divorce, it appears she continued to be depressed, splitting her time between bars and shooting galleries.

When mothers suffer from depression or postpartum depression, they often become sullen, lethargic and resentful. They are angry at their fathers, their husbands or the world, and they take out that anger on their infant sons. They feel that their husbands are off doing a job they love and getting rewarded by promotions, whereas they are left to perform what they see as a maid's job of changing smelly diapers and blowing driveling noses and ministering to a demanding and crying baby. Depressed mothers are preoccupied with their own misery, and they are unable to be attentive to their infants. They do not go to the child when he is crying, do not feed him when he is hungry and do not hold him when he is squawking to be held. Such mothers are in a funk, and they sometimes lie in bed for days at a time, weeks at a time and even months at a time. Their anger overwhelms them and they become intolerant of the baby's crying and may rock the crib too roughly to make him quiet down—which sometimes results in the "shaken baby syndrome," a syndrome that can cause permanent brain damage. Neglectful and angry mothering can go on for months, and when it does, the seeds of autism are laid. The infant learns that he cannot depend on his caretaker, that his caretaker is not interested in him. Thus, he turns away from her and from people.

Maternal depression can last a month or a year. When the depression ends, mothers typically feel guilty about the way they have neglected their baby. They snap out of it as they realize that their baby has been damaged, and they fear that others—doctors, their husband, their relatives—will find out about their neglect. Then they suddenly become very overprotective toward their child to make up for their previous neglect. When doctors meet such a mother, who is so eager to help her son, they cannot doubt that whatever ails the son could not have come from such a caring mother. There were many reports by experts—who treated Adam for his Asperger syndrome, obsessive-compulsive disorder and other disturbances—that Nancy Lanza was overprotective to Adam, of her refusing to follow a doctor's advice because she was afraid it would be hurtful to Adam, taking him out of school because she disagreed with the advice of the schools. She was overprotective and she was in denial. She did not want to hear what experts said about her son. According to reports, she and her son lived in a cocoon together, in which she enabled him and would not listen to anybody else, including her husband, about how to raise her child.

Nancy Lanza probably had some combination of depression and paranoia. She seemed to believe she and only she knew what medicine to give her son; she was convinced that she knew better than any medical authority. And she was suspicious about what doctors were doing, always quick to believe that it was harmful. In February 2007, when he was 14, Yale clinicians identified in Adam Lanza what they believed were profound emotional disabilities and offered him treatment that they said could give him relief for the first time in his troubled life. Nancy refused this advice and took him home to care for him in her way. A clinician from Yale wrote to Peter Lanza in desperation. She told him that "Adam has a biological disorder that can be helped with medication." She told him what the medicines are and why they can work. She told him that his son was "living in a box right now and the box will only get smaller over time if he doesn't get some treatment." Peter heard but could not get through to his wife. Since doctors determined it was a biological disorder, nobody tried to understand how the boy was feeling or why he was feeling it.

Nancy spent almost all her free time hanging out in a local bar, where people knew her to be happy-go-lucky Nancy. She drank away her sorrow in the bar and at other times went to shooting ranges, and nobody at the bar thought there was anything unusual about any of it. People in bars tend to enable other drinkers and all of their idiosyncrasies, and this seemed to be the case with her. Over the years, she collected an array of rifles, handguns, scopes, and other kinds of arsenal. She went to the shooting ranges frequently. She was obsessed with guns and shooting, and she most often took her son with her to the shooting range, apparently with no concerns about how being raised in shooting ranges would affect him. According to reports, she had the paranoid fear that she would not live long and that a disaster would befall her—for example, that bad people were out to kill her. Perhaps, on some unconscious level, she feared that her son, Adam, would kill her. And yet, by taking her son to the shooting range and teaching him all about shooting, she was unwittingly training him to be a shooter.

Ever since the age of three, when his developmental arrests were first discovered, she had protected him and given him everything he wanted. Every day she told him how much she loved him and how much she cared about him. Every day she smiled at him and told him everything would be all right. But the smiley face she showed him contradicted the fact that she was never interested in knowing about his deepest feelings. He was full of rage and loneliness, but she never asked about it. He was cut off and uncommunicative, but she never probed him about it; instead she smiled and coddled him. During his adolescence, he began collecting a library of information about mass killers, but she never inquired about it. She said she loved him, but she didn't know him at all and didn't want to know him. She appeased him, and this extreme need to appease him did not suggest to him that she loved him, but rather that she was afraid of him.

Once, when she hired a baby sitter to take care of him, she told the sitter, "Don't look at Adam in the eyes. If you do he will give you an evil eye." The more bizarre her son became, the more she tried to appease him. After a time, he began to see her as more helpless and more in need than himself. She looked at him with a smiley face that he did not believe and that he grew to hate, just as one can sometimes hate a clown's smiley face and be afraid of it. Later, he would shoot her in that face.

Once the father was out of the way, she developed an almost symbiotic relationship with her second son. She coddled him and catered to all his wants and whims. But after her divorce, she sank into another depression and was not really there for him emotionally. Instead, Adam seemed to have become her therapist-figure. When he was 16, after his mother had complained to him that she thought she had wasted her life, he wrote her an email:

> If you believe that you wasted your life, as you seem to have insinuated, you will gain nothing from regretting it and will only depress yourself; you cannot change anything from the past. There is something I can assure you of that will always be true: It does not matter if you live for the next one year … or even 100 years, the day before you die, you will regret ever worrying about your life instead of thinking of what you want to do. I am glad that I was born, and I appreciate your having taken care of me.

In this letter, Adam displays a verbal assurance that was in contrast to his social isolation, and it is perhaps a signal of his growing narcissism. It shows that while his mother took care of him, his job was also to take care of her and to be her surrogate therapist; and he would listen to her and, indeed, advise her like a wise mentor. In his narcissistic bubble, he apparently viewed himself as a superior being. His job was to listen to her woes and advise her, but meanwhile, he had to keep his darker and disturbed self from her and never talk of it. In reality, he needed her much more than she needed him, but he had to stroke her lagging self-esteem and be satisfied with what he got from her. She had probably never been loved or appreciated herself, and so she did not have true love to give.

After Adam's initial emotional difficulties were recognized by the

New Hampshire Birth-to- Three intervention program, his life became a series of dealing with one mental problem after another. At the age of three, he was referred to special education preschool services. From there he went into the first grade of elementary school, where he was diagnosed with a sensory processing disorder—a disorder that does not have official status by the medical community as a formal diagnosis but is a common characteristic of autism. Throughout elementary school, he had trouble not only with school work but with getting along with peers. He suffered from extreme anxiety, which affected his attendance at school, where he was being bullied. By the 8th grade, he was placed on "homebound" status, which is reserved for children who are too disabled—even with supports and accommodations—to attend school.

It wasn't until he was 13 that Adam was diagnosed with Asperger syndrome by a psychiatrist named Paul Fox. At 14, he was taken to Yale University's Child Study Center, where he was diagnosed with obsessive-compulsive disorder. He reportedly washed his hands and changed his socks 20 times a day, changed his underwear ten times a day, took five to ten showers a day, changed his towels and bed linen each time he showered, and generally ran through clothes and accessories from hour to hour—to the point where his mother did three loads of laundry a day. He also sometimes went through a box of tissues in a day because he could not touch a doorknob with his bare hand. He had phobias about germs and he also was fascinated by the topic of pedophilia, expressing the opinion that man-boy sex might be helpful for both the adult and the child. He may also have had homosexual tendencies, although there is no evidence that he ever engaged in sex with anybody.

At Yale, Adam was treated by Robert King, who recommended extensive support be put in place and prescribed the antidepressant Celexa. He took the medication for three days, then decided he couldn't stand it. "On the third morning he complained of dizziness," Nancy reported to Dr. King. "He was disoriented, his speech was disjointed, he couldn't even figure out how to open his cereal box." His mother told him to stop the medication. Medications often take a week or more to become effective, which she was told, but which information she disregarded. A later report from the Office of the Child Advocate found that "Yale's recommendations for extensive special education supports, ongoing expert consultation, and rigorous therapeutic supports embedded into (Lanza's) daily life went largely unheeded."

In 2013, Peter Lanza said in an interview that he suspected his son might have also had undiagnosed schizophrenia in addition to his other conditions. Peter said that family members might have missed signs of the onset of schizophrenia and psychotic behavior during his son's adolescence because they mistakenly attributed his odd behavior and increasing isolation to Asperger syndrome. He noted that autism advocates were concerned that published accounts of Adam's autism might result in a backlash against others with the condition, so they rushed to clarify that autism is a "brain-related disorder" rather than a mental illness. The violence Adam demonstrated in the mass shooting is generally not seen in the autistic population, and his psychiatrists, focusing on the autism, did not detect troubling signs of violence.

Peter Langman, wrote an article in *The Journal of Campus Behavioral Intervention* which diagnosed Adam with schizophrenia, noting that "The hypothesis that Lanza was schizophrenic originally was based on several behaviors and traits he exhibited that are associated with schizophrenia. These include the lack of expressed emotion (flat affect) and the failure to speak in situations where speech would be appropriate and expected (poverty of speech)." He added that "other aspects of his functioning are consistent with a diagnosis of schizophrenia. For example, he had an extreme sensitivity to lights and sounds, yet also had a marked decrease in sensitivity to pain." Peter Lanza, Adam's father, also believed he had schizophrenia, but he could not convince his wife.

A report by the Office of the Child Advocate detailed many of the vicissitudes of Nancy Lanza's relationship to her son and to the health providers who tried to treat him. Nancy Lanza lived with Adam in an affluent neighborhood in the east end of town. She did not have a job but received $289,800 a year in alimony from Peter Lanza. Her son seemed to be her main preoccupation, but, according to the report, she was an impediment to treatments he needed. In Adam's two most significant opportunities for meaningful psychiatric treatment—an evaluation at the Danbury Hospital emergency room in September 2005, and a complete work-up by clinicians at the Yale Child Study Center the following year—Nancy rejected expert advice and further isolated her son by keeping him at home and away from school. At Danbury Hospital, she declined an extensive medical evaluation and psychiatric examination of Adam, who was at the time suffering from overwhelming anxiety. Instead, she asked for a note excusing him from school indefinitely. When she didn't get her wish, she took Adam home anyway. At Yale in October 2006, a psychiatrist examined Adam at Peter Lanza's urging. The doctor noted Adam's social withdrawal and concluded that Adam suffered from OCD and severe social disabilities and would benefit from intensive therapy. The psychiatric nurse at the center reached similar conclusions about what she called his "increasingly constricted social and educational world." But Nancy, suffering from her own depression and paranoia, could not heed the experts.

"Mom, I don't want to go to that clinic anymore," Adam complained.

"Why?" his mother asked.

"They don't understand me. They haven't a clue as to who I am."

"Then you shouldn't go there anymore."

Nancy pulled Adam out of treatment at the Yale center, saying that the diagnosis "didn't fit" and that her son didn't want to go to the sessions.

Nancy also took Adam out of school and lived with him in isolation. Shunning the advice of the Danbury Hospital and Yale, she believed that she knew exactly what was best. She would only listen to one psychiatrist, who told her that Adam was a candidate for the "homebound" program, which would allow him to be tutored by her at home. In investigating the matter, the report stated that they found no evidence of a treatment or education plan for Adam, and that there was no record that he even received the 10 hours a week of tutoring required.

"In the face of disabilities that were so significant as to apparently justify [Adam's] lack of attendance for the entire school year," the report noted, "it does not appear that anyone questioned why, if he was so debilitated, he was never hospitalized or referred for specialized educational placement."

As mental health professionals tried to understand Adam's mental disturbances, they were not aware of his violent writings as a boy, which might have given them clues. A comic book he wrote in the sixth grade called "The Big Book of Granny," chronicles the evil adventures of a homicidal, gun-toting grandmother. There were eight chapters in the book, which could be summarized thusly: Chapter 1: Granny and Granny's son rub a bank. Granny shoots people with her rifle cane, and then blows up the bank with dynamite. After the robbery, Granny shoots her son in the head with a shotgun. Chapter 2: Granny and son go on a boat, she falls out, and the son tosses her a cement floatation device which causes her to sink to the bottom of the ocean. Chapter 3. Granny and Granny's son capture a boy and stuff him and put him on the fireplace mantle. Then Granny throws the boy into the fireplace and tries to burn him. The boy jumps out of the fire and punches her in the face. Then Granny shoots at the boy three times but misses him. Granny then throws an action figure at the boy and the boy says, "Yay, now we can hang it!" Chapter 5. Granny goes to Marine boot camp where she meets Dora the Beserker. Granny asks Dora if she will assassinate a soldier at midnight. Dora says she likes hurting people, especially children.

If we assume that Granny represented Adam's mother (who frequented shooting ranges and conveyed her anger at the world to her son), then one can surmise from the story how violent his thoughts were about his mother. He wrote other essays about battles, destruction and war during a short stint in the seventh grade at the St. Rose of Lima School in Newtown. These writings showed that Adam was deeply troubled by feelings of rage, hate and murder. A teacher at the St. Rose of Lima school said that "Adam's level of violence was disturbing. I remember showing his writings to the principal." He added that his "writing was so graphic that it could not be shared." When the school pointed out these writings to Nancy, she decided to take him out of the parochial school.

After spending a year in the homebound program, Adam returned to school as a freshman at Newtown High School. He spent two years there marked by some social progress and an effort by teachers and administrators to accommodate him in regular classes. Nancy convinced the school to cater to Adam's needs and they tried. The teachers there believed they were 'thinking outside the box' for Adam, and making great efforts to meet his needs through a careful partnership with his mother. But the partnership was a strategy of appeasement, without a skilled, therapeutic, expert-driven approach that would help Adam adapt to the world. Instead they adapted to Adam's world and enabled him to live his extremely introverted and unsocialized style of life. This approach of relating to a patient on his terms might have worked if they had gradually introduced, in a loving way, reality to him, but they did not; this was an approach that a psychoanalyst named Margaret Mahler used with much success during her study of Autistic children. However, after two years, Nancy took him out of this school.

The only thing that diverted him from this reclusive lifestyle was his passion for a video game called, Dance Revolution, in which the player dances in response to video cues. Adam had to go to the lobby of a movie theater to play this game, where he would dance "maniacally" for many hours at a time, neglecting to eat and stopping only to wipe off his dripping perspiration. The theater manager had to eventually unplug the game to get Adam to leave, because Adam "could become so lost in the activity that he would not respond to communication," the Office of the Child Advocate report said. Playing this game apparently served to partially discharge the anger he had inside him.

After leaving high school, he took classes at two local colleges but his increasing social phobias, declining physical health, and an argument with his father about his course load, drove him back home to a period of unparalleled isolation.

He appears to have had no contact with mental health providers after 2006. The report from the Office of the Child Advocate, written after the murders, stated: "In the course of Lanza's entire life, minimal mental health evaluation and treatment (in relation to his apparent need) was obtained." Nancy Lanza protected her son from what she saw as misguided health providers, and by doing so she kept him from the very help that might have saved him. Unfortunately, she herself may have been just as disturbed as her son, but nobody thought to suggest psychotherapy for her.

As she became obsessed with guns and going to shooting ranges, her main contact with her son was to take him shooting. She taught him how to shoot the arsenal of guns she had collected and instructed him on the need for protecting himself. They visited the shooting range regularly and during those visits she may have imbued him with her own anger at the world. When someone spends their life at shooting ranges: they are most often, in their mind, shooting down enemies over and over. His mother acted to all the world and to her son as if she was a loving, doting parent, but what her son saw when she presented him with her smiling face up close, was a lost woman whose bright smile covered her deep depression. She could not help him and could not know him.

In his teenage years, Lanza became fascinated with mass shootings, such as the Columbine High School massacre (1999), the Virginia Tech shooting (2007) and the Northern Illinois University shooting (2008). Among the clippings found in his room, there was a story from *The New York Times* about a man who shot at school children in 1891. His computer contained two videos of gunshot suicides, movies that showed school shootings and two pictures of Lanza pointing guns at his own head. A document titled "Selfish," describing Adam's belief in the inherent selfishness of women, was found on his computer. And, most telling, there was a comprehensive chart of mass killings in America, including who did the murder and what kind of weapon was used.

According to the report by the Office of the Child Advocate, Adam may also have had anorexia nervosa in his later teenage years. The report notes that "Anorexia can produce cognitive impairment and it is likely that anorexia combined with an autism spectrum disorder and OCD compounded Lanza's risk for suicide." While he was tall and skinny, it is not known if he took laxatives or had body dysmorphia. Once his mother had permanently taken him out of school, he was spending most of his time on the internet playing World of Warcraft and other video games. He descended into a dark place where his only communication with the outside world was with members of a cyber community that shared his dark and obsessive interest in mass murder. They would discuss the latest mass killing and express their thoughts about it and Adam expressed the idea that mass murders were going to increase. "In the future, there will be hundreds of them," he said.

During that time, he wrote in his journal, "I incessantly have nothing but scorn for humanity. I have been desperate to feel anything positive for anyone in my life." This was written in an email to his mother, and he seemed to be saying to her that he did not feel anything positive for her. Apparently, she ignored this letter.

In the weeks before the killings, Lanza's mother's infantilizing of her son reached a new level, as she was considering moving him to another town, believing it would be good for him to get away from Newtown. She planned to purchase a recreational vehicle for him to stay in. When she told Adam about this plan, which would take him out of the comfort zone of his room, this may have been the final factor that prodded Adam into action. James Knoll, a forensic psychiatrist at SUNY Upstate Medical University, was consulted about what motivated Lanza to kill. Knoll stated that Lanza's final act conveyed a distinct message: "I carry profound hurt — I'll go ballistic and transfer it onto you."

CULTURAL FACTORS

Adam Lanza was a disturbed boy who was further oppressed by a disturbed culture. America was the most violent culture in the world and in his teenage years it must have seemed as if there was a new mass killing each week. He became fascinated with these mass shootings and he was obviously affected by them. He found a cyber community that spent all its time discussing these mass shootings, almost as if they were casual events like baseball games, and the community followed the various mass shooters, saving clipping about them the same way baseball fans collect cards about their heroes. Mass killers were the heroes of these angry boys.

A year before he committed the murders, he called a radio station, according to a report in the *New York Daily News*. The radio show was discussing mass murders, focusing on the most recent one on January 8, 2011, in which U.S. Representative Gabby Giffords and 18 others were shot during a meeting held in a supermarket parking lot in Casas Adobes, Arizona. Six people were killed, including federal District Court Chief Judge John Roll; Gabe Zimmerman, one of Giffords's staffers; and a 9-year-old girl, Christina-Taylor Green. Giffords was holding the meeting, called "Congress on Your Corner," in the parking lot of a Safeway store when Jared Lee Loughner drew a pistol and shot her in the head before proceeding to fire on other people. Giffords was shot at point-blank range, and her medical condition was initially described as "critical," but she survived. Hearing the radio discussion of this event, in which the host expressed the hope that this would be the last shooting, Adam called in and said, "Hey listen, there is going to be another shooting, there is going to be another outbreak of violence." Nobody took him seriously.

Nothing in his life excited him more than mass killings. Each mass killing that he witnessed and the way in which the killings stunned and shocked the country no doubt gave him courage. He noted that most of the killers committed suicide after their deeds and went out in a blaze of notoriety. Their pictures were all over the headlines and everybody wanted to know who they were and why they had done what they had done. For as long as Adam had been alive, nobody had wanted to know him. He was full of rage, but nobody wanted to know about this rage. If he had told anybody he hated his mother, they wouldn't have taken him seriously. He had to keep his real personality hidden in the dark of his room, and the only outlet for his rage was to play the Revolution Dance Video game in the lobby of a movie theater and to fantasize about how he was going to someday shock the world by killing as many school children as he could and, like other shooters that he idolized, go out with dark glory. It was a comfort to him that there was a way for him to show how he felt. Only then would the world finally want to know him.

Adam was painfully aware of how disturbed American culture was and quite articulate about how that disturbance had affected him. He once wrote to his mother:

> Thinking of this society as the default state of existence is the reason why you think that humans would be 'not well' for 'no reason whatsoever.' Civilization has not been present for 99% of the existence of hominids, and the only way that it's ever

sustained is by indoctrinating each new child for years on end. The 'wellness' that you speak of is solely defined by a child's submission to this process and their subsequent capacity to propagate civilization themselves. When civilization exists in a form where all forms of alienation (among many other things) are rampant, as can be seen in the most recent incarnation within the past fifty years, children will end up 'not well' in all sorts of ways. You don't even have to touch a topic as cryptic as mass murder to see an indication of this: you can look at a single symptom as egregious as the proliferation of antidepressants. And look at your own life. You've said that you're afflicted by unrelenting anxiety, and you're afraid to leave your house. Do you really think that the way you feel is not symptomatic of anything other than your own inexplicable defectiveness?

This piece of writing might well be Adam's self-written obituary. It displays his brilliance at a young age, his capacity to think deeply about things and to articulate better than almost any of the so-called experts who attempted to analyze him after his death. In this piece, he offers an explanation for how he became who he was. "When civilization exists in a form where all forms of alienation…are rampant…children will end up 'not well' in all sorts of ways." He has clearly understood that his own "inexplicable defectiveness" is related to the defectiveness of American culture. He refers to symptoms such as alienation and to the proliferation of antidepressants. He knew that America's sick culture was a big part of the reason why he was "unwell"—a word probably used about him by the people who tried to treat him. Adam guessed that people who kept telling him he was unwell were too caught up in that sick culture themselves to be able to see the real causes of why he was unwell.

He followed each new mass killing in America and studied the shooter's personality. In an email to a fellow devotee from his cyber community, he wrote:

As far as the Holmies go [James Holmes], well the gif of him dancing on a llama was cute. I guess that's about all I can say about the Holmie thing since I don't really relate to it. I don't understand why there weren't the "he's just a poor misunderstood puppy who needs help" type flocking around Jerod Loughner since that spiel ostensibly applied to him more than James Holmes. And speaking more generally, I don't understand why the Aurora shooting was considered such a big deal all around, as if such a thing had never happened before. It's not like it's 1984.

His casualness about these shooters is a kind of gallows casualness, the function of which is to defend against the excitement and rage that the endless string of mass shootings had aroused in him. His preoccupation with it may have been due to the fantasies that had gone on in his own heart for many years and were constrained with great difficulty. The fascination with mass shooting heroes such as Holmes and Loughner held out hope for him. It kept the notion in his back pocket that he had an escape plan. He was lost, and wanted to be found and the happenings in culture reminded him there was one last way to be found. These mass killings may have told him that only by such an extreme act could he ever get people to listen to him. The constant strife in American culture added more turmoil to that which had already been aroused by his upbringing and gave him a direction to channel his rage.

He was a boy in a culture that had forgotten about boys, the son of a mother who tried mightily to hide her hate for him and a father who may have never felt anything for him at all. They both tried, but they were apparently held back by their own disturbances.

FINAL ANALYSIS

Killers are the products of childhoods and cultures that have conditioned them to kill. Boys born in mafia families and raised by male figures that are callous and matter-of-fact about killing, learn to be callous and matter-of-fact about it themselves. Soldiers are conditioned by military training and by their culture to kill the enemy without compassion. Those, like Adam, who become mass killers are also unwittingly bred to become killers. They have the childhood of an unwanted child, in which they are neglected and told they have not been neglected, abused and told they have not been abused, and laughed at and told they have not been laughed at. This causes the buildup of inner pain. When the boy cannot talk about this pain and there is no redress, the pain grows. Year after year the pain grows and turns inward. Eventually, the psychological pain is covered over by a psychological scab. The pain transforms into a numbness and to an absence of feelings. But beneath this numbness, the hidden pain festers. Eventually, this inner pain becomes intolerable and must find release in the form of an explosion: the mass killing.

Adam Lanza had the misfortune of being born into a dysfunctional family as well as a dysfunctional culture. It appears that his older brother, Bryan was the luckier of the two, being the first born, which meant his childhood happened when the marriage was still superficially all right. In the case of the Lanza family, it appeared to have been fairly functional for Ryan, who went on to be a somewhat normal child; but then a few years later, the Lanza family was quite dysfunctional for Adam. The crucial period of parental nurturing is in early childhood, from birth to about the age of seven. According to Bowlby and Mahler, during this period a child goes through crucial, formative stages of development that culminate in independence and autonomy. Ryan likely went through these stages and had a healthy start to life, but Adam did not.

What probably went on in Adam's early childhood, based on inferred data and knowledge of similar cases, was that Adam came along at the wrong time. When he was born, the marriage was apparently starting to fall apart. By all accounts, it appeared that Adam was an unexpected baby and of the wrong sex. Having had a boy, Nancy wanted a girl. By then, her anger at her father and husband had grown and she probably was caught in the grip of a rage-fueled depression. These factors may have caused her to be disappointed and also depressed during the months after delivery. Peter had become a workaholic and Nancy must have complained about his absence from home and about the fact that he was not being supportive of her. They may also have fought over parenting roles. She was an angry woman (as evidenced by her later obsession with shooting ranges), and the anger at that time may have taken the form of irritation at him for not helping her with the new baby. He, in turn, may have complained that she was coddling their younger son. The fact that Adam later developed symptoms of autism such as sensory processing difficulties, repetitive behaviors, dislike of physical contact and the delayed development of talking, indicated that Nancy may possibly have suffered from postpartum depression and had therefore not been attentive to the needs of Adam. When an infant does not get fed, receive physical contact and get changed by the mother or caretaker, the infant starts to turn inwards and go into a shell. The delay of talking was an indication of the formation of this autistic shell. "Nobody's interested in me, so I'm not coming out," such a child might be feeling.

Limited by her own disturbances and depression, she could not relate to her son as a separate being but only as an accessory to herself. As he grew older, Adam began to notice the neediness of his mother and played the role she recruited him to play, that of her caretaker. She could not take care of him the way he needed to be taken care of because she was too needy herself to take care of anyone else. She rejected the advice of psychologists at Yale and numerous other places, as well as the advice of his schools, because of her apparent need for him to be bonded with her and her only. She probably meant well and did what she thought would help him, but unconsciously, she may have kept him out of school and out of treatment centers because she wanted him dependent on her and attending to her. She was almost as reclusive as her son was. After the divorce, she seldom invited anybody to her house, and she lived in her house with him almost like a weird married couple. Her own depression fueled his depression and his depression in turn fueled hers.

He was an Oedipal conqueror (a boy who wins his mother's love from his father), but he was a damaged conqueror. And this situation may have hastened the separation of his parents. In a situation where the mother binds the son to herself and forms an exclusive club to which the father is not invited, the father is sometimes pushed away to the point of leaving the marriage. But his autism made him a conflicted Oedipal conqueror who was ambivalent about an attachment with Mom. He might have felt guilty about his exclusivity with his mother and come to believe, as happens in such cases, that his father's rejection was caused by his own closeness with Mom. If, as I have speculated, she suffered from depression during and immediately after Adam's birth, the Oedipal period with her son might have come during a brief respite in the depression. Later, out of guilt, she might have over-protected him, to compensate for the guilt she felt about neglecting him earlier. By then, any real bonding was no longer possible. It became an unreal relationship that was unconsciously geared for her convenience, not his.

His relationship with his mother was contradictory. She was the closest person to him, the one he confided in the most, and yet she was also the one he hated the most. However, he could never directly tell her about his deep hostility toward her. Telling her about that, he probably believed, would have sent her into a deeper depression, if not suicide. He wanted to spare her his wrath, but ironically, by not telling her about it, the wrath grew to the point where it could no longer be contained.

After Peter and Nancy Lanza separated and then divorced, Adam and his mother were each other's only significant relationship. And yet, he did not love her or anyone, as he noted when he wrote an email to her stating, "I have been desperate to feel something positive for anyone in my life." After the divorce in 2008, the relationship continued to be contradictory. Adam and his mother lived together but did not live together. He was cloistered in his room with the door locked, and she was in hers. And although they had their symbiotic relationship, it was conducted through emails. Nancy became increasingly depressed. During many evenings she hung out at a local bar and on others she went to a shooting range. She was in a depression that seemed to represent a congealed anger at her husband and perhaps went back to her own father, who may have abused her, and at the world. She was pulling away from her son while smiling lovingly at him and giving him everything he asked for, and he must have felt her pulling away and smiling away, and this may have hastened his plans for a mass killing.

Why did he want to kill little children? It was reported that he went through a period in which he was fascinated by pedophilia, but he also expressed to his mother his repugnance with doctors who had touched his penis as a boy. "Honestly," he wrote, "doctors touching my penis when I was a child was worse than it would be if I consented to an adult in a loving relationship with them," he wrote. "I don't see how I and every child was not raped by doctors: We did not consent to it. We only did it because our parents made us."

His early childhood was a nightmare of being touched but not cared about by doctors and of being neglected and overprotected and treated like a baby at home by his mother. His complaint about doctors touching his penis may have also been a disguised complaint about her emotionally incestuous relationship with him. Perhaps, therefore, he grew to envy privileged children at the Newtown Elementary School, who were all so happy and bright-eyed because they appeared to have been loved and understood in an appropriate way he never had. His mother volunteered at the school, and perhaps talked about these children in glowing terms while giving Adam her perfunctory fake smiles.

The story about Adam Lanza is a tragic one about a boy who did not get the attention he needed nor have a chance to find himself or to enjoy the gifts he had been born with. In a cautionary documentary about Lanza's life, Jeremy Veenstra-Vander Weele, MD, noted: "We need to be very conscious of what is going on in our children's worlds."

SOURCES

Bowlby, J. (1988). *A Secure Base*. New York: Basic Books.

Mahler, M., Pine, F., et al. (2000). Psychological Birth of the Human Infant: Symbiosis Individuation. New York: Basic Books.

Adam Lanza's Descent into Depravity. Documentary. Retrieved from: https://www.youtube.com/watch?v=Rwpb5VdG_u0

Sandy Hook Elementary School Shootings. In *Wikipedia*. Retrieved from: https://en.wikipedia.org/wiki/Sandy_Hook_Elementary_School_shooting

Adam Lanza. In Biography. Retrieved from: https://www.biography.com/crime-figure/adam-lanza

Adam Lanza, American Shooter. In *Britannica*. Retrieved from: https://www.britannica.com/biography/Adam-Lanza

Maya Salam, "Adam Lanza Threatened Sandy Hook Killings Years Before, Report Shows." In *New York Times*. Retrieved from: https://www.nytimes.com/2017/10/26/us/adam-lanza-sandy-hook.html

Ray Sanchez, "Unsealed FBI docs paint disturbing portrait of Sandy Hook Shooter Adam Lanza." In *CNN*. etrieved from: https://www.cnn.com/2017/10/24/us/sandy-hook-adam-lanza-unsealed-docs/index.html

Ralph Ellis, "Adam Lanza's Father in First Interview: He would have killed me in a "heart beat." In *CNN*. Retrieved from: https://www.cnn.com/2014/03/10/us/adam-lanzas-father-speaks/index.html

Scott Stump, "Adam Lanza's Father: 'I wish he had never been born.'" In *Today*. Retrieved from: https://www.today.com/news/adam-lanzas-father-i-wish-he-had-never-been-born-2D79346468

Mark Memmott, "Nancy Lanza, Gunman's Mother: From "Charmed Upbringing to First Victim." In *NPR*. Retrieved from: https://www.npr.org/sections/thetwo-way/2012/ 12/18/167527771/nancy-lanza-gunmans-mother-from-charmed-upbringing-to-first-victim

Michelle Welden, "Was Nancy Lanza a Monster or a Mother of One?" In *Women's News*. Retrieved from: https://womensenews.org/2012/12/was-nancy-lanza-monster-or-just-mother-one/

Nancy Lanza, Mother of Adam Lanza. In *Britannica*. Retrieved from: https://www.britannica.com/biography/Nancy-Lanza

Nancy Lanza. Biography. In. *IMDB*. Retrieved from: https://www.imdb.com/name/nm6954281/bio

Alaine Griffin and Josh Kovner, "Raising Adam Lanza: Who was Nancy Lanza?" In *PBS*. Retrieved from: https://www.pbs.org/wgbh/frontline/article/raising-adam-lanza/

"Report Reveals New Details about Newtown Shooter's History." In *CBS*. Retrieved from: https://www.cbsnews.com/news/adam-lanza-newtown-school-shooter-report-reveals-new-details-about-lanzas-history/

Peter Langman, "The Enigma of Adam Lanza's Mind and Motivations for Murder." In *The Journal of Campus Behavioral Intervention*. Retrieved from: https://cdn.nabita.org/website-media/nabita.org/wordpress/wp-content/uploads/ 2016/02/JBIT2015_Article1.pdf

Reed Coleman, "Adam Lanza Timeline." Retrieved from: https://cdn.nabita.org/website-media/nabita.org/wordpress/wp-content/uploads/ 2016/02/JBIT2015_Article1.pdf

Alaine Griffin and Josh Kovner, "New report on Newtown shooter: Parental denial, breakdowns, missed opportunities." In *Chicago Tribune*. Retrieved from: https://www.chicagotribune.com/la-na-adam-lanza-20141121-story,amp.html

Josh Kovner and Dave Altimari, "A Window into Shooter's Descent." In *Enewspaper*. Retrieved from: https://enewspaper.latimes.com/infinity/article_share.aspx?guid=caa7be37-02b1-40ab-a18b-c7462ff2f120

Shootings in Newtown, Connecticut. In *NPR*. Retrieved from: https://www.npr.org/series/167276841/shootings-in-newtown-conn

Sandy Hook School Shootings Fast Facts. In *CNN*. Retrieved from: https://www.cnn.com/2013/06/07/us/connecticut-shootings-fast-facts/index.html

Sandy Hook Shooting. In *PBS News Hour*. Retrieved from: https://www.pbs.org/newshour/tag/sandy-hook-shooting

Matthew Lysiak, "Why Adam Lanza Did It." In *Newsweek*. Retrieved from: https://www.newsweek.com/why-adam-lanza-did-it-226565

Adam Lanza, Emails to Mom. Retrieved from: https://www.google.com/search?q=Adam+Lanza+emails+to+Mom

CHAPTER 3

STEPHEN PADDOCK

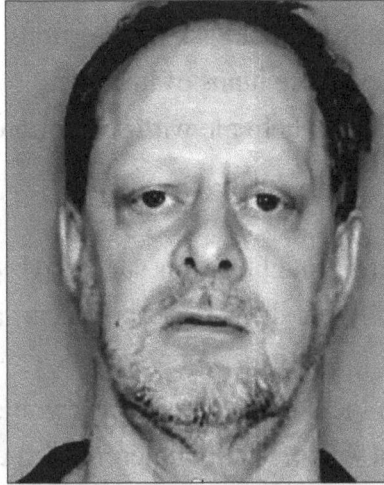

THE SHOOTING

It happened on October 1, 2017. Stephen Paddock, a tall, disheveled 64-year-old gambler of medium weight, began shooting at a crowd of young people attending the Route 91 Harvest Music Festival on the Las Vegas Strip in Nevada. He aimed his rifles out of the window of the hotel with a dull expression because he was emotionally dead and had been that way for months. He had ascended to stage 3 rage, and he was beyond anyone's reach.

Paddock arrived at Mandalay Bay about a week earlier in a deep funk, and booked Room 32–135, which he was given free of charge because of his reputation for going on expensive all-night gambling binges. Four days later, he also booked the connected Room 32–134. Both suites overlooked the venue at Las Vegas Village where the Harvest Music Festival was going on. In the days before the shooting, he had gambled all night in the hotel's casino and set things up for the shooting during the day, while being jovial with the hotel and casino staff. Nobody guessed what he was up to. The joviality was to cover up the deep depression and rage burning inside him. Outside he was smiling, but inside he was depressed and numb.

Hotel bellmen helped him bring 25 suitcases up to his suite in the days before the shooting without asking questions. Each day he would ask for help with a few more items of luggage.

"Excuse me, could you help me with some more suitcases," he said to the bellmen.

"Yes, sir, Mr. Paddock."

The suitcases were brought up on successive days. Each day the bellmen would politely put the suitcases on a cart and take them up to his room.

"Just put them in the corner there. Thank you so much," Paddock said in his calm, flat voice. The bellmen looked at the accumulating bags and did not say anything. He always tipped well, and that is probably all they cared about.

The suitcases contained his arsenal of weapons, ammunition and other equipment. The arsenal included fourteen AR-15 rifles (some of which were equipped with bump stocks—which enable the kind of rapid fire associated with automatic weapons. Twelve of the rifles had 100-round magazines). There were also eight AR-10 rifles, a bolt-action rifle, and a revolver. He also had four laptops and three cell phones. On September 30, the night before the shooting, he placed "Do not disturb" signs on the doors of both of his suites. He had been putting up the "Do not disturb" signs almost every day since he arrived.

He had reserved the second room under his girlfriend's name. However, his longtime girlfriend, Marilou Danley, did not accompany him to the hotel. Of Philippine origin, she took a trip, which he had arranged, to her country at the time of the shooting and did not return until two days after the shooting. When she was later questioned by police, she claimed she did not know anything about her boyfriend's plans. Paddock stayed quietly alone in his room and did not begin to set things up for the shooting until the night before.

On the day of his shooting, Paddock woke up at about 12 noon, after having gambled late into the night as usual. He did not shower and he did not shave—he often went around with several day's growth of beard—and dressed casually in a plain brown knitted short-sleeved shirt and black pants. He was known as a slovenly dresser and he did not dress otherwise on his last day. Nor did he take much time to comb his short-cropped, graying hair. He ordered a big meal which included a burger, a bagel, potato soup, a bottle of water and two Pepsis and stayed in his rooms the rest of the afternoon, preparing his arsenal for the shooting. He spent an hour loading and setting up his assortment of guns near the window where he would do the killing. As he prepared for the massacre, he may have imagined how shocked people would be when he started shooting them down, and that thought most likely excited him.

He had lived a sordid life of all-night gambling binges and waking up late and gambling all night again. For months he had not thought about anything else but shooting people down. The thought was in the corner of his mind as he gambled the nights away and kept himself inebriated with alcohol and tranquilizers. He had been depressed all his life and now he knew that his depression was finally breaking.

At around 9:45 p.m., Paddock screwed an L-shaped bracket on the doorframe of the door that allowed immediate access to the 32nd floor. Sometime around 10 p.m., he took a hammer and broke two windows of his hotel room. Country music singer Jason Aldean was performing on the stage and he was the last performer of the festival. Paddock had put off the shooting until the last minute. It was estimated that there were around 20,000 fans swarming around the stage. Without ceremony, Paddock stuck one of his AR-15 rifles out of the window and began firing at the crowd in the semidarkness.

He proceeded to shoot at the crowd for ten minutes. The crowd was about five football fields away and he needed to use a high-powered scope to aim correctly. He did not fire at the crowd in a random manner; he had written down calculations about where he needed to aim to maximize his accuracy. A note found by police contained the actual distance to the target, his own elevation, and the bullet trajectory relative to the line of fire. As he peppered the crowd with bullets, people began falling down. At first the audience did not know what was happening and thought people were falling down because they were ill. It was hard to hear the shots over the music that was blaring from loud speakers. When people *did* hear the shots, they at first thought it was fireworks. As people became aware of what was happening, they pointed to the window of the Mandalay Bay hotel, where sparks were coming from a rifle.

"Shooter! Shooter! Shooter!" people were calling out all over the crowd.

"Get down!"

"Run!"

"Get out of the way!"

Paddock shot a hundred rounds from one rifle, then picked up the next rifle and shot another hundred rounds. Each rifle had a 100-round magazine preloaded, and rather than stopping to reload, he went from one preloaded rifle to another. Even though he was a bit drunk, his eyes were sharp and he concentrated in a businesslike way on the task at hand, which was to kill as many of the crowd as possible before the police came. He did not care in the least about the young people falling dead in the yard below, or about those who were screaming and making a mad dash for safety. He was stupefied from the accumulation of anger and drugs that had built up in him over the years and to him, in his groggy state of mind, it was probably like shooting at mechanical bears in a shooting gallery.

Panic rippled through the crowd as people were falling down in clumps. The crowd began dashing this way and that, running over anybody who was in their way. People were trampled as the crowd spun in every direction, running for its life. In a panic, people in the crowd did not care who they ran over; they just wanted to get out of the line of fire as quickly as possible. Jason Aldean and the other musicians ran off stage when bullets began hitting the stage. People were scaling walls and hiding in any nook or cranny they could find. Some people were trying to help others but ended up getting shot themselves. Pandemonium set in.

Shortly before the shooting began, hotel security guard Jesus Campos was sent to the 32nd floor to investigate an "open-door alert." An open-door alert is hotel lingo for a door what won't open. He took the elevator and found that a door that provided immediate access to the floor would not open. He forced the door open and discovered the L-shaped bracket Paddock had screwed into the door and door frame. While reporting to the dispatch center, he heard a strange noise down the hall. "It sounds like there's a jackhammer in one of the rooms." He went to investigate the matter and found that the noise was coming from Rooms 32-135. He knocked on the door and hollered, "Hello? What's going on in there?"

Inside the room, Paddock heard the knock. He turned his AR-15 on the door and began shooting through it. Campos was hit in the right thigh by one of about 35 bullets that Paddock fired through the door. After Campos was hit, he took cover in the alcove between Rooms 32-122 and 32-124 and immediately reported back to the dispatch center by both radio and cellphone that he had been shot.

"Someone's in Room 32-135 shooting rifles. I got hit in the leg!" he said.

At first he believed he had been shot with a BB or pellet gun, because there was not much pain in his leg. At the same time, a maintenance worker named Stephen Schuck, who had been fixing the door that Campos had reported as being barricaded, also heard the noise in Room 32-135. Campos saw Schuck running by and yelled at him.

"Get down, get down! Somebody's shooting in there! I got hit in the leg. Take cover!"

Schuck ducked into the same alcove and called hotel dispatchers, informing them of the ongoing shooting, and telling them to call the police. They called the Las Vegas Metropolitan Police Department and the headquarters of MGM Resorts International, the owner of the Mandalay Bay Hotel.

Paddock continued firing at the crowd, aiming his rifles at those who were trying to run away. He was shooting approximately 490 yards into the festival audience. He was most likely smiling as he fired away, enjoying his hour of power. A security fence that surrounded the 15-acre concrete lot hindered concertgoers from fleeing, but some managed to climb over it. Paddock continued with hardly a pause, except when he turned to shoot at the door of his room. However, most concertgoers down below were able to find a way to escape.

In the midst of his shooting spree, Paddock fired eight bullets at a large jet fuel tank at the Harry Reid International Airport, which was about 2,000 feet away. Only two bullets struck the exterior of the tank and only one of them penetrated the tank. The fuel did not explode because jet fuel is mostly kerosene, which does not ignite when hit by a bullet.

Harry Reid International Airport was shut down for several hours as approximately 300 people escaped the festival grounds and sought shelter in the airport. This prompted officials to shut down the airport and all four runways. More than 25 flights were rerouted to ensure that no aircraft would be hit by gunfire, and other flights were canceled. The airport did not resume its normal schedule until 12:40 a.m. As word of the shooting hit the nearby casinos, gamblers stopped gambling and stood around watching television sets that were reporting the event even as it occurred. Eventually, the whole city of Las Vegas came to a stop and virtually all gambling came to a standstill. It may have been the only time in Las Vegas history that such a thing had occurred. Much of Las Vegas Boulevard was closed while police SWAT teams combed the venue and neighboring businesses.

Police began driving up in groups, responding to calls from members of the crowd. They were initially confused about whether the shots were coming from the Mandalay Bay, the nearby Luxor hotel, or the festival grounds. There were also multiple false reports of additional shooters at other hotels on the Strip. Finally, after about five minutes, the police spotted the flashes of gunfire coming from the northern side of Mandalay Bay and went to the hotel. Other police, responding to the emergency call from the Mandalay itself, went right to the hotel. Two officers arrived on the 32nd floor at 10:17 p.m. and, after searching the hall, found Campos hiding in his alcove.

"He's in Room 32-135!" Campos yelled.

"Which way is Room 31-135?"

"That way."

"Have you been hit?"

"In the leg."

"OK, before we break into the Room 32-135, we need to evacuate this floor."

Campos gave the police his master key and helped them to evacuate the floor. When they noticed how much his leg was bleeding, they told him to go down to the lobby to seek medical attention. The sound of shooting had by then paused for a while. The two police officers then heard a single shot, and afterwards the shooting stopped for good. They looked at each other.

"That shot sounded different," one said.

"You can't really tell," the other said.

Inside his room, Paddock had been listening to the voices outside in the hallway, and he knew it would only be a matter of minutes before police broke into his room. He could have shot at the door again, but he didn't. It's time, he probably thought. Just end it! He tossed aside the AR-15 he was using, picked up a revolver lying on the floor nearby and sat down on the floor in the middle of the room. Whether he had reached his kill point is not clear. He had run out of victims, since everyone had by now escaped from the venue below his window, and he heard the police outside his door and knew he did not have much time. He has spent a lifetime building up rage and there may have been a lot more inside him. But he had planned it all carefully and knew in advance that he would shoot himself when the time came, and now that time had come and he held the revolver to his face. Although he was a multimillionaire, his life had been a dark and miserable tunnel in which he slept during the days in hotel rooms and spent his nights staring at poker slot machines without enjoying a moment of it, some-times losing a million dollars a night. He was a monomaniac about gambling and apparently used it to distract himself from his misery, but it hadn't worked. Now, at that last moment, the hatred he felt for the world got turned on himself. "Let me out of here!" he may have muttered to himself. Without a further thought, he aimed the revolver at himself and stuck it between his eyes, blowing away the middle of his face. It seemed evident that he not only hated the world, but he hated himself as well.

Soon eight more officers got to the 32nd floor and joined the other two. The gunfire had stopped for a while, but the police moved down the hallway, room by room, to make sure everybody was evacuated. It was not until 11:25 p.m. that the police finally blew down the door of Room 32–135, using explosives. Paddock was found dead on the floor with blood all over his face, surrounded by his arsenal of weapons and a plethora of empty shells and laptops.

"The suspect is down," the police called in to headquarters. "It's over."

He had fired more than 1,000 bullets from his 32nd-floor suite in the Mandalay Bay hotel and ended up killing 60 people and wounding at least 413. In terms of the number of deaths, it was the largest mass killing ever recorded (outside of a war). The panic that caused people to run down other people in an attempt to find shelter, brought the total number of injured to approximately 867. The shooting spree had lasted a little over an hour.

STEPHEN PADDOCK'S FAMILY AND LIFE

Stephen Paddock was born in Clinton, Iowa on April 9, 1953, but he moved to Tuscan, Arizona a year later, growing up there and in the Sun Valley neighborhood of Los Angeles, California. He was the oldest of four sons of Benjamin Paddock and Dolores Hudson. His younger brothers were Patrick (born in 1957), Bruce (1959), and Eric (1960).

Stephen's father, Benjamin, was a bank robber who was arrested in 1960 when Stephen was seven years old. Benjamin was later convicted and jailed for nine years, until 1969, when he escaped from prison and subsequently appeared on the FBI's most-wanted list. According to reports, Stephen's father was a psychopath who regularly beat him. His mother, Delores, was a housewife who was not strong enough to stop these beatings. He was also later beaten up by his younger brother, Bruce.

Since it is known that Benjamin was arrested when Stephen was seven, we can assume that these beatings must have happened in early childhood, before the age of seven. When a child is beaten regularly at an early age, it is generally severely traumatic. The earlier the beatings occur, the more traumatic they will be. If a child is beaten as an infant or during the toddler years, such beatings are the most traumatic of all. A baby and toddler are almost completely defenseless, and if an impatient, psychopathic father cannot tolerate the boisterousness of a crying infant or a screaming toddler, he will not hesitate to shut the child down in any way, including slapping the child, violently shaking the child's crib, screaming at the child and, in short, smothering the child and terrorizing the child. Such terrorizing of a child can make the child fearful and afraid of life. The child must shut down completely in order not to provoke the father's wrath, and so he develops the habit of internalizing his anger.

Children who are physically abused can grow up to be seemingly nice people, and this was certainly the case with Stephen Paddock. But the repressed anger that lurked inside him during his formative years and throughout his adulthood would affect his personality forma- tion. In many cases the repressed anger comes out when the physically abused child grows up and has his own children. Research has shown that children who are physically abused often become abusers of their own children. However, if they do not have their own children and do not have weaker objects (such as a wife) on which to take out their repressed anger, it can come out in other ways, such as addictive gam- bling or mass murder.

A prime example of this was Adolf Hitler who, like Paddock, was also regularly beaten by his disturbed father from his earliest child- hood. Hitler also had a weak mother who could not provide a safety net for the child. Hitler seemed to be a nice guy in his early adulthood, a mild-mannered young man who was interested in being an artist. However, his father had severely and monstrously abused and beaten him, mocked him and tried to eliminate him during the long years of his childhood. Some disturbed fathers are like this: They view their son as a dangerous rival who must be destroyed. Later, when he took over Germany in the 1930s, Hitler found a way to channel the repressed anger into a cyclone of violence in which he started a world war and exterminated millions of Jews in concentration camps.

After he was arrested and convicted, Paddock's father, Benjamin, disappeared from Stephen's life and from his family. He escaped from prison in 1969 and moved to Oregon where he took the name Bruce Warner Erickson. He was described by a newspaper reporter in 1969 as a "glib, smooth-talking 'confidence man'," who was "egotistic and arrogant." His life was a series of deviant episodes: He was twice cited for traffic violations; operated an illegal bingo parlor for the Center for Education Reform, a non-profit organization based in Eugene, Oregon; was captured and arrested in early September 1978 in Springfield, Oregon; was released on parole; was charged by the Oregon Attorney General with racketeering related to his bingo business and fraud for an illegal operation of rolling back car odometers; and avoided a prison sentence by paying a $100,000 fine. Later in life, he had become so well-known for his bingo empire that his fame had earned him the nickname, Bingo Bruce. He died of a heart attack in Arlington, Texas in 1998.

Consciously or unconsciously, a boy's father serves as his first role model, and Stephen obviously did not have a good model.

From the age of seven, Paddock was raised by his single mother, who never remarried. It is not known whether she and her husband ever saw each other again after he was arrested, or whether they got a divorce. We do know that she raised her four sons by working as a secretary, and she never told them the truth about their father. She just said that he had left and never come back, and she didn't know where he was. The boys' mother raised them alone on a secretary's salary, the younger brother, Patrick Paddock, later reported. According to Patrick, the second-oldest brother, the brothers would fight over who would get the whole milk or the less tasty powdered milk. They were a single-parent, lower-middle-class family and Stephen experienced this economic instability as painful and he became determined to be rich. According to his younger brother, Eric, Stephen focused on gaining complete control over his life and not having to rely on anyone. He had learned from his early, abusive relationship with his father, to stay away from people.

Richard Alarcon, a former Los Angeles city councilman, who lived near the Paddocks, said the neighborhood in which the Paddock's lived was working class, with a Japanese community center and tidy ranch houses bought with money from the G.I. Bill. Alarcon recalled taking a science class with Paddock and remembered him as smart but with "a kind of irreverence. He didn't always stay between the lines." He cited as an example a competition in the class to build a bridge of balsa wood. The challenge was to build the bridge without staples or glue. Paddock cheated, Alarcon said, using glue and extra wood. "Everybody could see that he had cheated, but he just sort of laughed it off," Alarcon added. "He had that funny quirky smile on his face like he didn't care. He wanted to have the strongest bridge and he didn't care what it took."

He was not a great student, but he managed to graduate from California State University, Northridge, working nights at a nearby airport to pay for it. Afterwards, he looked for ways to make money as fast as he could. "He went to work for the IRS because he thought that's where the money was," Eric said. "But it turned out the money wasn't there. He went to the aerospace industry but the money wasn't there either. He went to real estate and that's where the money was."

When he turned to real estate, he began to accumulate wealth. Paddock started buying and refurbishing properties in economically depressed areas around Los Angeles and taught himself how to put in plumbing and install air-conditioning. In 1987, he bought a 30-unit building at 1256 W. 29th Street in Los Angeles, near the University of Southern California. Eric Paddock said the buildings were not "Taj Mahals, but they were nice safe places." They proved to be excellent investments, allowing Stephen to more than double his money on his

California holdings, which soon included at least six multifamily residences. Later, when he lived in Texas, he made money there, too. In 2012, he sold a 110-unit building in Mesquite, outside Dallas, for $8.3 million. He was reportedly a good landlord. He kept the rents low, responded promptly to his tenants' complaints, learned all their names and made sure they were happy. When one reliable tenant complained about a rent increase, he took half off the price. He designed the ownership structure so his family would profit and installed his mother in a tidy house just behind the apartment complex in Mesquite, Texas.

By the late 1980s, according to Eric, "We had cash flow." Eric confided that he had given his life savings to his older brother to invest and eventually became a partner in his company, because "that's the kind of guy he was. I knew he would succeed. He helped make my mother and I affluent enough to be retired in comfort." The younger brother looked up to the older brother, and Stephen took the role of the older brother and ran with it. He seemed to want to prove to himself and to the world that he could earn money in the right way, as opposed to his father, whom he assumed had not been able to earn money the right way and had abandoned the family to poverty. He was seven when his father was arrested for bank robbery, and he may have known more about who his father was than his younger brothers. He wanted to be the exact opposite of that father.

During his young and middle adulthood, he continued to accumulate wealth, but success in business did not correlate with success in his personal life. Paddock was married and divorced twice. He was first married from 1977–1979, in his twenties, and was married the second time from 1985–1990, in his late thirties. Both marriages were in Los Angeles County, California. He did not become attached to his wives and girlfriends; they were more like accessories that he added to his life for a while. His main attachment was to his mother, with whom he communicated on a daily basis. He was, like Adam Lanza, an Oedipal conqueror—a boy who had won his mother's love from his father. From the age of seven, when his father was arrested, he had become his mother's surrogate husband. Throughout his life he confided in her, calling her frequently, and discussing all aspects of his finances with her. He married twice, but his wives were never as important as his mother, and the wives apparently became tired of a man who was financially generous but emotionally distant. Family members said he stayed on good terms with his ex-wives.

He had become a narcissistic man, and like most narcissists, he had developed feelings of superiority to compensate for feelings of inferiority that were, to a large degree, due to the abusive way his father had treated him as a young child. With success in business came a lofty attitude and a rigidity and uncompromising attitude. Some who met him described him as arrogant, with a quiet attitude of dominance. People in his life bent to his will, even his mother and brother. He did not go out of his way for anyone. "He acted like everybody worked for him and that he was above others," said John Weinreich, an executive at the Atlantis Casino Resort Spa in Reno, which he saw Paddock frequently from 2012 to 2014. When Paddock wanted food while he was gambling, Weinreich said he wanted it immediately and would order with more than one server if the meal did not arrive quickly enough. "He would get irritated and uppity about it." His quickness to become irritated, his arrogance, and his sense of entitlement were early signs of the repressed anger and outward narcissism that would envelope him.

By the 2000s, with both of his marriages long over, Paddock turned to gambling. He liked living the high life, being waited on, seeing shows and eating good food. "He likes it when people go, 'Oh, Mr. Paddock, can I get you a big bowl of the best shrimp anybody had ever eaten on the planet and a big glass of our best port?'" his brother Eric said. Gambling made him feel important, and perhaps less lonely. "You could tell that being in that high-limit gambling environment would lift him up," Weinreich said. "He liked everyone doting on him." Paddock sometimes invited his brother Eric and his children for a free weekend in a luxury suite. But mostly he stayed alone. Soon, gambling became the mainstay of his life. At one point, Paddock stayed in a Las Vegas hotel, gambling for four months straight. An analyst at that time described him as a mid-level high roller, capable of losing $100,000 in one session which could extend over several days.

He preferred playing poker slot machines. He had reportedly developed an algorithm that enabled him to win at that game. Poker slots require skill and knowledge as well as luck. Players have to know the history of a particular machine and what it offers. They can do that by reading a pay table, which tells them what each possible winning hand pays out. One of the ways that video poker players get an advantage is to play casino promotions, which essentially pay out bonuses to winners, said Richard Munchkin, author of a noted book on gambling. A gambler like Mr. Paddock will often "lock" a machine, he explained, meaning he or she monopolizes it and makes sure no one else uses it during a gambling session.

For one casino promotion, Mr. Paddock showed up two hours early, locked up two machines and played them for 14 hours straight, Mr. Munchkin said, based on information he had compiled from other gamblers who were there at the time. The promotion lasted 12 hours, he said, "but he wanted to play for two hours before anybody got those machines. He knew they were the best machines based on pay tables." Munchkin added, "He knew the house advantage down to a tenth of a percent."

Year after year, Paddock spent more and more time in casinos and hotels, but he did have time to get a pilot's license to help him fly from casino to casino, and also to go on occasional cruises with his girlfriend. On his 60th birthday, April 9, 2013, he flew to the Philippines and stayed for five days. The family of Ms. Danley, his girlfriend, lived there and Paddock joined her while she was visiting her family. The couple visited her family again for his birthday the following year. These visits to the Philippines seemed to be his only respite from gambling.

When he lived in Texas, he used his plane to fly to Las Vegas to gamble. He became a certified private pilot on November 17, 2003, when he was given a document that said, "Airplane Single Engine Land," which meant he was allowed to fly a fixed-wing aircraft with a single-engine that landed on the ground. Paddock had his last examination for his license in February 2008. He had a "third class" medical classification, which expired in 2013. When he did not renew this medical certification, the FAA wouldn't let him fly without renewed medical information.

After losing the ability to fly, he moved to Nevada and bought a house in Reno and later in Mesquite. At that point his life became a cocoon of hotels and casinos, and neighbors rarely saw him at his homes. Colleen Maas, a neighbor of Paddock's in Reno, said she had not seen him once in a year and a half, despite walking her dog three times a day and going to line dancing events with his girlfriend, Ms. Danley, at the community center. When he did appear at his Reno home, he could be curt. Another neighbor, John McKay, recalled a day when he was hanging Christmas lights on a railing in his front yard when Mr. Paddock walked by. Mr. McKay greeted him and yelled out, "Merry Christmas!" but Mr. Paddock kept walking. "He said nothing," McKay said. "Not a word. No eye contact." McKay was baffled when he tried to strike up a conversation with Mr. Paddock about Donald Trump during that year's election campaign and got no response at all. Paddock reportedly liked Trump because the New York stock market went up after he was elected in 2016, but he almost always shied away from any discussion of politics.

Paddock bought his last house in Mesquite, a retirement community of 18,000 people about 90 minutes from Las Vegas. It was a community that attracted golfers and gamblers from around the country. He paid in cash and, as he did with other houses, spent very little time there.

While his neighbors added personal touches to their yards — trees, decorative pots, plants of all colors and sizes—Paddock's house was left unadorned. One of the few things neighbors remembered about him was the solid-panel fence he erected around the house. The message was clear: Paddock was a man who did not want to be seen.

In 2013—four years before his shooting binge—he brought a civil suit against the Cosmopolitan Hotel. The details are contained in a 97-page court deposition. Paddock was deposed October 29, 2013 as part of a civil lawsuit against the hotel, where he slipped and fell on a walkway in 2011. During the proceedings, he offered telling details about his lifestyle. At one point he said he was taking Valium, a tranquilizer, prescribed by an internist named Steven P. Winkler. "He's like on retainer, I call it, I guess," Paddock said of Winkler. "It means I pay a fee yearly ... I have good access to him." While Valium can help a person feel less anxious in the short term, in the long term it can sometimes cause depression.

He described the night of the incident in which he slipped and fell, saying he wandered into the casino in his favorite attire, black Nike sweatshirt, black pants and size 13 black flip-flops. He was on his way to the high-limit room when he slipped on some liquid and fell. He testified that he hurt his hamstring, which he said resulted in a lingering injury. Asked if he had been drinking that night, he replied, "I was my normal happy-go-lucky self. Perfectly sober."

This brought a laugh from the lawyers who were in the room, and then they continued with the interview.

He described himself as being the "biggest video poker player in the world." He was asked by the attorney, "How do you know that you're the biggest video poker player in the world?"

He replied, "How do I know that? Because I know some of the video poker players that play big. Nobody played as much and as long as I did."

He went on to testify about how big he played. "I averaged 14 hours a day, 365 days a year." Did he gamble during the day or at night? "I'll gamble all night," he said. "I sleep during the day." Asked if he ever visited the hotel pool, Paddock replied, "I do not do sun." Asked about his drinking, he said he rarely drank alcohol when he gambled, because "at the stakes I play, you want to have all your wits about you, or as much wit as I have." Asked about how much he gambled during an average night, he answered, "Each time I push the button, it will range from $100 to $1,350." Asked how much he would bet on a given night, he replied in a flat, almost boastful voice, "A million dollars."

"That's a lot of money," the lawyer said.

"No, it's not," Paddock said. The lawyer did not pursue his line of questioning.

This testimony tells us a lot about Paddock's personality. First of all, what comes across is a flippant anger and arrogance in the tone of his answers, as when he replies, "I do not do sun." He had become obsessed about gambling. He also indicates exactly to what extent he had become obsessed with it; he gambled 14 hours a day, 365 days a year—which means it was his entire life. Money meant very little to him; a million dollars a night gambling was just a million dollars. When he was asked if he drank when he gambled he said that he had to keep his wits about him—"or as much wits as I have." This qualifying phrase may have been an indication that he was aware, conscious or unconscious, that he drank more than that, and that his mental capacity was slipping away due to his obsessive lifestyle. Also, he would not want to admit to drinking on the night he slipped and fell.

During the last few years of his life, he used gambling and tranquilizers to contain the rage that always lurked inside him and to manage his loneliness and depression. He began stockpiling weapons and planning in his head (without ever telling anyone) what he was going to do. He searched out various festivals before settling on the one in Las Vegas. Toward the end, he began to drink heavily and to lose more money and hotel staff reported that they could smell alcohol on his breath. After years of throwing himself into gambling in order to take his mind off of his internalized rage and misery, gambling no longer worked. He tried gambling and drinking and that did not work. It was at this point that his repression broke. He could no longer contain the rage and the underlying loneliness that he had stuffed inside since he was a small child. That was the moment when he began to fantasize and make plans about ending his life with a big bang.

We tend to repress painful feelings, memories and thoughts, particularly those associated with a traumatic event. There is the unconscious, instinctive notion that by repressing painful memories—by putting them out of mind—we can forget about them and they will no longer affect us. But, in fact, the opposite is true; the more we try to push something away, the stronger it becomes. If we do not deal with trauma through some process like psychotherapy, the feelings from the trauma lurk in our unconscious mind and grow fat there. Repression takes a lot of energy, and the more we repress the more we lose our natural vitality. Sometimes repression can last a lifetime and we continue to function in a damaged state in which we can only use a fraction of our natural ability. Sometimes we die with our secret misery still locked inside us, never having lived even a small part of a full life. Sometimes the repressed anger breaks through along the way, as it did with Stephen Paddock.

Many of us, if not most, start out our lives as infants being loved and cherished. Infanthood, when it occurs as it should, is the primordial honeymoon. The first few years of our life, we are bathed in love and care. An infant and toddler is loved and held and changed and treated like a little king. He does not know any pain, because his mother and father rush forth to hold him and kiss him and rock him whenever there is the slightest discomfort. This is how early childhood should be, but that is not how it was for Stephen Paddock. He did not have a honeymoon, because he had a father who was mad. Can you imagine how you would feel if were two years old and you opened your eyes and you had a red-eyed monster yelling at you and pummeling your little body? Can you imagine how you would feel if you were being yelled at and pummeled every time you cried, and there was nothing you could do about it because you were too small and could not understand what it was or why it was happening? This is how young Stephen must have felt. He was a prisoner of this lunatic father and could not escape. Instead of a honeymoon, he was born into a nightmare. He was trained by this early conditioning to feel that he was helpless in the face of adversity, and that early training stayed with him the rest of his life. He never learned how to deal with emotional problems, never learned that he could ask for or receive help, and he therefore tried to manage his problems in a lonely, destructive way.

And so, at the age of 64, Stephen Paddock shot down 60 people, injured hundreds of others, and then took his own life in a final expression of rage.

CULTURAL FACTORS

Stephen Paddock was a boy who grew up under a violent father; then he became a man who lived in a violent society. He tried mightily to keep his inner rage and violent tendencies under wraps, but the exposure to the violence of American culture only served to provoke his rage and provide him with ideas of how to give that rage an outlet. From our study of Adam Lanza and other mass killers, we know that they pay particular attention to what is going on in culture, to devaluations of males, to the divisiveness and warfare between political factions and in particular to mass killings, which are a chief symptom of the disturbance of our culture.

Stephen had endured being bullied and beaten by a brutish father who never allowed Stephen to defend himself or speak out about this paternal terrorism. Later, his second youngest brother also bullied him, which indicates how vulnerable he had become. He had grown up to be a tall, skinny kid whose instinct for self-preservation had been squashed by his father and brother; therefore, he had no idea of how to defend himself. Later, as an adult, he had to witness the bullying tactics of various political leaders, groups and factions and that most likely had an irritating effect on him. When a child is bullied, he is extra-sensitive to any bullying he sees in society, just as a soldier who has gone through bombings develops PTSD and is extra sensitive to loud noises after he returns home. The bullying he saw in society must have seemed like a replay of what happened in his childhood, and triggered the same helpless rage response.

The culture we live in is like an extended family. In the nuclear family, if one member is behaving in such a way as to disrupt the family, that member roils the whole family. If a son is constantly acting out, cutting classes at school, taking drugs and screaming at his parents about some complaint or another, it affects the feelings and behavior of the rest of the family. If the parents are constantly fighting and even coming to blows on occasion, that affects the feelings and the behavior of the children. Families need a harmonic relationship between parents and a balance throughout the family in order to function well. Culture is the same; it is a large, extended family. If the two parties that run America's extended family are constantly fighting with one another, this affects the feelings and behavior of the whole family or society. And if various groups in society are at war with other groups, that affects the feelings and behavior of the whole extended family or society, especially if groups are perceived as bullying people into seeing things the way they want them to see things.

As a citizen of America, Paddock could not help but be stirred up by what was going on in American society, particularly the bullying. He seemed to make it a point to live far away from the mainstream, in the dark halls of casinos and the rooms of casino hotels. He was also affected by the mass shootings. One after another, week after week, the shootings kept relentlessly occurring. Each shooting set an example for other raging people such as Paddock to follow and each was a dramatic, compelling event that drew attention to the shooter. Everybody wanted to know all about the shooter: Who was he, what was he thinking, what was he feeling, how did he get that way. Paddock, like most shooters, had kept things locked inside of him all his life, and had thus lived a sad, lonely life in which nobody ever knew what he was feeling down deep. He was afraid of being known, because when he tried to be known by his father—when as a toddler he cried and screamed out for comfort—he was probably yelled at and beaten. His craving to be known had to be kept down, but when he saw one shooter after another becoming the center of national attention, this observation offered him a way out.

His last girlfriend, Marilou, was a Philippine woman who seemed to be mild-mannered and easy to get along with, like his mother. After the failures of his previous marriages with American women, he may have sought out an Asian woman, thinking that she would be easier to control, and observers testified about his controlling manner. Employees at a Starbucks in Mesquite, Nevada, located inside the Virgin River Casino, described Paddock's relationship with his girlfriend, Danley, as troubled. A supervisor at the coffee shop claimed that Paddock often berated Danley when they were together in the store. "It happened a lot," Esperanza Mendoza said. He claimed Paddock would verbally abuse her when Danley asked to use his casino card to buy food or other things inside the casino, Esperanza said. "He would glare down at her and say—with a mean attitude—"You don't need my casino card for this. I'm paying for your drink, just like I'm paying for you." Esperanza added, "He was so rude to her in front of us." Paddock's mother was a mild-mannered woman who was too timid to prevent his mad father from abusing him. It may be that Paddock was to some degree transferring his unconscious anger at his mother to his girlfriend. He was full of repressed anger and that anger was leaking out, primarily on his girlfriend, but also on others.

Darlene McKay, a neighbor of his in Reno, said that she would usually get up early each morning to watch the sunrise, and he would always ignore her. When Paddock was at his home, she would see him dressed in his gym clothes walking to the community center for a workout. Ms. McKay recalled something peculiar: If she waved he wouldn't wave back and if she smiled he wouldn't smile back. "He always walked across the street and would never pass in front of our house," she said.

Paddock was reportedly riled by the anti-male attitude of feminists, and his anger at his girlfriend and at women may have been exacerbated by the cultural events. Feminism had dominated the headlines for years, and he had witnessed men being accused of saying the wrong thing about women, being fired from jobs and cancelled from culture. I was familiar with this response because during those years, many of my male patients vented anger toward feminism. They saw feminism as one-sided, only concerned about the feelings of women, but not sympathetic about the feelings of men. One angry male client scoffed at feminist slogans such as, "a woman should be believed," "men have toxic masculinity," and "one out of five women is raped," calling them, "feminist bullshit." "Nobody's listening to men anymore!" Perhaps Paddock had similar feelings about feminism, which may have contributed to the hostility he expressed to his girlfriend.

Another type of cultural violence that he reacted to was the riots of Blacks that were often happening in cities during the 1990s. During the riots in Los Angeles of 1992, he became so incensed by the fear that the riots would spill over to the apartment complex he owned, he ran up to the roof of his building, dressed in a flak jacket and armed with a gun, waiting for the rioters to appear. He stood on the roof all night long, with an AR-15 in his arms and a glare in his eyes, waiting for the rioters to appear in his neighborhood. He told his girlfriend, Marilou, "They won't get my building."

FINAL ANALYSIS

Stephen Paddock was not a typical older brother. His other brothers described him as the least angry of the brothers, and they were shocked when the news of the Las Vegas shooting came out. Even though he grew up to be a tall man—six feet two inches tall—he was skinny and awkward and so passive that his third-youngest brother picked on him as they were growing up. He was a big lug who seemed to have no idea how to defend himself.

He had become awkward, quiet and passive because of his reported abuse in his early childhood by his antisocial, hot-tempered father. There are some severely disturbed parents who take out all their frustrations in life on a particular child, and this seems to have been the case with Paddock's father, Benjamin. Stephen apparently became his father's scapegoat from an early age—perhaps even from birth on—and he was emotionally and physically battered for seven years. His younger brothers probably received some degree of abuse from the father as well, because all of the brothers were reportedly troubled except for the youngest. This father was out of their lives when Steven was seven, and his younger brothers did not experience paternal abuse to the same extent as Stephen did. Steven got the brunt of the abuse. As a toddler, he probably fought with all his might against his demon-father, but the father completely squashed the child and he never tried to defend himself again.

What happened to Stephen Paddock seems to fit the description of "soul murder," a term created by Leonard Shengold. He defined it as the perpetration of brutal or subtle acts against children that result in a kind of emotional bondage and in their psychic and spiritual annihilation. Children who are soul-murdered lose their emotional grounding—that is, they lose their identity. This is probably because their abuse starts very early in life, before the age of three, before a child's ego is fully developed. When children are abused before their ego is fully developed, their sense of themselves is stripped away before they even have a chance to find themselves. The ego, which is the part of the mind that runs things, remains a rudimentary ego. It never has a chance to develop, but remains stunted. A person with a weak ego is like an army with a weak general. In the end, Paddock became a fragile, infantile character, who lived in a cocoon (womb) of hotels and casinos in search of relief for his misery.

Another psychoanalyst, Martin Seligman, is noted for his theory of learned helplessness, a theory which also perhaps applies to the case of Stephen Paddock. Seligman did research with dogs, who were put in cages and deliberately shocked. In one experiment, the dogs were shocked while standing in a cage and there was nothing they could do to stop the shock. Finally, they gave up and stood shivering. Later they were put in another cage in which the floor was shocked, and they could have escaped the shock by jumping over a small partition. But the dogs had learned from the previous experiment that they couldn't stop the shock; that is, they learned to be helpless. Paddock may have learned to be helpless when his father abused him at a young age and he was not able to do anything to stop it. Later, his younger brother beat him and he could not do anything to stop that either. As an adult the only way he could defend himself was to stay away from people. He did not like to be with people and certainly did not like to ask for help from people. He depended only on himself.

Alice Miller wrote about how children are prisoners of childhood, and that theory also relates to Paddock. During their early childhoods, children are completely under the sway of parents. Most parents are fairly healthy and treat their children well. But some can be brutal and their children are like prisoners of sadistic guards. Sadistic guards, such as the ones in Nazi prison camps, can cause prisoners to end up feeling depressed, ashamed and humiliated. Children of sadistic parents can turn out the same way.

Paddock's mother was apparently a weak and ineffectual mother. She too was probably afraid of her terrorizing husband and could not stand up to him or protect her son from him. But she was the only relatively sane parent and Paddock may have clung to her like a drowning swimmer to a buoy. Yet, while he loved her because she was his only somewhat loving parent, unconsciously he may have resented her. But he could never express anger to her because of how hard she worked as a secretary to support the family and because she may have favored him as her oldest son.

Looked at in psychoanalytic terms, Stephen was a man with a weak ego and an overblown id that needed the instant gratification of gambling and also needed to control all aspects of his life. Eventually his id, the primitive part of his mind, caused him to go completely out of control. His need to be wealthy and later his gambling was an attempt to compensate for the sense of powerlessness and helplessness that resulted from his early domination by his father—as well as his mother's inability to save him from the father. In a healthy family, the father's primary job is to provide stability and discipline and the mother's main job is to maintain love and safety. Stephen did not feel safe in his early childhood environment. He probably longed for his mother to save him, but she could not, and so—fatherless and motherless—he had to become his own man.

Paddock's life was not really his life. His life had been taken away from him in early childhood. He attempted to carry on despite the emotional damage done to him. He was an intelligent man and he managed to accumulate some wealth and to live what appeared to be a quietly successful life. Power in the form of wealth had to substitute for real connections. In order to keep his rage under control, he had to restrict his life. He did not have any friends, and his relationships with women were short-lived; both of his marriages lasted only a few years. He was a man of few words and preferred to be alone than to be with people. He did not trust people—why would he, when his first experience with a person was a madman who completely betrayed him?

Many so-called experts have theorized that sociopaths are born that way; that it is a genetic condition. Babies are not born sociopathic, although some babies are crankier than others. Thomas, Chess and Birch clarified this when they did a study of newborns and found three types of babies at birth: easy babies, cranky babies and slow-to-warm-up babies. They concluded that the cranky babies had either been genetically determined or that they were made to be cranky by conditions—such as a mother's anxiety—during gestation. One might theorize that a baby's crankiness is the precursor to antisocial personality development, which might be so, but we do not know for certain if Paddock was a cranky baby. We do know that he became cranky very early on due to his father's physical abuse.

Environmental cause and effect is a thing that can be readily observed. If someone pushes you, you want to push back; if someone yells at you, you want to yell back; if you are starved for 10 days, you want to eat a horse; and if a child is neglected for two years, he may then neglect everyone else for the rest of his life. This is the root of physics and of human psychology: Every action has an equal reaction. In Paddock's case, he was the toddler who was beaten by his father and wanted to beat him back, but he was beaten and shut down. Hence he learned to hold his anger in. If this happens over a period of years, the individual will be like a clogged pipe that builds up water until it breaks.

Paddock lived his life as best he could, but once he had attained a compensatory power—once he had attained some wealth and a modicum of stability—he began to implode. For many years he kept taking care of his family and particularly his mother, toward whom he remained loyal, but then he started to go downhill. He started to distance whatever friends or acquaintances he had established and to be surly toward those around him, such as the workers at casinos. His last girlfriend, Marilou Danley, said he was loving and even romantic in the beginning, but that toward the end he became more and more despondent, uncommunicative and abusive. At that point he was running out of the energy to keep his rage down, and he ascended to stage 2.

He started to gamble, at first in bits and pieces and then obsessively and addictively. Eventually, as he put it in his testimony for his law suit against the Cosmopolitan Hotel, he was gambling 14 hours a night, 365 days a year. The quiet depression that was always there became full-out depression. He was a man who was not in touch with his feelings, and a man who is not in touch is a man who is dominated by those feelings. He had been squashed by his father and did not want to focus on that inner pain, but rather to escape it. He did not trust others and so he did not trust any kind of help, such as psychotherapy. Instead, his focus was outward, not inward, and what he saw outside—such as the rising incidence of mass killings and the demonizing of men that was going on in American culture—only served to stoke his depression and the rage underneath it. In the final years of his life, it was all he could do to maintain the status quo.

Paddock developed an addictive personality. Freud's understanding of how an addictive personality develops was more or less the same as B. F. Skinner's behavioral perspective: An addictive personality was something that is conditioned during the oral stage, before the age of three. If a mother feeds her baby every time he cries (whether the baby is crying because it needs a hug or it needs to be changed or for some other reason), that baby learns to relieve stress via oral gratification. Primary addictions all have do with oral gratifications such as drinking or smoking. Secondary addictions such as gambling or pyromania are not instant gratifications and therefore not as strong. It may be that Paddock's mother coddled him to compensate for the cruelty of his father, and one of the ways she coddled him was to put her breast in his mouth to stop him from crying, no matter what he was crying about. Thus, he might have been fed physically but not emotionally. Hence, the habit of oral gratification had been set, and he spent his life seeking gratification to relief his stress, but never succeeding in nurturing himself emotionally.

In the last few years he began to collect guns and to plan for his great escape. Gradually, quietly, he collected an arsenal, but he did not tell anybody what he was doing—it was a surprise and even a shock to his girlfriend and members of his family. He kept it all to himself to the very end because of the distrust for people that began with his distrust of his father. He did not want anybody to know about the darkness that he harbored inside. When the repression broke, he could not hold the rage down anymore and it began to manifest itself. In the last weeks of his life, the rage grew to a point where he could no longer control it, and he broke into stage 3 rage. Even when his rage was right at the surface, he managed to hold it down until the last minute, when he aimed his rifles through the window of the Mandalay Hotel.

He probably did not connect that rage to his mad father or his weak mother, because he was not in touch with what the rage was about. He was probably only aware that he wanted to kill as many people as fast as he could. He was not at all particular about it. He was not aiming at people of a certain type or of a certain race. He was in his hotel room firing away at the crowd, killing and killing, caught up in the deep pain of complete hatred for all of humanity and unrelenting hatred for himself.

SOURCES

Stephen Paddock. In *Wikipedia*. Retrieved from: https://en.wikipedia.org/wiki/Stephen_Paddock

2017 Las Vegas Shooting. In *Wikipedia*. Retrieved from: https://en.wikipedia.org/wiki/2017_Las_Vegas_shooting

Tavernise, S., Kovaleski, S. and Turkewitz, J. (2017). "Who Was Stephen Paddock? The Mystery of a Nondescript 'Numbers Guy'". In *The New York Times*. Retrieved from: https://www.nytimes.com/2017/10/07/us/stephen-paddock-vegas.html

"Stephen Paddock, a High Roller and 'Psychopath.'" In *BBC News*. Retrieved from: https://www.bbc.com/news/world-us-canada-41472462

Grinberg, E. (2017). "Something went 'incredibly wrong' with Las Vegas gunman, brother says." In CNN. Retrieved from: https://www.cnn.com/2017/10/02/us/las-vegas-attack-stephen-paddock-trnd/index.html

Del Real, J. and Bromwich, J.E. (2017). "Stephen Paddock, Las Vegas Suspect, Was a Gambler Who Drew Little Attention." In *New York Times*. Retrieved from: https://www.nytimes.com/2017/10/02/us/stephen-paddock-vegas-shooter.html

Becket, S. (2017). "Stephen Paddock: What We Know About the Las Vegas Gunman." In *The New York Times*. Retrieved from: https://www.cbsnews.com/news/las-vegas-shooting-stephen-paddock-what-we-know-about-gunman/

Las Vegas Shooting. "Gunman was on losing streak and 'germophobic', police say." In *The Guardian*. Retrieved from: https://www.theguardian.com/us-news/2018/jan/20/las-vegas-shooting-police-report-gunman-motive-mystery-stephen-paddock

Marilou Danley. In *Wikidata*. Retrieved from: https://www.wikidata.org/wiki/Q41731955

Marilou Danley. In. Everipedia. Retrieved from: https://everipedia.org/wiki/lang_en/marilou-danley-nevada

Associated Press. "Vegas gunman Stephen Paddock inspired by criminal father's reputation." In *U. S. News*. Retrieved from: https://www.nbcnews.com/storyline/las-vegas-shooting/vegas-gunman-stephen-paddock-inspired-criminal-father-s-reputation-n964066

Romo, V. (2017). "FBI Finds No Motive in Las Vegas Shooting, Closes Investigation." In *NPR*. Retrieved from: https://www.npr.org/2019/01/29/689821599/fbi-finds-no-motive-in-las-vegas-shooting-closes-investigation

Kloor, K. (2018). "Anatomy of a Conspiracy Theory." In *Politico*. Retrieved from: https://www.politico.com/magazine/story/2018/11/16/conspiracy-theory-las-vegas-shooting-dangerous-222576/

Romano, A., Nelson, L., Abad-Santos, A. and Lopez, G. (2017). "Las Vegas Shooting: What We Know So Far." In *Vox*. Retrieved from: https://www.vox.com/2017/10/2/16395600/las-vegas-shooting-updates

Thomas, A., Chess, S. and Birch, H. C. (1968). *Temperament and Behavior Disorders in Children*. New York; New York University Press.

Shengold, L. (1991). Soul Murder: The Effects of Childhood Abuse and Deprivation. NewYork: Ballantine Books

Seligman, M. (1976). Learned Helplessness and Depression in Animals and Men. New York: General Learning Press

Schoenewolf, G. (1991). *The Art of Hating*. Northvale, NJ: Jason Aronson

Miller, A. (1981). *Prisoners of Childhood*. New York: Basic Books

Freud, S. (1990). *The Ego and the Id*. New York: W. W. Norton (Revised Paperback).

Skinner, B. F. (2020). *The Behavior of Organisms*. New York: B. F. Skinner Foundation (Revised Paperback)

CHAPTER 4
SEUNG-HUI CHO

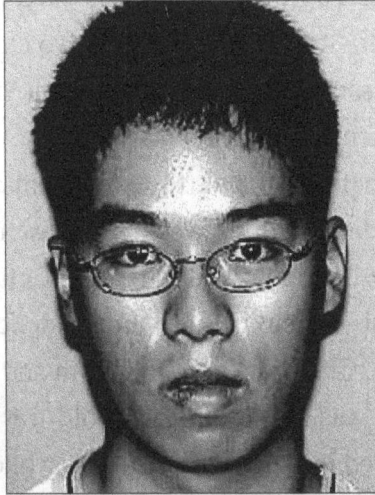

THE SHOOTING

On April 16, 2007 at about 6:47 a.m., a Virginia Tech student named Seung-Hui Cho marched up to the entrance of West Ambler Johnston Hall. He was an angry loner, slight of build, standing about five feet six inches and weighing only 130 pounds, who had lived an isolated life on the campus of this college in Blacksburg, Virginia. He had been born in South Korea but had grown up in America from the age of eight, and now, as a student at Virginia Tech, he had been stalking a girl named Emily Hilcher. A few days before, he had gone into her room, uninvited, and introduced himself with, "Hi. I'm Question Mark," and she had been freaked out and told him to leave. She called the campus police after he left and they went to his dorm room to warn him to cease and desist.

As he stood looking at the door of her dormitory on that cloudy morning, wearing his bullet-proof vest, a pistol in each hand, he remembered the note he had left in his own dormitory room, in which he criticized "rich kids", "debauchery" and "deceitful charlatans." The note included the sentence, "You caused me to do this." He had become obsessed with Hilcher and disgusted by American culture and the party life on the campus of Virginia Tech. He checked both pistols to see if their safeties were off—two revolvers with two extra magazines, a .22 caliber Walther P22 semi-automatic pistol and a 9mm Glock 19 semi-automatic pistol—then inserted his card into the door. Normally, the hall was only open before 10 a.m. to its residents, who had magnetic key cards. Cho's student mailbox was in the basement of the building, and he had a key card that allowed him access after 7:30 a.m., but he found a way to use his card to get into the residence earlier.

A little after 7 a.m. Cho broke into the dorm and entered the room of Emily Hilscher. She was a pretty 19-year-old freshman who was still asleep when he walked into her room and she woke up with a start and sat up in her bed, wiping her eyes, most likely stunned by seeing Cho in front of her bed with two guns aimed at her.

"What are you doing here?' she asked.

"I'm here," he said. He gazed at her with a dark, calm expression, as if he were looking at a worm. Without further ado, he shot her once in the head with the Glock 19, the pistol he used throughout his shooting spree, and she fell back on her dorm bed.

After hearing the gunshots, a resident assistant, 22-year-old senior Ryan C. Clark of Martinez, Georgia, dashed from his room down the hall and burst into Hilsher's room. He said, "What's going on in here." Before he could say another word, Cho shot him in the head and he fell forward on Hilsher's bed on top of her. He died instantly, but Hilscher remained alive for three hours after being shot. When police arrived about five minutes later, they found Hilscher on the bed, bleeding, and took her to a nearby hospital.

Cho left the West Ambler Johnson Hall and returned to his room in Harper Hall, a dormitory a block away. While he heard police and emergency medical services units responding to the shootings in the dorm next door, Cho changed out of his bloodstained clothes, logged on to his computer to delete his emails and his student university account, and then removed the hard drive. He also finished a 20-page "manifesto," which he left on his computer after printing it. Then he put the printed copy of the manifesto and some writings and video recordings into a package and addressed the package to NBC News. About an hour after the attack, Cho, dressed in the usual black shirt and pants, strode up to the duck pond a block away, and threw his hard drive into the pond. Directly afterwards, he walked into a nearby post office and mailed the package of writings and videos to NBC. The package was postmarked at 9:01 a.m.

Cho then strolled around with a backpack on his shoulders for about 30 minutes. The backpack contained his two handguns, 400 rounds of ammunition, heavy duty chains and locks, a hammer and a knife. He apparently kept strolling aimlessly around the campus, trying to decide whether to proceed with the rampage that he had been planning for months. Should I go on? he probably asked himself, and wavered back and forth. Finally, he made the decision to keep killing, indicating that he had not yet reached his kill point. He pivoted sharply and hurried toward Norris Hall.

At around 9:40 a.m., Cho entered the Norris Hall doorway, the building where the Engineering Science and Mechanics program was housed. He chained shut the three main entrance doors and placed a note on one, saying that attempting to open the door would cause a bomb to explode. A few minutes later, a faculty member found the note and took it to the third floor to notify the school's administration, at which time police were called. Cho continued into room 200, which was empty, and took out his two handguns and his extra rounds and stuffed the extra magazines into his pockets. After he had geared up, he went back into the hallway and began opening doors and peeking inside to see how many students were in each classroom.

Erin Sheehan, a student who was in Room 207, told reporters later that "the shooter peeked in twice" in her classroom and that "it was strange that someone at this point in the semester would be lost, looking for a class." She was lucky that he did not see many students in her class. He went to the next classroom, saw more students and began shooting. From then on, Cho entered one classroom after another on the second floor, methodically shooting all the students in each classroom.

His first attack occurred in an advanced hydrology engineering class taught by G. V. Loganathan in Room 206. Thirteen registered students were inside. Cho swung open the door, stood in the doorway and looked at the students, some of whom he knew, with blank eyes. He did not smile and he did not frown. He just looked and shot at the students as if he were a surgeon making an incision. He shot and killed the professor and nine of the thirteen students and injured two others. Two students lay on the floor pretending to be dead and were unharmed.

After leaving the classroom, Cho caught two students running down the hall, fleeing from Room 207. He aimed his Glock 29 at them and fired, but they managed to escape down the stairwell across the hall. He also fired at another student and a substitute professor from Room 205 who were peering out from the door, but they survived. He then went into Room 208, where instructor Jamie Bishop was teaching Introductory German. "I think he may be coming this way," Bishop told the class. Cho opened the door, shot Bishop and some students near the door, then walked into the classroom and shot at other students inside, who were running for the corners and dropping on the floor or behind the teacher's desk. Cho fatally shot Bishop and four students, then wounded two others. Cho moved on to Rooms 211 and 204 but he was initially not able to push the doors open because students had set up barricades against the doors.

Hearing the commotion from below, professor Kevin Granata guided twenty students from a classroom on the third floor into his office, where the door had a lock. Granata then went downstairs to investigate along with another professor, Wally Grant. Cho, who was now in the hall, glanced up and saw them. "What in hell are you doing?" Granata said, just as Cho opened fire. He shot both men as they came down to the second-floor hallway. Grant fled into a bathroom, where he survived, but Granata died within minutes. Cho tried to open Granata's office but could not, and none of the students locked in the office were harmed.

Next Cho calmly walked down to Room 211, methodically checking room to room. Inside Room 211, Intermediate French professor, Jocelyne Couture-Nowak, peeked out and saw Cho heading toward her doorway. She and student Henry Lee quickly ducked inside and barricaded the door with a few desks while she yelled at students to get down on the floor and under their desks. "Call 911!" she called out to them. Cho pushed through the barricade and entered the room. Lee called out, "Why are you doing this?" Cho did not answer. He simply aimed his pistol and shot and killed Nowak and Lee, with two shots and they fell behind the door. A student named Matthew La Porte, who was a trained Air Force ROTC cadet, charged toward Cho and attempted to tackle him. "Aaaaaaah!" La Porte growled as he drove toward Cho, but Cho shot him seven times as he rushed forward. Of the 22 students enrolled in the class, 18 were present at the time of the shooting. Cho shot a total of eleven students and injured five more. The sole uninjured survivor, Clay Violand, played dead and he and a wounded female student were the only two people to walk out of the room when police arrived.

Cho's pattern was to open doors, stand in the doorway and fire into classrooms from the doorways, then walk up and down the aisles of the classroom and methodically target potential survivors as they tried to hide. He did not say a single word throughout the shooting. In between shootings, he reloaded in the hallways, then reentered rooms to make sure everybody was dead.

He returned to Room 206 and found that a student named Waleed Shaalan was trying to move. He had been wounded and Cho, without a word, shot him a second time and killed him. Another wounded student named Guillermo Colman was shielded from Cho by the body of student Partahi Lumbantoruan, who had fallen on top of him. Although Cho entered Room 206 three times, these students and two others who were playing dead managed to get out alive.

After Cho left Room 207 a while earlier, several students barricaded the door and had begun tending to the wounded. Cho returned minutes later, pushed the door open again and found that Katelyn Carney and Derek O'Dell were holding the door. He shot through the door, injuring them, but the remaining students survived. In Room 205, students had already barricaded the door with a large table after graduate assistant Haiyan Cheng, who was substituting for the professor, saw Cho coming. Cho shot through the door about seven times, but failed to force his way in. Finally, he gave up and no one in the classroom was wounded or killed.

Across the hall in Room 204, Professor Liviu Librescu, a holocaust survivor from Romania, prevented Cho from entering his room by holding the door with his body until most of his students escaped through the windows. After kicking open the window screens, the students successfully escaped. Some suffered leg injuries while landing on the ground two floors below, others survived after landing on the shrubbery just below the window and then ran either to some ambulances pulling up or to the nearest bus stop. Cho shot Librescu through the door four times, including through his wrist watch. Two students who were lying in a corner near the windows were also hit and injured. Cho finally forced his way in and saw Professor Librescu and student Minal

Panchal lying on the ground next to the door. He shot both, execution style, in the temple, then turned to two other students who were hiding behind desks and critically injured them before going back out to the hallway.

At 9:50 a.m., ten minutes after the Norris Hall shooting began, a SWAT team entered the building. They couldn't shoot their way through the chain-locked entrances, but they managed to find a separate door and ran up to the third floor, where they found student Emily Haas, who was wounded and hiding in one of the empty rooms. She said that the gunman had been in her Classroom (211) and she had escaped to the third floor. As police started to descend the stairwell to the second floor, Cho heard their footsteps from the hallway.

"Police!" one of the officers called out.

"Throw down your guns!" another said.

As soon as he saw them, Cho ducked into the next classroom, Room 211.

The police walked down the stairs toward the room. "Come out of there with your hands up!" they shouted.

They waited for a few minutes and then they heard a shot.

When he heard the police, Cho looked out of the room where he had paused to reload. He peered down the hallway to check on where the voices were coming from. When he saw the police, he closed the door and backed into the center of Room 211. Students outside saw him stare out the windows for a moment as if they were thinking about escaping into the nearby woods. Then he heard the police yelling outside the door, lifted his Glock 19, shot himself in the temple and fell backward onto the floor. He died instantly. The expression in his face was blank. When police arrived, they saw Cho lying on the ground with his guns beside him. Some students in nearby classrooms, who were either injured or playing dead, heard the officer's first words:

"Gunman down!"

State Police Superintendent William Flaherty told a state panel later that officers had found 203 remaining rounds of ammunition and noted that "the armed aggressor" was well prepared to continue on. During the two attacks, Cho killed five faculty members and 27 students (two students in West Ambler Johnston and twenty-five teachers and students at Norris Hall) before he committed suicide. A Virginia Tech Review Panel later reported that Cho's gunshots wounded seventeen others; six more were injured when they jumped from second-story windows to escape from Librescu's classroom. Sydney J. Vail, the director of the trauma center at Carilion Roanoke Memorial Hospital, said that Cho's choice of 9 mm hollow-point bullets increased the severity of the injuries, since hollow-point bullets make a wider hole when they enter a body. Twenty-eight of the victims were shot in the right or left temple.

Later, when police searched his apartment looking for clues about Cho's motive, they found a note scrawled in frenzied handwriting: "You have vandalized my heart, raped my soul, and torched my conscience. You thought it was one pathetic boy's life you were extinguishing. Thanks to you, I die like Jesus Christ, to inspire generations of the weak and defenseless people."

CHO'S FAMILY AND LIFE

Functional families—families that are wholesome, healthy, loving, honest and well-adjusted—are transparent. They have nothing to hide. They are sociable people who are friendly and known in their neighbors and by the communities in which they live. Their children go to school with smiles on their faces, make friends who often become lifelong pals, and do well in school. Such families are positive models and an inspiration to all. Dysfunctional families—families that are unwholesome, unhealthy, dishonest and poorly adjusted—are secretive and their family life is shrouded in mystery. They are not sociable people nor particularly friendly, and they remain uninvolved and unknown by their neighbors and by their communities. Their children go to school with frowns on their faces and do not make friends or do well in school—and, quite the opposite, are often outcasts. They live behind closed doors and it is difficult to know what exactly has gone on behind those doors. Parents in such families do not acknowledge to themselves and others the horrors they may have committed against their small children, but instead pretend that all is well.

Following the Virginia Tech killings, Seung-Hui Cho's family withdrew from public life and seemed to become just as mute as their prodigal son had been. A year after his killing spree, his parents had virtually cut themselves off from the world. Relatives from South Korea had not heard from them. The blinds were always drawn at their home in Centreville, Va., and several windows were papered over.

"They continue to live in darkness," said Wade Smith, a North Carolina lawyer who was assisting the family. "I think there will come a time when they are able to speak; for now, they have made it clear to me they just want to be quiet and not say anything."

The family was still in hiding as of this writing.

The family had seemed to be in hiding from the time Seung-Hui Cho was born. He was born on January 18, 1984, in Asan, a remote, hardly known outpost in South Korea's South Chungcheong Province. Not too long after he was born, the Cho family moved from one dark place to another, from the isolated village to a dingy, basement apartment in Seoul. Neighbors hardly knew they were there. Cho had an older sister named Sun-Kyung who was the family's "golden child," while Cho, who was an unwanted kid, became the pariah. His father, Sung Tae, was an introverted intellectual who ran a bookstore, from which he made little money. His mother, Hyang Im, was a frustrated housewife.

The Cho family was not a happy family. Cho's mother was forced into an arranged marriage with a man she detested, who was ten years older than her and from a poor blue-class family from the south. She had been born into a well-educated family of North Korean landowners, who had been forced to flee without their possessions during the Korean War. Desperate to marry their daughter off, her parents found a man who had made enough money to support her by working in Saudi Arabia for 10 years on construction sites and oil fields. Relatives noted that Cho's mother bitterly resented having been forced by her father to marry Sung Tae, a man whom she considered beneath her.

The Cho family immigrated to the United States in 1992, when Seung-Hui was eight years old. The family first lived in Detroit, then moved to the Washington metropolitan area after learning that it had one of the largest South Korean expatriate communities in the U.S. They settled in Centreville, an unincorporated community in western Fairfax County, Virginia, near Washington, DC. Cho's father and mother opened a dry-cleaning business, where eventually they applied for, and became permanent residents on the basis of being South Korean refugees. His parents were devout Christians and soon became members of a local Christian church. Seung-Hui was raised as a Christian, although, in a note found in his apartment, he railed against his parents' strong Christian faith.

While his older sister thrived, Seung-Hui did not. From the beginning he did not seem to listen or look or talk to his family. Some members of Cho's family who had known him in South Korea had concerns about his behavior during his early childhood. They thought that he was mentally ill. According to Cho's uncle, Cho "didn't say much and did not mix with other children." Cho's maternal great-aunt described Cho as "cold." According to this great-aunt, who only met him twice, Cho was extremely shy and "just would not talk at all." Although he was otherwise considered "well-behaved," readily obeying verbal commands and cues. The great-aunt said she knew something was wrong after the family's departure for the United States because she heard frequent updates about Cho's older sister but no news about Cho. During a TV interview after Cho's mass killing, Cho's grandfather reported his concerns about Cho, pointing out that he never made eye contact, never called him by his name designation, grandfather, and never embraced him.

Soon after the Cho family had moved to America, Cho was diagnosed with mutism. Mutism is a disturbance defined as an unwillingness or refusal to speak, and is said to arise from psychological causes such as depression. During his preschool years in South Korea, Cho exhibited what relatives called selective mutism, causing him to speak to some people but not others, and not speak to anybody at all on other occasions. If he entered a room of people with whom he was uncomfortable, he would not speak and nothing would inspire him to speak. There were certain people, like an aunt, to whom he would always speak, and others, like his grandfather, to whom he would occasionally speak, and others with whom he would never speak. He learned to speak Korean and then, at eight years old, English, but would typically have a long response time. If someone asked him a question, he would sometimes pause for 30 seconds while the questioner waited with furrowed brows for an answer.

A family acquaintance reported that when Cho attended the Poplar Tree Elementary School in Chantilly, Virginia, "Every time he came home from school he would cry and throw tantrums saying he never wanted to return to school." It is common for young children to cry on their first day of school, but for Cho the shock of elementary school was made worse by the fact that it was full of strange-looking people (white people) who did not speak Korean.

Research has also shown that the more insecure a child's attachment is with his family, the more he will fear leaving it. Mary Ainsworth, an influential researcher, studied mother-and-child interactions and concluded that there were three major styles of attachment: secure attachment, ambivalent-insecure attachment, and avoidant-insecure attachment. Cho seemed to have the avoidant-insecure attachment. Children with such an attachment, according to Ainsworth's follow-up studies, were usually not able to establish secure attachments later in life when it came to finding a mate if they had not established a secure, trusting attachment in their first relationship with a maternal figure. Another researcher, John Bowlby, came to the same conclusion. In studying many infants and mothers, he found four stages of attachment. During the first stage, from birth to six weeks, a baby is indiscriminate in its attachments; in the second stage, from six weeks to about six months, the child begins to attach to familiar people; in the third stage, attachment proper, six months to 18 months, a child develops a firm and exclusive attachment to mother; in the fourth stage, after 18 months the child learns reciprocal behavior (a give-and-take relationship) with mom and others. Bowlby emphasized the importance of the third stage, noting that if children did not establish this firm attachment with mom—because, for example, their mom died at that stage), they would suffer a trauma that could sometimes result in lifelong depression.

In order to understand the effect of attachment on humans, one can look at cats. It is well known by trainers and cat owners that if a kitten does not get enough handling by humans at the earliest cat infant and toddler stage, the kitten will grow up shying away from handling by humans. It is not because of any chemical imbalance or biological factor. It has to do with kitten attachment. It is the same with humans. If they are not handled and lovingly cared for by a caretake during this early stage—from six to 18 months—they will not want to be attached to people later on.

Notwithstanding his attachment issues and mutism, according to a former fifth grade classmate of Cho's, he eventually adjusted to the Poplar Tree School and finished the three-year program at the school in one and a half years despite having to learn a new language. He was even complimented as a good example by teachers. In this first

American school, he got along with other students despite his mutism. By the eighth grade, Cho had been officially diagnosed with selective mutism and would no longer communicate with teachers or students. This was the point at which he began to be bullied by certain students in his classes, who seemed to be annoyed by his standoffish attitude.

"Hey, what's wrong with you, Choo-choo," the bullying kids would likely have said when they saw him standing awkwardly in the corner. "You can't speak? Or you don't want to speak?"

"Maybe he doesn't like us," another boy might say.

"Maybe he thinks he's too good for us white people," another would say.

"Maybe if I pull his nose, he will speak?" The first boy might pull his nose and Cho would stand frozen. "No, that doesn't work. He still can't talk."

"Maybe you need to pull something else!" The two boys might giggle in Cho's face, and Cho would stand there and say nothing.

"Should we pull something else, Choo-Choo?" The boy might reach down. "I would pull it, but I can't find it! Hey, it's not there!"

The students might laugh and laugh and Cho would simply stand there and look blankly out into space.

This bullying continued throughout middle and high school. Students laughed at his extreme shyness and his unusual speech mannerisms, and singled him out as an oddball with a funny Korean accent. Former classmates who tried to be friends with him noted that he was a loner who did not seem interested in interacting even when teachers or other students tried to include him. Girls in his classes treated him as if he were a joke, and boys—especially those with sadistic tendencies—teased him unmercifully. He walked around the halls of the school in what appeared to be a daze.

During Cho's ninth-grade year, in 1999, he suddenly snapped out of his daze. The Columbine High School massacre made international news and Cho was transfixed by the news, and began to talk. He talked about the incident and began idealizing Eric Harris and Dylan Klebold, the Columbine shooters. The incident seemed to inspire the angry part of him, which he usually tried to keep hidden. "I remember sitting in Spanish class with him, right next to him, and there being something written on his binder to the effect of, you know, 'Fuck you all, I hope you all burn in hell,' which I would assume meant us, the students," said Ben Baldwin, one of Cho's classmates. Cho also wrote in a school assignment about wanting to "repeat Columbine". The school contacted Cho's sister, who reported the incident to their parents. Cho was sent to a psychiatrist, but nothing came of it.

In high school, Cho was placed in special education under the "emotional disturbance" classification. Teachers were sympathetic because of his mutism and excused him from oral presentations and class conversation. He was assigned to speech therapy, which was totally irrelevant to his mutism. He continued to receive misguided therapies that did not address his real issue—his anger—until the end of his junior year.

According to two of Cho's family members and one family friend, the Cho family had been told that Cho's mutism was a symptom of autism; however, no known record exists of Cho ever being formally diagnosed with autism. A clinical psychologist and expert in selective mutism said that based on Cho's videos, Cho "was not autistic. He clearly has the capability of talking to people." However, a paper published in 2017 in *The Journal of Psychology*, years after Cho's shooting spree, stated that there was "strong evidence suggesting Asperger's syndrome for Cho." The debate still goes on. It appeared that mental health experts were called in throughout Cho's childhood but were not able to help him. This is a theme found in most of the cases of mass killers that I have studied, and it indicates a failure of America's mental health system.

When Cho left for Virginia Tech at 18 years of age, the family lost control of him. Cho's mother, a devout Christian, was increasingly concerned by reports of his inattention to classwork, absences from school and run-ins with campus police. She sought help for him during the summer of 2006, before he left for college, from various churches in Northern Virginia. According to Dong Cheol Lee, minister of One Mind Presbyterian Church of Washington, Cho's mother was frantic about her son's situation and asked about spiritual healing. "She thought that her son's problem needed to be solved by spiritual power ... that's why she came to our church—because we were helping several people like him." Members of Lee's church even told Cho's mother that he had "demonic power" and needed deliverance, and they planned on some kind of exorcism. Before the church could meet with the family, however, Cho returned to school to start his senior year at Virginia Tech. A Federal law prohibited church officials from disclosing his condition or treatment without Cho's permission, and therefore the Virginia Tech admission office was not told anything about it.

In his freshman year at Virginia Tech in 2003, Cho majored in business information technology, but he reportedly did not get along with students or professors in the business technology school. By his senior year, Cho changed his major to English, professing a desire to be a writer. He began writing bizarre stories, plays and poems.

In a screenplay called *Richard McBeef,* which he wrote as a class assignment, a young man accuses his stepfather of murdering his father in order to possess his mother. The young man later derides the stepfather for committing pedophilia when he puts his hand on the young man's leg, apparently in a friendly gesture. "What are you, a Catholic priest," the boy rails at the stepfather. "I will not be molested by an aging, balding, pedophilic stepdad named Dick. Get your hands off me, you sicko. Damn you, Catholic priest. Just stop it, Michael Jackson." At the end of the play, the stepfather punches the 13-year-old stepson, killing him. This play is, of course, a lose takeoff of Shakespeare's *Hamlet.*

"Nobody took too much notice of him except for, oh, that's the kinda weird quiet kid who never talks," said Steven Davis, 23, a senior who was in a drama class with him. "Until we read his work. And then it was like whoa, something is off."

Nikki Giovanni, a professor, told about teaching Cho in a poetry class in the fall of 2005. She said she found his poetry and behavior so menacing that she was scared of him. She recalled that Cho had a "mean streak" and described his writing as "intimidating." Giovanni reports that Cho wore sunglasses in class and that when she tried to get him to participate in class discussion, Cho remained stubbornly silent. She related how in her class, Cho had angered female classmates by photographing their legs under their desks and by writing violent and obscene poetry about "depraved sluts who deserved to be killed." By the fall of 2005, Giovanni told the then department head Lucinda Roy she would resign before she could continue to try to teach Cho. After this, Roy removed Cho from the class."

Roy had taught Cho in her Introduction to Poetry class the previous year. She described him as "actually quite arrogant and could be quite obnoxious, and was also deeply, it seemed, insecure." She stated that she had told him numerous times to go to counseling, to little avail. She said that Cho hardly spoke in class and took cell phone pictures of her while she taught, which unnerved her. After she became concerned with Cho's behavior and the themes in his writings, she developed a special, motherly interest in him and started meeting with him privately to help him adjust to American life. Sometimes they would study art together.

"Tell me, what does that drawing mean to you?" she may have asked.

He might simply look at her without answering.

"Look at the drawing, not at me."

He might have kept looking at her.

Mostly he would not smile. Sometimes he would suddenly smile at her in a strange way.

Roy soon became concerned for her safety, and she arranged that if she spoke a certain name of a beloved former professor to her assistant, who would accompany her when she tutored Cho, the assistant should call security. After Roy notified authorities of Cho's behavior, she again urged Cho to seek counseling, again to no avail. Roy described Cho as seeming "extraordinarily lonely," and said that Cho, in a moment of lucidity, even admitted he was lonely and didn't have friends. Roy says that she found Cho's writings to be very disturbing and his behavior menacing, and she asked for help from the police and the university administration. However, the police took no action, since Cho did not make any explicit threat.

As the years at Virginia Tech passed, Cho became more peculiar and deluded. At the time of the attacks, Cho lived with five roommates in a three-bedroom suite in Harper Hall. They reported odd incidents such as the night he sat in the corner at a party and repeatedly stabbed the carpet in a girl's room with his pocket knife. Karan Grewal and Joseph Aust, two of the males who shared a room with him, stated that Cho was so reclusive and unpredictable that they mutually avoided any relationship with him. They claimed that Cho had an imaginary girlfriend named "Jelly." Aust related that during the period leading up to the killing spree, he noticed that Cho's sleep schedule became unusual; he would be up all night and dozing during the day, sometimes mumbling the name, "Jelly." Andy Koch and John Eide, roommates with Cho at Cochrane Hall during 2005 and 2006, also spoke about how they became aware of his imaginary girlfriend. Koch told about how Cho, under the influence of alcohol at a party, provided a description of Jelly:

"She's a supermodel living in space," he said.

Koch and Eide tried to pin him down. "What part of space? Is she on Mars?"

He thought for 20 seconds before answering. "No, not Mars."

"Is she in a black hole?"

Another long pause. "No, she's here on earth but she's living in space!"

Koch described other incidents of disturbing behavior. Once, Cho stood in the doorway of his room late at night taking photographs of Koch. Koch was trying to study and did not say anything to Cho about it, having become used to such behavior; but Koch felt afraid, as Cho was aiming the camera at him like a gun. Later, Cho began calling himself "Question Mark." He would sign in to classes with a question mark instead of his name, and Koch recalled how Cho repeatedly made harassing cell phone calls to Koch. "It's Cho's brother, 'Question Mark'." Koch also described a telephone call that he received from Cho during the Thanksgiving holiday break from school, during which Cho claimed to be "vacationing with Vladimir Putin" in North Carolina." Koch and Eide, who had earlier tried to befriend him, gradually stopped talking to him and told their friends, especially female classmates, to stay away from their room.

On one instance, Cho told his roommates, "I frightened a girl when I went to her dorm to look her in the eyes."

"What did you see in her eyes?" they asked.

Cho remarked, "I saw promiscuity in her eyes."

Koch and Eide related that Cho had gotten in trouble because of two incidents involving two different female students, which resulted in verbal warnings by the Virginia Tech campus police. The two students, one of whom was probably Emily Hilsher, felt Cho was stalking them, but did not press charges. According to Koch, "Question Mark" was Cho's online persona which he used to talk with girls. Koch stated that Cho also used to call him on the phone using the alias, Question Mark. Koch and Eide said that on at least two occasions, police came to their room to investigate a woman student's complaint about Cho's behavior online. According to Koch, after one such incident police came at night to Cho and Koch's dorm and banged at the door after a complaint that Cho had been talking to a woman online about wanting to commit suicide."

On November 27, 2005, a student called the campus police, stating that Cho had sent her annoying messages and made an unannounced visit to her room. Two campus police officers visited Cho's room at the dormitory later that evening and warned him not to contact the student again. The student may have been Emily Hilsher.

Things all came to a head on December 13, 2005, when Cho appeared in Emily Hilsher's room. In the preceding days, Cho had both sent her an AOL message, and written on her door, a line from the Shakespeare play *Romeo and Juliet*. Hilsher was initially unconcerned by the AIM messages and the quotation from Shakespeare until she was contacted by her friend, Koch, informing her of Cho's previous stalking incidents. Koch speculated that Cho had schizophrenia. Hilsher contacted the campus police, who again warned Cho about further unwanted contact. Later the same day, Cho sent an email to Koch stating, "I might as well kill myself now." Worried that Cho was suicidal, Koch called home to talk to his father for advice. Both contacted campus authorities.

The campus police went to his dormitory and escorted Cho to New River Valley Community Services Board, the Virginia mental health agency serving Blacksburg. There, Dr. Crouse, the physician in charge, declared Cho to be "mentally ill and in need of hospitalization." He noted that Cho had a flat affect and depressed mood, and that Cho "denies suicidal ideation" and "does not acknowledge symptoms of a thought disorder." The physician also noted: "His insight and judgment are normal." He speculated that Cho was in "imminent danger to himself or others." Cho was then detained temporarily at Carilion St. Albans Behavioral Health Center in Radford, Virginia, pending a commitment hearing before the Montgomery County, Virginia district court. On December 14, 2005, Cho was released from the mental health

127

facility and on the same day Virginia Special Justice Paul Barnett ordered treatment for Cho as an outpatient. However, Cho did not receive the treatment and neither the court, the university nor community services officials followed up on the judge's order. He was set free.

During February and March 2007, Cho began to prepare for his grand finale. He started purchasing the weapons that he later used during the killings. On February 9, Cho purchased his first handgun, a .22 caliber Walther P22 semi-automatic pistol, from TGSCOM Inc., a federally licensed firearms dealer based in Green Bay, Wisconsin. On March 13, Cho bought his second handgun, a 9mm Glock 19 semi-automatic pistol, from Roanoke Firearms, a licensed gun dealer located in Roanoke, Virginia. Because Cho was not involuntarily committed to a mental health facility, he was still legally eligible to buy guns under Virginia law.

Soon after, on April 16, 2007, Cho went on his killing spree, murdering Hilsher and Clark and 30 other people. In between shootings, he paused to mail a package of his videotapes, photos and writings to NBC.

In one videotaped message he said, "You had a hundred billion chances and ways to have avoided today. But you decided to spill my blood. You forced me into a corner and gave me only one option. The decision was yours. Now you have blood on your hands that will never wash off." In another videotape, he discussed "martyrs like Eric and Dylan" referring to the Columbine High School gunmen Eric Harris and Dylan Klebold, who killed thirteen people and then shot themselves on April 20, 1999, in Littleton, Colorado. In yet another videotaped message, he railed against the wealthy. "You had everything you wanted. Your Mercedes wasn't enough, you brats. Your golden necklaces weren't enough, you snobs. Your trust fund wasn't enough. Your vodka and cognac weren't enough. All your debaucheries weren't enough. Those weren't enough to fulfill your hedonistic needs. You had everything."

The package included an 1,800 word "manifesto," 27 QuickTime videos of Cho talking to the camera while discussing religion and his hatred of the wealthy, and several photographs of Cho posing and pointing handguns at the camera, at his head, and a knife to his throat.

CULTURAL FACTORS

Seung-Hui Cho was caught between two cultures, the South Korean one into which he was born, with its roots in the Christian religion, and the American culture into which he was transported at the age of eight, which he perceived as emphasizing sex, drugs and violence. He was a boy who lost himself in the first years of his life and retreated into a shell from which he hid from the world. At the same time, he seemed to want to protect the world from his dark self. Later he became a young man who was struggling to fit into American culture, looking for his identification in that culture, but feeling shut out and inferior. He had been left mute by the mysterious trauma that happened in his early childhood, and hence ill-equipped to deal with the most basic issues of living, taking care of himself, going to school and dealing with his biological needs.

He railed against the rigid Christianity of his parents and he at first thought that American culture might offer a way out. But while he railed at his parents' fundamental Christianity, that fundamental indoc-trination also came to permeate his perspective and colored his reaction to what he saw as the hedonism of American culture. It provided him a sense of moral superiority and provided him with an excuse for not being able to make the leap and handle the chaos of American culture. Hence, he displaced all his anger about his childhood neglect onto this wild new culture. He could not allow himself to feel or express his rage against his parents, which had been stirred up before he could talk or think, and which was forbidden by the Christian faith. ("Thou shall honor thy father and mother.") But he could direct this rage in his thoughts and through his writings at America and at the students at Virginia Tech, who were proxies of American depravity. He focused on what he saw as the sinfulness of American culture as exhibited by the students at Virginia Tech, and he managed thereby to bolster his low self-esteem by turning his wrath on his fellow students. He wanted desperately to be accepted by them, but his personality had already become so damaged by the way his life got started and how it was limited by his mutism, that he was not acceptable to himself or anyone. Hence, he rejected the people whom he felt rejected by, and looked at them with loathing and degraded them in his mind.

"You had everything you wanted," he uttered in one of the video-tapes in the package he sent to NBC. "Your Mercedes wasn't enough, you brats. Your golden necklaces weren't enough, you snobs!" It is clear in this message how deep was his anger toward his fellow stu-dents. He had begun to see them as evil, as part of a culture he had tried so hard to be accepted by, but had instead only found rejection. He projected his own unconscious feelings of shame and self-hatred onto those who shamed him. It was not Cho who was loathsome and hateful, but the sinful hedonists out there. Unconsciously, the rage was toward his parents, but on a conscious level, it got redirected to his sinful fel-low students. Eventually, his hatred of Virginia Tech and of America became a self-fulfilling prophecy: Virginia Tech and America became the monsters he assumed they were.

When the news of the Columbine High School mass shootings ex-ploded into the media, he took particular notice. The Columbine shoot-ing may have been the catalyst that sent him over the edge into stage 3 rage. According to reports by fellow students, he became obsessed by this incident and began speaking to whoever would listen about "another Columbine." It was clear that he had found an outlet for his locked-up anger and it was perhaps at that point that he had begun making plans for his own mass shooting. Like other mass killers, he found inspiration in a violent incident that was alarming and sad to most others.

The violence in American culture, as evidenced by the ongoing mass shootings, seemed to go straight to Cho's heart. These mass shootings brought out the violence he secretly harbored, which until then had found expression only in his obstinate refusal to respond to or talk to other people or in his strange writings. Had it not been for the violence of American culture, he might never have gone on his mass shooting spree. Instead, he might have spent his life in his shell or he might have ended up committing suicide. Homicide and suicide are two sides of the same coin. If one is an intropath (that is, if one takes out his mental disturbance on oneself) then suicide is the solution. If one is an extropath (that is, if one takes out his disturbance on others), then the answer is homicide. Cho was apparently in the middle of this range. When a young man like Cho witnesses one mass shooting after another and observes this to be a "grand event" in which someone just like him becomes a gigantic antihero and is given a kind of negative, but intense international attention, he is provided the perfect antidote to his misery.

American society, moreover, was rife with daily putdowns of males, and he had probably been required to take a seminar in college to help him get rid of his toxicity toward females. He would have heard the slogans about "toxic masculinity" and "rape culture" and "the sins of patriarchy." I can make an educated guess about how he felt because of my experiences with my male therapy clients; these attacks and accusations of males affected my male clients deeply. In order to understand how the anti-male culture affected Cho and other young men, consider the opposite: How do you think young females would react if they heard slogans about "toxic femininity," and "female abuse of men" and "female sexism"? What if young females were required to take sensitivity training courses to guide them in being more sensitive to men? Would they not be infuriated? Cho was already full of shame and self-hatred, and the anti-male sentiment of American culture could not help but exacerbate such feelings.

A young man like Cho, who has lived in a shell all his life and has had to listen to his angry inner thoughts and deal with the inner pain such thoughts bring, will feel trapped in his own tormented self. When one is in extreme pain, he will do anything it takes to end that pain, even if it means jumping off the highest cliff in the world, diving into the deepest ocean or killing a hundred people. By killing himself and 26 others, he could not only gain revenge in one big bang on the world, but he could also finally assert himself as he had never been able to do before.

He wanted to be a writer, he wanted people to know that he had deep thoughts and feelings and he wanted people to know that he was someone to be respected. He did not choose to be the way he was, but rather he believed he was made to be that way by a corrupted culture. In the 23-page manifesto he delivered to NBC News, he addressed the "terrorists" of American culture, saying:

> Are you going to admit the truth or are you going to stand resolute on your mission to eternally fuck the Weak and the Defenseless and lie about it? Are you still going to use your power and manipulate the truth to end up with some sort of profit as you have always done? Are you going to skip over all the crimes you've committed and act as victims to the world so you can suck in millions of donation money to turn the situation into a profit?...I am the antiterrorist of America.

He was not in touch with the original childhood trauma that set him up for a fall. His first trauma, and the deepest trauma, was caused by his parents, but it was so far back in time it was beyond memory. Instead, he focused on the indignities he suffered from American culture. He did not and could not remember the earliest part of his childhood. It was easier to get mad at Virginia Tech.

FINAL ANALYSIS

From an early age, Seung-Hui Cho suffered from mutism, a condition in which a person withdraws into a shell and selectively does not speak to certain people or only occasionally to some people and occasionally to other people. It is not known when the mutism began, but it seemed to have started before the age of three, when Cho had begun to talk. Although mutism is viewed by experts as a condition that is related to psychological trauma, experts in this case did not look for psychological trauma. Instead, they concentrated on how this mutism affected his life.

Cho's parents did not have a good marriage. His mother, Hyang Im, came from a wealthy family that had lived near the border between North and South Korea. When the war started, the family lost its wealth and had to move to the south of Korea. When Hyang Im was 29, her father was anxious to get her married—females in Korea at that time generally married by the age of 20—so he arranged a match with a poor, shy bookstore owner who was ten years older than her. She was a strong-willed 29-year-old who did not want to get married at all. She felt angry and resentful when her father forced her into this marriage to a man she did not like. Korea, at that time, was a patriarchal society, and men ruled their households with an iron fist. So Hyang Im had no choice but to marry this man that she loathed. In the first few years of the marriage, she tried to make it work and did her best to be a good mother to her first-born, a daughter named Sun-Kyang. She was able to moderate her resentment about her marriage and embrace her daughter. Seung-Tae also lavished his daughter with love, and this daughter became the focal point of both parent's attention. Hence, she flourished and became a somewhat healthy woman.

Seung-Hui did not flourish, as his beginning in this life was just the opposite of his older sister's. By the time he was born, Hyang Im's resentment about her father's arranged marriage with a poor man against her will had grown to a point where she harbored a deep hatred for both her father and the man he made her marry. Neither her father nor her husband paid any attention to her feelings of resentment, so her feelings remained pent-up inside her. When she had a boy child, her hatred found a suitable object; it was directed at her Seung-Hui, her new son. From my studies of this type of situation in dysfunctional families, I have found a certain prevalent pattern. I speculate that Cho's mother likely suffered from postpartum depression when this male child was born—a depression brought about by the combination of her hatred of her husband and of her father. She was angry with her husband for forcing her to have two children in a row, when she hadn't wanted to marry him or have any children at all. Each new child may have caused her to feel further entrenched in an unsavory situation. Now, suddenly, she was weighed down with the child-rearing of two children, which to her case may have seemed like she had been sentenced to a prison sentence with a man with a cheery prison guard. She was able to tolerate the first child, a girl, but not her second child, a boy. Giving birth to and having to care for an offspring of her unwanted husband and detested father may have sent her into a deep and bitter depression.

If Hyung Im suffered from postpartum depression (which seems likely) she would not have been a happy mother. She would be a mother who has no interest in taking care of her baby or in anything else. She will be unable to get out of bed or even brush her teeth, take a shower or eat a meal. The baby lies in its crib crying for hours at a time without relief. If the mother does pick up the infant, she is often rough with it, does not speak to it and does not look at it. The mother sometimes does not want the child to exist. She sees the child is an evil thing that has ruined her life and crushed her aspirations. The source of her anger was her father, primarily, and her husband, secondarily, but she could not directly express her anger at them, for they were too powerful. While she may have been neglectful of her son, her husband was neglectful of her. The anger at her father, her husband and at men in general, was probably completely displaced onto her son.

An infant is the most vulnerable of human beings. An infant's ego is not yet formed, so the infant has no means of psychological defense. Whatever harm is done to the infant has a much deeper and lasting effect than harm done to a seven-year-old and an even deeper effect than harm done to a 14-year-old. What little information we have suggests that Cho's mother suffered from guilt and depression but nevertheless believed that demonic spirits, not her upbringing was the cause of his misery—as when she desperately took him to a local church to be exorcised. If she had postpartum depression, she might have severely neglected him. This caused the infant Cho to be deeply hurt. An infant cannot think it out, cannot say to himself, "Something rotten is being done to me! Look at me, Mom! Love me! Help me!" But he can feel these things on an unconscious, physical level. He has what psychoanalysts call a "body ego," and he reacts on a physical, rather than an intellectual level, to what is being done. The mother refuses to talk to him, and when he later learns to talk, he refuses to talk to her or to anybody else. The mother refuses to look at him and he later refuses to look at her or anybody else. The mother does not care about him, so later he does not care about her or anybody. The mother does not want him to exist, and later he does not want her or anybody to exist. The mother has been a monster to her baby, and so she ends up raising a monster. Early traumas are the deepest and longest-lasting traumas.

Cho apparently received a major blow to his development at the moment he was born and during his first months of life, and this blow was an arrest that he could not overcome. From infancy on, he closed up like a clam. He thus started out life in the most disadvantaged way and had to look on while his older sister was going through life in a much more advantaged way. Then, later, after he could talk, he had to look on while his mother, filled with guilt about her early abuse and neglect, went overboard to try to find a cure for his malady, which she was sure had come from some "Devil seed." He had to look on while his parents went from doctor to doctor trying to find a cure, but perhaps craving all the while that they would just sit down with him and be honest about what happened at the start. But parents such as this are not able to be self-honest; they are interested in covering up and saving face.

His life, from the beginning of his childhood was a miserable one. He tried valiantly to find acceptance somewhere—in his family, in his elementary, middle and high schools, from his college roommates, from the young women he approached without having the confidence and social skills to successfully court. On some unconscious level, he sensed that he had superior intelligence and talent, but the emotional damage that he had received rendered his intelligence or talent ineffective. His parents and relatives could see how he was, but they could not help him. They took him to health care professionals and the professionals could not help him either. They tried giving him medication that could only maintain him at a low level but not cure him. Only years of intense psychotherapy by a dedicated psychotherapist could have altered the course of his severe disturbance, but that never happened.

In college, his disturbance blossomed into what appeared to be schizophrenia. There were many signs of his withdrawal from reality and inability find an identity. He began to introduce himself in his classes, on social occasions, and to various women, as "Question Mark." His use of that phrase to name himself indicates his sense of having no direction and no settled sense of himself. He had begun his college career by majoring in business technology, but later changed to English. He initially craved acceptance from fellow students and when he couldn't get that he reviled them. His life was a struggle between his id, which demanded almost unconditional love and acceptance by his peers, and his superego, influenced by his Christian fundamentalism, which caused him to judge these same peers as morally inferior. There was very little ego to mediate between the out-of-control id (his inner child) and a harsh superego (his moral system), and he remained a boy without a compass.

At some point during his college years he developed a seeming delusion of having a girlfriend named Jelly, whom he described at one point as a supermodel living in space. He spoke of this girlfriend on numerous occasions and seemed convinced of her existence. However, in a story called, "The Adventures of Spanky," written for one of his classes, he fantasized about a girlfriend named Jelly and, in this story, he was aware she was a fantasy. He fantasized being a superior man who had a supermodel girlfriend, and who was morally superior to all the bullies from elementary school onward who looked down on him, insulted him, teased him, laughed at him and roughed him up. His fantasies also contained magical thinking about people becoming his friends even though he completely shut himself off from them and acted in ways that were peculiar, obnoxious and threatening to them (taking pictures of the legs of girls under their desks). He also seemed to have paranoid features, linked to his projections onto his peers, in which he blamed their hatred for his misery (they made him that way) but saw his own hatred as justified by his victimhood. Some have thought that he had delusions and other indications of schizophrenia, but he did not seem to have delusions, only fantasies which did not indicate a complete break from reality.

Year after year, he internalized his rage at Virginia Tech and at the world. This rage did not come out directly until the end. Instead it leaked out in his odd behavior and in his writings. He could not feel anger at a mother who had been overly devoted to him since the time he became aware of himself and of what was happening to him—from the age of three onward. He had no memory of his mother's original neglect before the age of three, during her likely postpartum depression, nor any access to the anger connected with that neglect. So, he protected his parents from his rage, even though they were the original cause of it. All his rage was displaced on the students at Virginia Tech.

Cho's relationship with his mother and father was ambivalent. The information we have about her resentfulness about her forced marriage inclines me to the supposition that she suffered from postpartum depression, particularly when Cho was born, and that she was a neglectful mother who lay in bed all day and did not address his infantile needs. Later she may have felt guilty about it and that guilt then caused her to swing from being neglectful to being overprotective. While he may have liked her guilt-ridden overattentiveness, underneath his positive feelings toward her lurked his free-floating anger. Meanwhile, his mother's binding him to her may well have stirred up a fear of his father's jealousy. This theme came up in his short play, *Richard McBeef,* in which the stepfather kills the son. That he called the character McBeef was a way of parading him (The "beef" in the stepfather's name may have represented his beef against the boy, who had taken the mother's attention from him, or it may have represented his larger penis. This entanglement in an Oedipal world with his parents was another reason his rage had to be displaced to Virginia Tech; it was a forbidden and sinful entanglement. His parents were the only mother and father he had, and so he needed to protect them from his anger and divert the anger to the "sinful" students of Virginia Tech.

Hyang Im probably developed a reaction-formation toward her son; that is, she behaved in the extreme opposite to the hatred she felt down deep. On an unconscious level, she resented and hated him. But having been raised as a devoted Christian, she could not admit this hatred to herself or anybody else, so she became an extremely caring, supremely conscientious mother. Every day she told him how much she loved him. Every day she searched her brain for ways to make him come out of his shell. Every day she contacted one doctor or another or one church or another. She convinced herself that she loved her son with all her heart, but since that love was a reactionary, guilt-ridden love and not a real love, it only went so far.

Cho struggled mightily to find out who he was and to assert himself, but he could only do so in a twisted way. He took pictures of females, teachers and roommates, symbolically shooting them. He wrote Oedipal plays in which a mean stepfather kills his son, hoping the teachers who read his works and would understand his misery; instead, they saw him as bizarre and menacing. He attempted, unsuccessfully, to form relationships with his roommates and, indeed, seemed to have opened up to them more than to anybody he had ever been involved with in his life, but that did not succeed. He tried, in his clumsy way, to court a few young women at Virginia Tech but ended up scaring them away due to the twisted way he approached them. Sometimes his delusion of moral superiority caused him to reject women before they could reject him, as when he entered a female student's room and saw "promiscuity in her eyes." He had no idea of how to love himself, much less how to love a young, desirable female.

Toward the end, although he had strived mightily to keep his rage in, he had reached stage 2 rage and it started to spill out in bits and pieces, as when he wrote an angry poem or play or when he harassed roommates on the phone or stalked various females. During his freshmen year at Virginia Tech he tried for a while to fit in, but when he could not succeed, he gave up trying to fit in and began to revel in his victimhood, particularly in his stories about an outcast. His play, *The Adventure of Spanky,* started out with a poem titled "a boy named LOSER," who lived in his fantasies and dreams.

a boy named LOSER
walks off the sidewalk, shudders into his house,
and lays his weary head to sleep and dream.
In his dream, he lives two lives,

> because in this world he has no life,
> no class, no friends—just a Moron in this world.

The poem is followed by a collection of interrelated stories that reveal his image of himself as a sweet guy. The first story is about Spanky and his girlfriend, Jelly. Why did he call the protagonist Spanky? Does it denote how in his upbringing he had been spanked (punished) and therefore was awkward with girls? Jelly is a sweet, warm girl with pink hair who loves to kiss and hug Spanky. She wants to kiss him but he hesitates because he hasn't brushed his teeth. They spend a happy day doing innocent, playful things like riding on a merry-go-round and soaring to the sky on swings—it was a day of hugs and kisses and the activation, so it seemed, of childhood fantasies, not of adult sexuality. He was still a child-man and had not yet truly reached adulthood. When she undresses to take a shower, he goes home in order to be polite and not see her naked body. This story conveys the fantasized normal relationship with young women he wished he could have had.

This is followed by another story in which the lead character is named Bud. Bud wakes up and finds a car idling on the street and steals it. He drives to a field where he has hidden some guns and then puts on his black jeans and black vest and stuffs the guns into his pockets. He drives to a nearby school, where he intends to shoot the students. "Bud stands in the middle of the empty hall. He stands there for a moment, then turns and goes to an arbitrary classroom, and stands in front of the door." This story is obviously a rehearsal of what he has been planning to do in real life. But this time he can't do it. He watches a class where "everyone is smiling and laughing as if they're in heaven-on-earth, something magical and enchanting about all the people's intrinsic nature that Bud will never experience." He is about to open fire on this class, but sees a gothic girl, who gives him a sympathetic, knowing look, and he changes his mind. The gothic girl may be another version of Jelly, a woman who knows what he is going through because she, a gothic girl, has known that same pain.

His poem and fiction display his self-hatred (calling himself a LOSER), his fantasy life of an ideal world wherein Jelly was in love with him, and his later hatred and jealousy toward the students in the class who are smiling and laughing as if they're in heaven-on-earth. He acknowledges that this was a way he would never be. He knew he would never have Jelly or anyone like her, and he knew he would never be released from the excruciating pain of his alienated existence, so he had to live in his fantasies.

His anger was brought over the top on December 13, 2005, when Emily Hilsher rejected him and called the campus police. He was taken by the police to a psychiatrist, who found him to be a danger to himself and to others, and to a judge, who ordered him to undergo outpatient psychotherapy. However, he was let go and not required to do any psychotherapy. This was the moment where the system truly failed, and this was a turning point for Cho. Had the system reeled him in at that moment and put him in a hospital for his own and other people's sake, things might have been different. If someone, anyone, would have finally sat down with him and taken the time to really talk to him and find out what was boiling up within him, he might have been able to snap out of his funk.

Instead, from that point on Cho seemed to know that if he wanted to do any killing, he would have to do it soon. He probably knew that he had been given one last chance to execute his plans and he did not know how long that chance would last. So, he began to buy the guns and to plot the details of the shooting spree. He most likely began his manifesto during those last days and finished it on the morning of his killing spree.

The stories of this mass killer and all mass murderers are the stuff of tragedy. Their traumatic childhoods render them too broken to function in even a somewhat healthy manner. Cho and other mass killers often have higher than average IQs, many talents and abilities and an unusual sensitivity and perceptiveness. But they cannot activate any of these abilities, talents or skills. Having such potential and knowing they are too emotionally crippled to use it must be doubly frustrating for them. That is the ultimate tragedy of the mass killer.

Mass killers like Cho are men who might have been geniuses, but instead they are derailed by the unfortunate circumstances of their lives and the unwell cultures in which they grow up. They strive mightily to compensate for those circumstances by reinventing themselves according to some form of heroic vision but they end up in a revenge killing spree that does not heal them, but they only succeed in passing their misery back to the world.

SOURCES:

Virginia Tech Shooting. In *Wikipedia*. Retrieved from: https://en.wikipedia.org/wiki/Virginia_Tech_shooting

Seung-Hui Cho. In Wikipedia. Retrieved from: https://en.wikipedia.org/wiki/Seung-Hui_Cho

Seung Cho. The Adventure of Spanky. Retrieved from: https://schoolshooters.info/sites/default/files/Cho_Fiction_Poetry.pdf

Seung-Hui Cho (Oct. 14, 2014). In Biography. Retrieved from: https://www.biography.com/crime-figure/seung-hui-cho

Seung-Hui Cho. In *Incels Wiki*. Retrieved from: https://incels.wiki/w/Seung-Hui_Cho

Seung-Hui Cho. In *Murderpedia*. Retrieved from: https://murderpedia.org/male.C/c/cho-seung-hui.htm

Seung-Hui Cho's Manifesto. Retrieved from: https://schoolshooters.info/sites/default/files/cho_manifesto_1.1.pdf

Somashekhar, S. and Horwitz, S. (April 12, 2008). "A year later, family of Virginia Tech g https://www.spokesman.com/stories/2008/apr/12/a-year-later-family-of-virginia-tech-gunman-still/unman still lives 'in darkness'." In *The Spokesman-Review*. Retrieved from

Seung-Hui Cho. In *The Conserapedia*. Retrieved from: https://www.conservapedia.com/Seung-Hui_Cho

Watts, J. (April 19, 2007). "Gunman's Brooding Disturbed his family." In *The Guardian*. Retrieved from: https://www.theguardian.com/world/2007/apr/19/usgunviolence.usa4

"Police: Cho Stalked 2 Women in 2005." In *CBS News*. Retrieved from: https://www.cbsnews.com/news/police-cho-stalked-2-women-in-2005/

Drogin, B., Fiore, F. and Kang, C. K. (April 22, 2007). "Bright Daughter, Brooding Son, Enigma in the Cho Household." In *Los Angeles Times*. Retrieved from

https://www.latimes.com/archives/la-xpm-2007-apr-22-na-cho22-story.html

Seung-Hui Cho. In *The Famous People*. Retrieved from: https://www.thefamouspeople.com/profiles/seung-hui-cho-40993.php

Seung-Hui Cho. In *Criminal Minds Wiki*. Retrieved from: https://criminalminds.fandom.com/wiki/Seung-Hui_Cho

Virginia Tech Shootings. In *Encyclopedia Virginia*. Retrieved from: https://encyclopediavirginia.org/entries/virginia-tech-shootings/

Mass Shootings at Virginia Tech. In *Virginia Tech Review Panel*. Retrieved from: https://scholar.lib.vt.edu/prevail/docs/VTReviewPanelReport.pdf

Virginia Tech Shootings Fast Facts. In *CNN*. Retrieved from: https://www.cnn.com/2013/10/31/us/virginia-tech-shootings-fast-facts/index.html

Staff Writers. "For Some Locals, Cho Family was 'Like Ghosts." In *Tampa Bay Times*.

Retrieved from: https://www.tampabay.com/archive/2007/04/22/for-some-locals-cho-family-was-like-ghosts/

Kleinfeld, N.R. (April 22, 2007). "Before his Slaying, His Life." In *Orlando Sentinel*. Retrieved from: https://www.orlandosentinel.com/news/os-xpm-2007-04-22-vatechnyt22-story.html

Shapiro, A. (April 18, 2007). "Cho's Behavior Troubled Those Who Knew Him." In *NPR*.

Retrieved from: https://www.npr.org/templates/story/story.php?storyId=9642190

Timeline of the Virginia Tech Shooting. In *Wikipedia*. Retrieved from: https://en.wikipedia.org/wiki/Timeline_of_the_Virginia_Tech_shooting

Schoenewolf, G. (2022). "The Banned Theory of Autism." In *Forbidden Psychology: A Book for Dark Minds*. Bushkill, PA: Living Center Press

Ainsworth, M. D. S., et. al (1978). *Patterns of Attachment: A Psychological Study of the Strange Situation.* **New York: Psychology Press, 2015**

Bowlby, J. (1988). *A Secure Base*. New York: Basic Books

CHAPTER 5

JAMES OLIVER HUBERTY

THE SHOOTING

On July 15, 1984, 41-year-old James Oliver Huberty took his wife, Etna and their two daughters, Zelia and Cassandra, aged 12 and 10, to the San Diego Zoo. After walking through the zoo, they had lunch at a nearby McDonald's and returned home early in the afternoon, at which time he checked his answering machine. He was expecting a call from a mental health clinic, which he had contacted the day before, asking for help with his "mental health problem." When he did not receive an answer from the clinic, he became enraged, and he said to his wife, "Well, society had their chance."

Huberty, who was of medium height and build, had been recently fired from his job as a security guard and had been in a rage ever since the firing. He had been in a stage 2 rage most of his life. After the firing, he slid into stage 3 rage, which propelled him to bouts of physical abuse toward his wife and children. On this particular day he had been jolted deep into stage 3 and he could hardly contain himself. He yelled at Etna about hypocritical people before getting dressed in a maroon T-shirt and a pair of green camouflage slacks and prepared himself to execute the escape plan he had been mulling over. His wife lay resting in bed, keeping silent as she had learned to do when he got into his moods. He leaned toward Etna and said, "I want to kiss you goodbye."

She let him kiss her and asked, "Where are you going? I'll be starting dinner soon."

"I'm going hunting…hunting for humans," he replied. He gave her the menacing smirk that had become his trademark over the years of their marriage.

She looked at him and said nothing. He had been sniping and yelping since the firing, and while this statement about hunting for humans shocked her, it did not surprise her. She did not report it to the police. She most likely did not even give it a thought. She was angry herself and at her wit's end—so over it that she no longer cared what he did or what the result was.

Holding a rifle across his shoulder and carrying a bag of ammunition in one hand and a shotgun wrapped in a checkered blanket in the other, he walked out of the bedroom. As he went toward the front door of their home, he glanced toward his oldest, ten-year-old daughter and said, "Goodbye, Zelia. I won't be back."

He then drove down San Ysidro Boulevard, looking for a place to do his "hunting." He felt a little feverish but otherwise he felt calm. Do it, he probably thought. Just do it and get it over with!" He first drove to a Big Bear Supermarket, passed it by, and headed toward a branch of the U.S. Post Office. He considered the Post Office for a few minutes, then changed his mind again and entered the parking lot of the McDonald's restaurant across San Ysidro Boulevard where he had eaten a Big Mac an hour before. The building was a little over 100 yards from his apartment, and Zelia and Cassandra were able to watch their daddy through the back window of their house.

"What's Daddy going to do," Cassandra probably asked her older sister.

"Something bad," Zelia answered.

It was approximately 3:56 p.m. when Huberty parked his Mercury sedan and took out his arsenal of weapons. It included a 9mm Browning HP semi-automatic pistol, a 9mm Uzi carbine, a Winchester 1200 12-gauge pump-action shotgun and a bag filled with hundreds of rounds of ammunition for his weapons. He strode from his car and looked through the window inside the restaurant. There were about 45 customers inside the restaurant, gobbling down hamburgers and French fries with no idea that a killer was about to enter. He flung open the door and walked toward the counter, aiming the shotgun at a 16-year-old employee named John Arnold. As he did so, the assistant manager, Guillermo Flores, pointed to Huberty.

"Hey, John, that guy's going to shoot you!"

"Really?" Arnold answered.

Huberty pulled the trigger, the shotgun clicked, and nothing happened. Arnold, who thought Huberty was joking, began to walk away. As Huberty checked out his gun, the manager of the restaurant, 22-year-old Neva Caine, dashed toward the counter. "What's going on?" she asked. Huberty fired his shotgun toward the ceiling to check it out, shooting a hole in the ceiling, before aiming the Uzi Carbine at Caine, hitting her once beneath her left eye. She sank to the floor and died in a few minutes. Huberty smiled, relieved that the gun had worked, and fired the shotgun at Arnold, wounding him in the chest and arm. By this time customers were jumping up from their chairs.

"Oh, my God!" someone shouted.

"He's got a rifle!" someone else yelled.

"Everybody down!" Huberty yelled back. "Get down on the floor, you morons!" He waved his two rifles around the room like some rebel from the deep woods and began to rant. "You're all a bunch of filthy jerks! You're a bunch of Vietnam assholes. I have killed thousands like you in Vietnam and I'm going to kill a thousand more today! You're nothing but a lot of human trash. You're worthless! You all think you're hot shit, and you're not! You're just a bunch of worthless trash! Yeah, look at me, that's right! You're nothing but trash! And you know what has to happen to human trash? You got it! It has to be disposed of!"

When Huberty paused in his rant, one of the customers, 25-year-old Victor Rivera, tried to persuade him not to shoot anyone else. "Listen, you don't have to do this," Rivera said. "Whatever is going on with you, it can be resolved..."

"Shut up!" Huberty replied. He shot Rivera four times and screamed, "Shut up! Shut up! Shut up!" and shot him ten more times. River's body jerked here and there and he fell to the floor as he cried out in pain.

At that point staff and customers were diving under tables and hiding behind the counters. Huberty turned his attention toward six women and children huddled together in a corner of the restaurant. He shot and killed 19-year-old María Colmenero-Silva with a single shot to the chest and followed that by shooting nine-year-old Claudia Pérez in the stomach, cheek, thigh, hip, leg, chest, back, armpit, and head. He then wounded Pérez's 15-year-old sister Imelda in the hand with the Uzi and fired upon 11-year-old Aurora Peña with his shotgun. Peña—wounded in the leg—had been shielded by her pregnant aunt, 18-year-old Jackie Reyes. Huberty shot Reyes 48 times with the Uzi, seeming to be particularly angered by a pregnant woman. She held her stomach as she died. Eight-month-old Carlos Reyes sat up and wailed, whereupon Huberty shouted at him, "Shut up, you little piece of trash!" Huberty killed the toddler with a single pistol shot to the center of the back.

Huberty then shot and killed a 62-year-old trucker named Laurence

Versluis, who was having lunch before continuing on his route. Then he found a family huddled near the play area of the restaurant. Blythe Regan Herrera, the 31-year-old mother, was shielding her son, Matao, who was eleven, beneath one booth, while her husband, Ronald Herrera, 32, was protecting Matao's friend, 12-year-old Keith Thomas, in a booth.

"Don't move," Herrera whispered to Thomas.

Huberty aimed his guns and started shooting in rapid fire. He shot Thomas in the shoulder, arm, wrist, and left elbow, but Thomas was not seriously wounded. He shot Ronald Herrera six times but he survived. His wife, Blythe, and son, Matao, were both killed by numerous gunshots to the head.

Nearby, three women were also attempting to hide beneath a booth. Twenty-four-year-old Guadalupe del Rio lay against a wall; she was shielded by her friends, 25-year-old Gloria Ramírez, and 31-year-old Arisdelsi Vuelvas Vargas. Huberty hit del Rio several times but she was not seriously wounded and shot Vargas once in the back of the head and she was critically wounded. She died of her wound the next day. Ramirez was unhurt. At another booth, Huberty killed 45-year-old banker Hugo Velázquez Vasquez with a single shot to the chest. He squirmed on the floor in pain and expired.

It wasn't until about 4 pm that emergency calls starting coming into police headquarters. Unfortunately, the dispatcher mistakenly directed officers to another McDonald's two miles from the San Ysidro Boulevard restaurant. This delayed the arrival of police by about ten minutes, and the only warnings to civilians walking, riding, or driving toward the restaurant were given by people waving their hands and shouting on the street.

"Stop! Don't go to McDonald's! Someone's shooting!"

At approximately 4:05 p.m., a Mexican couple, Astolfo and Maricela Félix, not paying attention to the people shouting on the street, drove toward the take-out window of the restaurant. Noting the shattered window, Astolfo initially assumed renovation work was in progress and that Huberty—who was standing inside the shattered window—was a repairman. No, he was not a repairman, he was a grim reaper in a maroon T-shirt. Huberty, who had shot at everybody in the restaurant was now stalking the new arrivals. He raised his shotgun and Uzi and fired at the couple and their four-month-old daughter, Karlita,. striking Maricela in the face, arms and chest. He critically wounded the baby in the neck, chest and abdomen, and shot Astolfo in the chest and head. All three survived.

Next, three 11-year-old boys rode their bikes into the parking lot to purchase sundaes. Huberty stepped forth and shot the three boys with his shotgun and Uzi. One boy survived and two others did not. Huberty then noticed an elderly couple, 74-year-old Miguel Victoria Ulloa, and 69-year-old Aida Velázquez Victoria, walking toward the entrance. As Miguel was opening the door for his wife, Huberty fired his shotgun, killing Aida with a bullet to the face and wounding Miguel. Miguel cradled his wife in his arms, wiping blood from her face, and shouted curses at Huberty.

"You monster! I'll kill you! I'll kill you for this!" he shouted at Huberty.

"No you won't, you piece of shit," Huberty said, and snuffed him with a shot to his forehead.

About ten minutes after the first call had been placed to 9-1-1, police finally arrived at the McDonald's restaurant. The first officer on the scene, Miguel Rosario, rapidly determined the location and cause of the actual disturbance and relayed this information to the San Diego Police Department while Huberty fired at Rosario's patrol car.

Officers immediately imposed a lockdown on an area spanning six blocks from the site of the shootings. They established a command post two blocks from the restaurant and deployed 175 officers in numerous strategic locations. These officers were joined within the hour by several SWAT team members, who also took positions outside of the restaurant. There were police cars in parking lots all around the six-block area and more coming with their sirens blaring. An officer was waving furiously at drivers on San Ysidro Boulevard, "Move on! Just move on!" But some drivers stopped to get a look at McDonald's.

Huberty, inside the restaurant, was still firing rapidly and alternating between firearms when police arrived. They initially could not tell how many people were inside the restaurant, because most of the restaurant's windows had been shattered by gunfire and reflections from shards of glass provided an additional difficulty for police trying to see what was happening inside. At first they could not determine if the gunman (or gunmen) might be holding hostages, and only after one individual who had escaped from the restaurant informed them that there was a single gunman holding no hostages could police properly assess the situation. At 5:05 p.m., all responding law enforcement personnel were authorized to "kill the perpetrator(s) should you obtain a clear shot."

Several survivors reported seeing Huberty walk toward the counter and adjust a portable radio, apparently searching for news reports of his shooting spree. He could not find a news station so he turned the dial to a music station. He selected one that had rock music and then resumed shooting out of the window at police cars. For several minutes he was shooting and dancing to the music. He was smiling and kicking his legs and swinging his hips, then stopping to shoot through the window once more, and then dancing and smiling and whirling around. He looked as if he were in a disco somewhere, not in a McDonald's surrounded by dead bodies. It was apparent that not only was Huberty in the throes of stage 3 rage, but also giddily celebrating the release of that rage. After dancing a while, with no more targets in sight, he suddenly decided to search the kitchen area, where he discovered six more employees.

"Oh, there's more," he said, grinning, as he pushed open the swinging door. "You're trying to hide from me!"

Paulina Lopez, a 19-year-old cook, cried out in Spanish: *"Por favor, no me mates! ¡No me mates!"*

Huberty laughed and opened fire, killing López, 19-year-old Elsa Borboa-Fierro, and 18-year-old Margarita Padilla, and critically wounding 17-year-old Albert Leos. As Huberty had begun shooting, Padilla grabbed the hand of her friend and colleague, 17-year-old Wendy Flanagan, and the two began to run. Huberty fatally shot Padilla. Flanagan and four other employees and a female customer hid inside a basement utility room. They were later joined by customer, who had crawled to the utility room after being shot five times.

When a fire truck drove up, Huberty opened fire and pierced the vehicle with bullets, wounding one of the men. Huberty heard a wounded teenager, 19-year-old Jose Pérez, moaning behind him; he shot him in the head, and the boy fell dead in a booth. He also shot his neighbor, 22-year-old Gloria González, and a young woman named Michelle Carncross. At one point, 11-year-old Aurora Peña, who had lain wounded beside her dead aunt, baby cousin and two friends pretending to be dead, noticed a lull in the firing. She made the mistake of opening her eyes, only to see Huberty staring right at her. "You fucking little piece of trash! You think you're going to live? Is that what you think!" He threw a bag of French fries at her, then lifted his shotgun and shot the child in the arm, neck, and jaw. Aurora Peña survived, although she would remain hospitalized longer than any other survivor.

At around 5:17 p.m., Huberty sat on the counter for a minute resting and perhaps contemplating his next move. After a while, he walked from the counter toward the doorway and paused at the drive-in window of the restaurant. The window had been shot out and afforded a clear view of him. At that point, a 27-year-old police sniper named Charles Foster lay on the roof of the post office directly opposite the restaurant with an unobstructed view of Huberty's body from the neck down. This post office had served the neighborhood for years; it was a place where people rushed in and out of the doors to send or pick up mail. Now is was in a war zone and the roof served as a vantage point for conducting the war. Foster aimed and fired a single round from about 35 yards. The bullet entered Huberty's chest, severed his aorta just beneath his heart, and exited through his spine, sending Huberty sprawling backwards onto the floor directly in front of the service counter, killing him almost instantly. "I never did see his face," Foster said excitedly, afterwards. "The first time I was actually able to see him, he was sitting on a counter in about the middle of the building. Then he got up and started walking toward the door, where we had a better view of him from the neck down. He stopped about six feet from the door, so I took the shot. He dropped the Uzi and was thrown back a few feet." By the end of the shooting spree, Huberty had managed to kill 20 people and injure 21 more.

There are many ways to commit suicide. There is the direct way of killing yourself via gun, jumping off a bridge or—as Cleopatra did it—unleashing a poisonous snake upon yourself. There are many indirect ways of suicide such as drinking yourself to death, smoking yourself to death, working yourself to death or over-eating yourself to death. And there is the deferred method that Huberty used. He simply stood near the shot-out window and waited for the SWAT team to do its job. Consciously or unconsciously, he knew he would be killed sooner or later. He heard the sirens, saw the fire engines and police cars pulling up in the parking lots across the street. He knew it would just be a matter of time. Unlike many other mass killers, he decided to let somebody else pull the trigger. He stood smiling defiantly, like a soldier in his last, glorious stand.

"I never saw his face at all," Foster, his sniper said. "I could only see his neck and chest, so I shot him there. It was so easy."

HUBERTY'S CHILDHOOD AND LIFE

James Oliver Huberty was born on October 11, 1942 in Canton, Ohio, the second of two children born to Earl Vincent, a quality inspector, and Icle Evalone Huberty a homemaker and later a missionary. His sister, Ruth, was 4 years older. Both parents were devoutly religious, and the family regularly attended local United Methodist churches. No information is available about what kind of mothering he got during his first three years of life. However, we know that when Huberty was three years old, he contracted polio. This was apparently the original traumatic jolt of his early life, and for several years he went through the shock and pain of dealing with polio. He had to wear steel-and-leather braces on both legs. He recovered from the illness, but the three-year episode left him with a slight limp and a not-so-slight emotional scar along with a bitter chip on his shoulder that festered through the years.

When Huberty was seven, his father purchased a 155-acre farm in Mount Eaton, Ohio—an Amish community. Icle refused to live in a rural community and would not even look at the property. Husband and wife bickered endlessly about this as their children looked on. To make matters worse, Icle felt "called" to become a Christian missionary, and one day she abruptly abandoned her family, leaving James and his younger sister in her wake. She went on to perform sidewalk preaching as a Pentecostal missionary in Tucson, Arizona and later worked with Indians on the Island of Jamaica. Huberty's father would later remember finding his son slumped against the family chicken coop, sobbing away.

If a mother and father never really get along, the friction between them will often prevent them from paying attention to their children's needs. In Huberty's case, they were not able to pay attention to their polio-infected child's heightened needs. When a child gets polio at three years old and is required to wear steel and leather braces, this will be in and of itself traumatic for a boy. When the parents are embroiled in constant bickering, they will most likely not pay proper attention to that traumatic event, and should they also find the son's polio and his neediness to be an unwanted demand, the trauma will be much worse. The parents were involved in their important bickering, let us say, and their child's cries were viewed as loud, relentless interruptions. "Shut up! We're fighting!" And when the mother abandoned the boy four years later, it was like one trauma piled on another. He must have felt cursed. Indeed, his mother's abandonment of her son at such a young age might have been the deepest hurt of all. It told him that he was worth nothing in her eyes.

After his mother left, he had nobody to turn to but his father, and his father was, according to observers, a religious nut. If the boy complained about his polio or about having to wear the braces or about his mother's abandonment, the father could probably only answer in a pious voice, "God works in mysterious ways." Or perhaps he would tell the boy to "be a man." This would not assuage a boy's hurt, and the boy would become increasingly bitter. Not only did Huberty have to deal with his mother's abandonment, but also with his fundamentalist father's authoritarian parenting. We do not know exactly what went on behind the family's closed doors, but we do know that as soon as he got married, at the age of 23, he never spoke to his father again.

Huberty was a sullen child with few friends, whose primary interest was target practice. A family acquaintance would later describe him as a "queer little boy who practiced incessantly with a toy pistol." He was seen to constantly run around his house shooting at imaginary villains with his toy pistol. "Pew! Pew! Pew!" His toy pistol shot rubber bullets and he would sit in his backyard all day shooting the rubber bullets at a target. By his teens, Huberty had acquired real guns and real bullets, and he was something of an amateur gunsmith. Collecting and shooting guns were his main preoccupations, and he stored them in his basement. Later he set up a shooting range in his basement and would spend hours in the basement practicing shooting the guns. It is not known whether his father knew of his collection of guns or his shooting practice, but Huberty was undeterred. It was as though, even as a teenager, he had begun practicing for the shooting spree that would end his life with a bang.

Due to his limp, his family's religious extremity (which set him apart from his peers), and his social awkwardness, he became a favorite of bullies. The bullies were his schoolmates in middle school and high school. He would typically stand around during recesses not talking to anybody, not joining into activities.

Some of the students at his schools interpreted his standoffishness as a conceit as disdain for them.

"Hey, Huberty, what's the matter, you can't talk? You think you're better than us," they might taunt him.

He would scowl at them and try to walk away, but they would catch up with him and shove him hard. Two or three of them would surround him.

"Don't do that!" he would say, but without conviction.

"What are you going to do about it?"

He had developed taciturn pride to compensate for inner shame, and bullies saw through it. Sometimes, when he limped by them, they would trip him up and have a good laugh as he fell. He would get right back up and limp away with his patented grin, as though to say, "You can't hurt me." But inside, he was incensed.

"That's right, walk away, loser!" they would laugh.

In Waynedale High School in Apple Creek, Ohio, he remained an outsider all four years and the bullying not only left him bitter at those who bullied him but also at people in general. Ever since he had gotten polio at three and had seen his little friends running and playing while he was trying to maneuver around with the heavy braces on his legs, he had felt jealous of other guys and angry about his situation. This jealousy of other guys stayed with him throughout middle and high school. If he went to his father to complain about the bullies, his father would simply tell him to "turn the other cheek," hence he got no real help in dealing with adversity. He railed at bullies in an ineffectual way and gave them disdainful looks, which made them keep coming. In order to stop bullies, you have to give them only neutral looks and just go on your way; you can never give them the satisfaction of thinking they have gotten to you. Body language is everything. He could not be neutral because he was too angry and bitter to do that. The bullying became a nightmare, and it became his whole world, affecting his ability to function. Academically, he barely got by, graduating 51st out of a class of 77 students in 1960. It is hard to do well in school when you are being constantly bullied. Like other mass killers, he internalized his anger during these years and tried to take it in stride.

In 1962, Huberty enrolled at Malone College, a private Christian University in Canton, but he only lasted a semester. Soon after, he opted to study at the Pittsburgh Institute for Mortuary Science. He graduated with honors from this institute in 1964, earning a funeral director's license and, the following year, an embalmer's license. His interest in mortuary science and in embalming can perhaps be seen as a proxy for his preoccupation with death and suicide, which would plague him all his adult life. In early 1965, Huberty met Etna Markland at Malone College. They were alike in that they both came from dysfunctional families, and she apparently took a maternal interest in him. They were soon married, and shortly afterwards, he got a job at a funeral home in Canton. Although proficient at embalming, Huberty's caustic personality caused him to have problems in dealing with members of the public and also led to conflicts with his superiors. He lasted for only two years on this job before suddenly going into a completely different direction—becoming a welder for a firm in Louisville. Two years later he quit that job for a better-paid position at Babcock & Wilcox, a company known for manufacturing steam boilers.

Gradually, Huberty's finances began to grow. Being a welder did not require him to deal with others, and although he was reclusive and taciturn, he was a good worker. His employers considered him reliable, and he willingly took overtime, earned promotions and by the mid-1970s, he regularly earned between $25,000 and $30,000 per year ($121,000–$145,000, adjusted for 2021 inflation). Shortly after Huberty was hired by this firm, he and his wife moved into a three-story home in an affluent section of Massillon, Ohio. In the winter of 1971, this home was destroyed by a fire. How this fire started is a matter of speculation. However, shortly thereafter, James and Etna bought another house on the same street. They later built a six-unit apartment building on the grounds of their first home, which they managed together. Daughters Zelia and Cassandra were born in 1972 and 1974, respectively. In the beginning, he expressed love for Etna and she became a calming force. All went well for a few years.

Soon he began to physically abuse his wife and later his two daughters. When Etna later reflected on her relationship with her husband, she confessed, "I always figured there was a strong chance he'd kill me one day." Considering he once threatened her by pointing a gun at her, she had a reason to be worried. After giving birth, she became worried for her daughters. "I didn't become afraid for the girls until after February," Etna said. This was when her husband got angry with their oldest daughter Zelia. "He went flying into her bedroom with an Uzi pointed at her," Etna confessed.

Huberty frequently yelled at his daughters, slapped them, punched them, held knives to their throats and pointed guns at their heads. He treated his wife and two daughters as if they were disobedient prisoners in his own private concentration camp. Mostly Edna took the brunt of his domestic bullying. On one occasion, Etna filed a report with the Canton Department of Children and Family Services stating that her husband had "messed up" her jaw, although she later insisted that on the majority of occasions he only struck her once. Edna was also known to become physical with Huberty at times, but that was probably done to defend herself. Beginning in 1976, Etna repeatedly attempted to persuade her husband to seek counseling to alleviate his sources of stress.

"You need help, Jim," she would tell him again and again.

"I don't need therapy. Other people need therapy," he would tell her.

"And I don't need to walk on egg shells around you all the time," she replied.

Like other mass killers, he saw himself as an innocent victim of a corrupted society. In her efforts to pacify his anxiety and rage, Etna took great efforts to minimize any possibility of agitating him. Occasionally, she would read his future on tarot cards, always predicting success and happiness, as a way of calming him down. Huberty believed her tarot readings and they would produce a temporary soothing effect in him, and he would usually follow the advice his wife gave him during these readings. She seemed to become his surrogate mother, replacing the mother he had lost at seven, but he also transferred the ambivalence he felt toward his mother onto his wife.

Huberty was seen by his neighbors and coworkers as a sad, irritable, and paranoid guy preoccupied with firearms. He was said to keep a mental record of every setback, insult, or general source of frustration—real or perceived—that had ever happened to him or his family. In psychology such a person is called an "injustice collector." This is often a feature of the self-defeating personality disorder. On several occasions, James' neighbors were alarmed when they heard gunshots coming from the Huberty's basement, where James had set up his makeshift shooting range. "No Trespassing" signs were posted all around the house, and he also had a security dog to which he apparently had no emotional attachment.

His lack of attachment to the dog was highlighted one day when one of James' neighbors informed him that his dog had damaged his car. Within minutes, James had taken the dog to the back of the house and shot it dead. The neighbor was furious.

"What are you doing?" the neighbor said. "There was no need to do that!"

"I believe in paying my debts, both good and bad," he replied.

A conspiracy theorist and survivalist, Huberty believed an escalation of the Cold War in the 1970s was inevitable and that President Jimmy Carter and, later, Ronald Reagan and the United States government were conspiring against him. Convinced of an imminent increase in Soviet aggression, he believed that a breakdown of society was fast approaching, perhaps through economic collapse or nuclear war. He devoted himself to surviving this perceived collapse by stuffing his house with ample supplies of non-perishable food and guns and other weapons—some purchased from co-workers[71]—which he intended to use to defend his home during what he believed would be a holocaust. According to one family acquaintance named Jim Aslanes, Huberty's home was bedecked with loaded firearms to such a degree that wherever Huberty was sitting or standing in his home, whether it be a bedroom, bathroom or kitchen, he "could just reach over and get a gun." Each firearm was loaded, with the safety catch disabled. In all, he collected over 300 guns of various types.

In November 1982, Huberty was laid off from his welding job at Babcock & Wilcox, causing him to become despondent over his dire financial situation and general inability to provide for his family. Upon being notified of the impending closure of this firm, Huberty angrily told a coworker, "If I can't provide for my family, I'll just kill myself and "take everyone with me." According to Etna, shortly after her husband became unemployed, Huberty began hearing voices, a possible symptom of paranoid schizophrenia and a feature of stage 3 rage. In early 1983, he sat in his living room before his family and placed a loaded pistol against his temple, grumbling that he was going to end it all. Etna successfully dissuaded her husband from ending his life, although he later remarked to her: "You should have let me shoot myself."

As his economic situation went up and down, so did his emotional and physical state. Unable to find lasting employment in Ohio, the Huberty's sold their six-unit apartment building for $115,000. Shortly thereafter, Huberty obtained another welding job with Union Metal Manufacturing Company but this job lasted only five weeks before the closure of the plant. In the weeks following this incident, Huberty complained of an aggravation of neck pains he had endured since childhood and of a nerve tremor in his hands and arms. It is common for people who suffer from severe anxiety and depression to have associated physical symptoms. In a state of high agitation, he looked for a quick way out by moving to another locale.

In the summer of 1983, the Hubertys applied for residency in Mexico, believing the money obtained from the sale of their apartment building would financially sustain the family longer in Mexico than in America. Having also sold their home for just $12,000 in cash in September (with the buyer assuming their $48,000 mortgage), they were off. Before leaving for Mexico, he confidently told neighbors, "We're going to show them who's boss."

Huberty and his family moved from Ohio to Tijuana, in October 1983 but was unable to find employment there. Within three months, the family relocated to San Ysidro, a largely poor district of San Diego just north of the Mexican border. In San Ysidro, Huberty rented an apartment in the Cottonwood Apartments, and he and his family were the only White Americans within this apartment complex. This irritated Huberty, who would often complain to his wife and daughters about how his Hispanic neighbors looked and how they smelled. "They should all be shot down before they have a thousand more babies!" he would snap. "All they do is have babies and steal from the government! Maybe I'll just go outside and stand on the street some day and shoot about a hundred of them down." Shortly thereafter, Huberty replied to a newspaper advertisement offering security guard training in a federally funded program. He completed this course on April 12 and soon obtained employment with a security firm in Chula Vista, California, assigned with guarding a condominium complex. The money earned there enabled the family to have their furniture shipped from Ohio, and the family soon relocated to a two-bedroom apartment on Averil Road.

On July 10, after only three months, Huberty was summarily dismissed from this latest job. He was a moody worker who would sometimes show up for work and sometimes not. When he did show up, he had a belligerent attitude. When he was fired, he grinned at his boss.

"Just for the hell of it, could you tell me why you are firing me?" he asked.

His boss, a man who had learned to choose his words carefully when talking with Huberty, answered, "You have a poor work performance and a general physical instability."

"Physical instability? What does that mean? You mean because I limp?"

"No, it's not that." The firing was the last straw, the event that sent him to the highest stage of rage. A few days after the firing, he went hunting for humans.

In 1986, three years after Huberty's shooting spree, Etna Huberty tried to sue both McDonald's and Babcock and Willcox for $7.5 million, claiming that the MSG (a poisonous chemical) in chicken McNuggets mixed with poisonous metals in the welding materials that Huberty used at work sparked delusions and homicidal tendencies. She alleged that his heavy appetite for McNuggets and his years of inhaling fumes on the job were triggers for his homicidal rage. When it was found that these accusations were scientifically baseless, Mrs. Huberty's attorney advised her to drop the charges. This law suit was perhaps a manifestation of her own paranoia. It is sometimes the case that two people may be attracted to one another because they are both lost souls who try as best they can to help one another, but because of their mental and emotional damage they cannot succeed in doing so.

CULTURAL FACTORS

The first culture that Huberty came into contact with was the fundamentalist religious culture of Ohio. His parents were both brought up in this culture, particularly the culture of the Methodist Church to which they belonged. Later, Earl Huberty took his two children to the Amish community of Ohio, a community that was even more fundamentalist. This fundamentalist religious indoctrination had a lasting influence on Huberty's development. When he began to attend regular schools, such as Waynedale High School, his religious fanaticism put him at odds with almost all of the other students in the school and made him the target of bullies. In this respect, his situation was similar to Seung-Hui Cho, whose fundamentalism put him at odds with the mainstream culture at Virginia Tech, and who ended up railing against this culture in the writings that were discovered after his rampage. Huberty's indoctrination in fundamentalist culture continued to have an effect on him throughout his life, causing him to have various prejudices toward groups that he regarded as sinful and morally inferior. His chief delusion was that he was morally superior to almost everybody in America, a moral superiority—a holier-than-thou attitude—that became evident when he killed his dog after his neighbor complained about him, saying, "I always pay my debts." This allowed him to compensate for deep-seated feelings of hatred, shame and inferiority.

The cold war of the 1960s and 1970s between Russia and the U.S.A.

was a cultural event that affected everyone, and it had a large influence on Huberty. He was said to have stockpiled weapons, food, and other items to prepare for the final nuclear holocaust. He was a person who had never felt safe in the world, and perhaps never felt loved. When he was still a three-year-old toddler—an age when a child wants a world that is safe and stable—his world was shattered by the discovery that he had polio. It was shattered again with the breakup of his parents and by his mother's abandonment of him. Each of these events was threatening to his existence. The cold war, with its dark shadow of nuclear annihilation, portended an even more horrific event. During this time his paranoia about being an innocent in a corrupt world bent on destroying him developed full scale and he collected over 300 guns and engaged in rampant thinking about conspiracy theories. In such a fearful culture, one's own fears are exacerbated. All of his anger about what he perceived as the immorality of American society and his fears of people outside of his family were made worse by the nuclear culture, in which people anxiously began building bomb shelters in their basements and hoarding food and drink supplies. The irony is that he viewed himself as an innocent that was corrupted by a corrupt society while he himself was physically and emotionally abusing his wife, daughters and many others.

The 1960s and 1970s were also the starting point of political unrest in the U.S.A. Various political movement sprang up and began to rebel against the American government. There was a slogan that became prominent in those years: "Don't trust anybody over 30." It was the beginning of divisiveness in America between liberals and conservatives, and Huberty was clearly in the conservative camp. Fundamentalists like Huberty saw mainstream liberal society as corrupt and hedonistic. This mainstream took drugs like marijuana, LSD and cocaine, which he believed were evil drugs; they were promiscuous and had serial relationships and divorces, which he viewed as depraved and sinful behavior, and they cared more about their rights than their responsibilities, which he saw as selfish. He believed in being loyal to his wife and family, although his loyalty was filled with abuse. Toward the 1980s, he began to hear himself and other religious and conservative people referred to as "white supremacists" and was bombarded by people angrily complaining about "gun violence" and "bigoted gun owners." The stuff that was going on in American culture—the divisiveness, the political unrest and the persecution and alienation of conservatives and Christians—was bound to exacerbate Huberty's feelings of isolation and probably served to ramp up his rage response.

America culture had become divided and generally violent, where race was pitted against race and ethnic groups were at odds with other ethnic groups. Hence, when he lived in an Hispanic neighborhood, he became easily incensed at the Hispanics. Not too long later, he shot up a McDonald's that was known to cater to Hispanic clientele.

Finally, the escalation of mass shootings no doubt provided a model for how he could discharge his rage. He could not help but notice the constant mass killings in America, and these shootings gave him a way out of his misery. Like other mass shooters that have been studied here, the mass shootings suggested a direction in which to point his rage, and the successive mass shootings probably inspired him. He witnessed these shootings and noted how the shooters went out in a blaze of drama, if not twisted glory, in which they were, at last, given the notice they had always craved. Mass shooters modelled for him—and probably all other potential mass killers—a quick fix for his depression and a way to finally discharge his pent-up rage.

FINAL ANALYSIS

There were two major traumas in Huberty's early childhood that established his personality from that time on. The first one happened when he was three years old, when he contracted polio. A disease like polio is bad enough in itself, but its effect can be complicated by the attitude of the caregivers toward the child with that disease. Not only did he go through the disease, but he also had to go through it alone, without much support from his bickering parents. Afterwards he had to wear heavy metal and leather braces on both legs and watch his three-year-old mates run and jump and enjoy their laughs. To a three-year-old, the ordeal of getting sick and succumbing to the symptoms of polio—a sore throat, fever, tiredness, nausea, headache, stomach pain, loss of muscles, deteriorating breathing and sleep, and eventually paralysis—is like a living nightmare. He was in the honeymoon of infant life, lulled by freedom of concern, and then all at once he was falling into an emotional abyss. Then there was the fear of losing his legs and the requirement to wear the braces on his legs at a time when he had just learned to walk. How did it feel to have all of this suddenly interrupt his toddler paradise? From then on, he limped and felt alienated from others because of polio. Did the renegade feature of his personality begin with these early experiences?

How did his parents react to this ordeal? Some parents provide healthy empathy and support during such a disease and its outcome. Knowing what we know of Vincent and Icle Huberty, we can speculate that they were not able to offer much of that kind of support. Vincent's fundamentalist religion and stoicism would likely cause him to be prone to preaching rather than empathizing. Icle's anger at her husband and apparent abhorrence of family life might have caused her to be equally distant to her son. Healthy parents would tell a son with polio, "We will always be there for you and you can grow up to be just as happy and even better than normal people!" Icle, who abandoned her boy when he was seven and never looked back, demonstrated by such an action a lack of caring toward her son and daughter. Perhaps she was as cold as her name, Icle, suggested. She seemed to be not caring about his polio and also not caring about her husband. Earl, on his part, was probably emotionally distant toward his wife and children. Hence, Huberty would likely have had a strong feeling of being abandoned at three, when his life fell apart. The ordeal of polio and his neglectful parents may have left him with bitter feelings of abandonment. I have known of parents who resented a child for having some disability at birth and bemoaned their fate at having such a child, but at the same time smiled it up and pretended to be loving. This does not work. A child reacts to their parents' vibes, not to their words. How lonely and hurt would Huberty have felt when both his parents were not there for him? This initial loneliness and pain, this feeling that nobody in his child's world really cared about him, seemed to become an aspect of the chip on his shoulder.

Later, when his parents quarreled over the father's decision to buy a farm in Amish country and planned to move there against his wife's will, the boy again felt left out and abandoned. His mother suddenly scrammed when he was seven and went off to be a missionary, giving her attention to Indians in Jamaica but none to her son. Huberty again felt abandoned and uncared for. One can imagine the goodbye scene as she was about to leave.

"Mom, please don't go!"

"I'm sorry, Jimmy. I can't stay with your shit-head father. Please try to understand. I need to do the Lord's work. I will always love you!"

His father said he saw Huberty crying in the chicken house on the farm. He probably heard his father ranting about how selfish his wife was, but that was not helpful to Huberty, and he was left to deal with the aftermath of his polio and his parent's separation by himself. There was nobody to teach him how to accept his polio and how to function in society. His father was no help with any of that; he was a man who could relate to a God in the sky better than to a struggling son here on earth.

His subsequent experiences of being a pariah in his family and an oddball in elementary, middle and high school because of his bitter personality, his limp, his low self-esteem and the chip on his shoulder, attracted bullies to him. These bullying experiences would have exacerbated his feelings of loneliness and of being one against the world. Again, his father was no help with the bullying, just as he was no real help with the polio or with his mother's abandonment. A healthy father would have been more attentive to the son to make up for his lack of a mother, would have spent time with him and would have guided him toward a successful life: "Son, if you want to be a doctor, we'll make that happen." Instead, Huberty did not get the guidance he needed. As a result, once he reached adulthood and got married, he stopped speaking to his father for the rest of his life.

Huberty became who he was because of these early traumas and the ongoing harmful parenting and the bullying in school. As the result of all this, he suffered from lifelong depression, anxiety, self-defeating personality disorder and, perhaps, later, paranoid schizophrenia. These disturbances were clearly not because of a chemical imbalance or any other biological or genetic factor, but because of the vicissitudes of his childhood. It would be a stretch to suppose that an imbalance of serotonin would cause all this. To paraphrase Voltaire, man is not born sick, but he is made to be sick by his conditioning.

Psychiatry, unfortunately, with its misguided attitude toward mental illness, has done a lot of harm. It foisted propaganda about chemical imbalances that has since proven to be wrong. It has encouraged parents to put a whole generation of children on Ritalin and other drugs from an early age and guide them toward lifetime addictions rather than dealing their very real psychological problems. Through lucrative deals with the pharmaceutical industry, psychiatry has advised patients to take more and more opioids, ending up addicting millions of adults, rather than trying to understand the complicated psychological wellsprings of mental disorders. It deemphasized the importance of good parenting and emphasized feel-good medicines as the cure-alls and thus led Americans to look to medicines for all their psychological problems. In short, the psychiatric establishment has taught people to rationalize their immaturity and chase instant gratification.

Without any real aid with his mental health issues, Huberty became a defiant loner who could not get along with others. He got married soon after he crossed over into adulthood to a woman who was also caught up in her emotional problems. The two of them clung to each other in an isolated, dysfunctional coupling, later bringing two children into the world that Huberty would not be able to take care of any better than his parents had taken care of him. He struggled mightily to establish a normal life, despite his physical and emotional handicaps, but he could only go so far. He flew from job to job, from country to country, trying to find a solution to his misery. But the misery was internal, not external. He was depressed, homicidal and suicidal all of his life.

In his early twenties he studied to be a mortician and embalmer. This interest fit in with his depressed and morbid ideology. His thoughts were often about violence and death—his own and other people's. Most likely, when his mother deserted him, Huberty went into a deep depression and thought about committing suicide right then and there. He probably thought there was nothing left to live for. This preoccupation with violence, death and suicide would became a strong feature of his personality. He spent almost all of his life flipping from stage 1 to stage 2 rage. This was evident when his neighbor came to him and complained to him about his dog and Huberty immediately got out his rifle, took the dog to the back of the house, and shot it. The neighbor was rightfully upset, because the attack on the dog was a symbolic attack on the neighbor. It was as though Huberty was saying, "You just made me kill my dog. Would you like me to kill you? Leave me alone!"

People who are in a rage often displace their anger on weaker people, rather than expressing it to those who caused the anger. His parents were the ones who originally made him embittered and angry, but he ended up taking it out on the people who loved him the most and who were most dependent on him—his wife and children. Huberty had a history of domestic disputes and domestic violence with his wife and with his daughters, and he frequently got into huge brawls with his wife that would end up in violence. She claimed he would only hit her once and that he never battered her, and there were also claims by some that she also hit him at times, but he probably did much more to her, since she had to take on all his accumulated anger. He was also violent with his daughters. Etna described an incident when Huberty chased his oldest daughter Zelia into her bedroom with an Uzi carbine. He did not have any love to give to his family, only hate. He was a tyrant as a father and husband, just as his father had probably been in his own childhood.

Years later, Zelia spoke to reporters about the day her father left their house to "hunt humans." Zelia Huberty was just 12 years old then and watched the bloody tragedy from her bedroom window. The MacDonald's was a hundred yards from her window. "I had a perfect view of it," she said later. "I saw the car there. I saw everything. I saw people I knew, who I went to school with. I wasn't thinking anything that time, except: 'Better them than me.' I know that's a horrible thing to say, but as a 12-year-old, that's the sort of thing you think." Zelia said that if she could turn back the clock "I probably would have killed my father before any of this would have occurred." She had by the age of twelve lived in a state of violence and terror for years, and when she saw her father shooting down people in the McDonald's parking lot, what she mainly felt was relief that his anger was finally being directed on somebody other than herself. She went on to become a nurse and said that being a nurse—taking care of people rather than killing them like his father did—was therapeutic for her.

Of note was that most of the people that were killed in Huberty's shooting spree were Hispanic. A few years earlier, he had lived in a Hispanic neighborhood and had developed a loathing for his Hispanic neighbors—so much so that he quickly moved his family into a different neighborhood. It may well be that he was targeting Hispanics on that day. America had become a divided country. Violent behavior was rampant. Blacks shoved Asians onto subway trains; Whites assaulted Blacks: Hispanic gangs roved the streets. America was rife with unrest and distrust. Martin Luther King's often repeated quote about his wish that people would focus not on "the color of one's skin but on the content of one's character," had been all but forgotten.

When Huberty was fired from his last job as guard, he unraveled completely and was thrown into stage 3 rage. From that point on, his superego, which in psychoanalysis is defined as the mind's center of morals and standards, lost control of his morality and his ego could no longer regulate his emotions. The pent-up rage that had festered inside him all his life exploded out of its socket and the rage took control of him. He became a human killing machine, almost like a soldier on the front lines of a war who has been trained to kill and to feel no emotions about those he kills. During that shooting spree, Huberty regurgitated all the "injustices" he had collected over the years. He went on an orgy of violence, chewing people out with his words as he murdered them with his guns.

Finally, at last, he had the power that made up for the feelings of powerlessness caused by his early and later traumas. Perhaps everything streamed through his mind at that moment—his polio at three, having to wear leg braces, yearning to walk like other four-year-olds, fighting with bullies in elementary school, his mother's abandonment and his father's religiosity, getting fired from jobs, hearing the societal putdowns of gun owners like himself—all of this may have jammed his brain and passed through as he fired at the crowd. He fired here and fired there, and not only did he enjoy his power to end people's lives,

he was having a ball. He was dancing to the music of a radio and celebrating a happiness, perhaps even giddiness, that he had never before
felt. All his life he had felt controlled by others and victimized by the
cruelty of his parents, employers and people in general; now at last he
was the one who was completely in control and he was enjoying the
payback. Most people are happy at least some of the time, but Huberty
probably never felt a moment of happiness until the very last hour of
his life, when his true self finally became activated.

Then, after his violent pity-party, his life came to an end. He had
reached his kill point, and he sat on the counter for a moment to take
in what had happened, relish the moment, and prepare for suicide. By
then, he was no longer planning to do it himself. He sat on the counter
waiting to be shot down. Let them have the satisfaction of shooting me,
he may have thought. I had my fun, let them have theirs. Doing that
was a bit easier than aiming the pistol at himself, which, as a Christian,
was a sin. And he could die a martyr.

The windows were all cracked and foggy and the snipers on the
surrounding buildings could not get a clear sight of him as he sat on the
counter. So, he obliged them by ambling over to the take-out window
which had been shot out. As he stood by the drive-in window smiling about his afternoon of good work, a sniper named Charles Foster
looked through the scope of his rifle, aimed it at the figure in the window, and took one shot that hit Huberty in the heart. The bullet did not,
as the saying goes, put him out of his misery. Instead, it most likely put
him out of his ebullience.

SOURCES:

San Ysidro McDonald's Massacre. In *Wikipedia*. Retrieved from: https://
en.wikipedia.org/wiki/San_Ysidro_McDonald%27s_massacre

James Oliver Huberty. In *Murderpedia*. Retrieved from: https://murderpe-
dia.org/male.H/h/huberty-james.htm

James Huberty/Mass Murderer/San Ysidro McDonald's Massacre. In *WickedWe*. Retrieved from: https://wickedwe.com/james-huberty/

The 1984 McDonald's Massacre. In *YouTube*. Retrieved from: https://www.youtube.com/watch?v=XzpefFXjsOg

Brisbane, A. S. (July 21, 1984). "To Father of Mass Murderer, Son's Violence is Inexplicable.

In *The Washington Post*. Retrieved from: https://www.washingtonpost.com/archive/politics/1984/07/21/to-father-of-mass-murderer-sons-violence-is-inexplicable/377d77bd-97ff-4f22-b2a3-15c747f70ea3/

James Huberty. In *Criminal Minds Wiki*. Retrieved from: https://criminal-minds.fandom.com/wiki/James_Huberty

Barabak, M.C. (July 19, 1984). "James Huberty, the Loner Who Killed 21 People at…" In *UPI*. Retrieved from: https://www.upi.com/Archives/1984/07/19/James-Huberty-the-loner-who-killed-21-people-at/2102459057600/

Baker, D. (August 23, 2016). "Daughter of McDonald's Killer Has Advice for San Bernardino Baby's Killer." In *The San Diego Union-Tribune*. Retrieved from: https://www.sandiegouniontribune.com/opinion/the-conversation/sdut-daughter-mcdonalds-killer-james-huberty-interview-2015dec15-story.html

Rose, C. (October 21, 2021). "The Man Who Went Hunting for Humans." In *Medium*. Retrieved from: https://medium.com/@chelsea.rose/the-man-who-went-hunting-for-humans-ec520338dfe4

James Oliver Huberty. In *123 Helpme*. Retrieved from: https://www.123helpme.com/essay/James-Oliver-Huberty-256430

James Oliver Huberty. In *Real Life Villains Wiki*. Retrieved from: https://reallifevillains.miraheze.org/wiki/James_Oliver_Huberty

Special Report (July 30, 1984). "The Massacre at McDonald's." In *McLeans*. https://archive.macleans.ca/article/1984/7/30/the-massacre-at-mcdonalds

The San Ysidro McDonald's Massacre. In *My Blog*. Retrieved from: https://diaryofapartimewriter.wordpress.com/tag/mass-shooting/

Murfin, P. (July 18, 2020). "Heretic, Rebel, a Thing to Flout." In *An Eclectic Journal of Opinion, History, Poetry and General Bloviating*. Retrieved from: https://patrickmurfin.blogspot.com/2020/07/mass-murder-at-mcdonaldsa-preview-of.html

Express Web Desk (August 4, 2022). In *The Indian Express*. Retrieved from: https://indianexpress.com/article/world/florida-us-worst-mass-shootings-timeline-5065426/

San Ysidro McDonald's Massacre. In *The Reader Wiki*. Retrieved from: https://thereaderwiki.com/en/San_Ysidro_McDonald%27s_massacre

San Ysidro McDonald's Massacre. In *Pipiwiki*. https://pipiwiki.com/wiki/San_Ysidro_McDonald%27s_massacre

Archive. "Life Hasn't Gotten Easier, Gunman's Widow Says." In *AP News*. Retrieved from: https://apnews.com/article/d91276f1e42fe5248e-4a7417c5af456b

Matthews, J. and Sherwood, T. (July 20, 1984). "Death, Blood, in a Place of Laughter."

In *The Washington Post*. Retrieved from: https://www.washingtonpost.com/archive/politics/1984/07/20/death-blood-in-a-place-of-laughter/a5bb422b-fc48-4289-ab47-0f63d88676cd/

Schoenewolf, G. (2021). The Rise of Feminism: A Psychoanalyst Probes the Meaning of a Movement. Bushkill, PA: Living Center Press

CHAPTER 6

GEORGE HENNARD

THE SHOOTING

At 5:30 Wednesday morning, October 16, 1991, 35-year-old George J. Hennard walked into a convenience store in Killeen, Texas and bought a sausage-and-biscuit sandwich, an orange juice, a candy bar, a newspaper and a pack of Old-Fashioned Dunkers Doughnuts. He had been buying breakfast at the store six mornings a week for months, but Wednesday there was something different about the tall, grim, muscular son of an army doctor.

"George never smiled when he came in here," a clerk at the store, Mary Mead, said. "He just seemed like he had the world on his shoulders. He was a loner. He never talked. But yesterday he seemed almost calm, even a little friendly, for the only time I can remember. Usually, I was scared of him."

"Good morning, Mary," he said on that particular morning, addressing her by her name. "I'll have the usual." He almost smiled as he paid for his goods and went back out to his blue pickup truck to eat alone. He stayed in the parking lot for about an hour eating his breakfast and reading the newspaper as usual.

Seven hours later he was driving around looking for a place where he could kill a lot of people. In his pockets he was carrying the semi-automatic Glock 17 and Ruger P89 pistols he had recently purchased from a neighborhood gun store. He had been driving around all day, fuming to himself in the car because of his latest rejection. "Fuck you!" he yelled at the Merchant Marines. "Fuck you to hell! I made one mistake and that's it!" He had been trying for some time to be reinstated in the Merchant Marines and had just been denied for the second time. "You are going to pay!" he yelled as he squealed around a corner. "You are going to pay for not taking me back. Today you'll see what you made me do!"

Hennard had been in a rage for weeks while he tangled with the Merchant Marines over getting reinstated. After a lifetime career there, he had been fired because of some run-ins with another worker and with the higher-ups, and he was now on the outside looking in. His rage put him in excruciating pain, which was accompanied by a burning sensation and a tightening of his whole body that had stung for so long it had become intolerable. For a year, each time another mass killing hit the news, he had contemplated a mass killing of his own, and now he had gone into stage 3 rage and he was ready to execute his final plan.

It was Boss's Day at Luby's Cafeteria and the cafeteria was unusually crowded with around 100 people. Hennard drove around the cafeteria looking in the windows. He drove around once, twice and three times. He saw a lot of women inside and he thought: Yes! That will do. He had a history of bad relationships with women and it was women in particular he wanted to kill, but he wasn't going to be choosy. He would kill anything that moved. "Look at that?" he mumbled. "Look at all the vipers in there! They all look so smug and in love with themselves!

Let's see how they feel now?" Without giving it any more thought, he sharply turned his blue 1987 Ford Ranger pickup truck, stomped on the gas pedal and roared the truck toward the side of the cafeteria. It crashed through the plate-glass window and jumped into some tables of people who were munching down their meals. Shards of glass flew everywhere as the truck landed. Those sitting near the nose of the car jumped up and backed away. People everywhere leaped up and began screaming and scrambling for cover.

Once his truck had landed, he turned off the motor and sat in the driver's seat for a moment grinning at the "morons" who were happily living their lives while he himself was miserable. And then, without warning, he took aim at the people in the cafeteria and began to shoot. He gazed at them with a slight grin and felt nothing at all for them.

Seated around a table in front of the truck were Sam Wink, 47, an attendance officer at a nearby school, and some of his coworkers, who were treating their boss to lunch. "I leapt into the aisle," says Wink. "Then I heard sounds like light bulbs popping." Hennard was firing from inside the truck and the first person he saw was veterinarian Michael Griffith. He leaned out of the side window and shot the veterinarian dead. Then he stepped out of the truck and began shooting randomly at people—a pistol in each hand, a cigarette dangling from his mouth, his shirt pockets bulging with clips.

He stood spread-legged just outside the door of his truck and yelled, "All women of Killeen and Belton are vipers! This is what you've done to me and my family! This is what Bell County did to me, this is what the Merchant Marines did to me, and this is payback day!" He then opened fire with both pistols. "I heard him snap his third clip into his gun," says Wink. "He was about 12 feet from me. When he turned, our eyes met for a second. They were mean. There was a smirk on his face, as if he was thinking, 'I've been waiting for this a long time.' He was very intense, well-prepared, almost as if he had practiced at home. And even though he was yelling, he was very calm. The contrast between the fire in his eyes and the calm on his face was unbelievable."

Hennard circled around the cafeteria, selectively picking out women to shoot. "You bitch!" or "You viper!" he would yell at each woman, and then he would shoot them point blank in the head. He went from women to woman, but sometimes, if a man got in his way, he would shoot the man. At one point he saw a woman hiding underneath a bench near the serving line and he walked over to her.

"Hiding from me, bitch?"

The woman looked up at him with pleading eyes. "Please?"

"No bitch can hide from me today!"

He leaned down and shot her in the temple.

Hennard then approached Steve Ernst, who was huddled underneath a nearby table, and shot him in the stomach with one of his semi-automatic pistols. Steve rolled over, holding his stomach. "What's wrong with you?" Steve called out, in pain.

"Nothing's wrong with me," Hennard said. "Something's wrong with you."

He then approached a woman holding a baby. "You with the baby," he barked. "Get out before I change my mind." The woman dashed out of the cafeteria, holding the baby in her arms. After the woman went out the front door, Hennard turned around and shot Steve Ernst's wife in the arm. The bullet broke through her arm and killed 70-year-old Venice Ellen Henehan, Ernst's mother-in-law.

During a brief lull in the shooting, during which he reloaded, Hennard approached the table of 28-year-old Tommy Vaughan, who was squatting in the rear of the cafeteria, next to a window. When he saw Hennard coming toward him, the six-foot-four-inch Vaughn threw himself through the window and galloped away. By doing that, he created an escape route for others, and immediately afterward, one person after another pushed, shoved, and knocked each other down as they made their way to the open window to jump out.

As people went toward the window, Hennard continued to single out women.

"Die, bitch!" he kept saying.

Or, "Why should a viper like you live?"

Or, "Sorry, slut, this is not your day."

In many cases, he shot the women execution style through the temple.

He continued to walk around, looking for prey. Police did not arrive for about 14 minutes, and when they arrived, they pulled up on all sides of the cafeteria and positioned themselves behind their cars. The captain of the force jumped out of his car and spoke to Hennard through a speaker.

"Drop down your weapons!" he ordered.

"No, no, no!" he yelled out in a sarcastic voice. "This is fun! I'm going to shoot some more people!"

The police opened fire and he fired back. He was wounded, but not fatally, and retreated to a hallway between the men's and women's restrooms. He tried to open the restroom doors, but people were hiding inside and had locked them. He remained in the hallway, shooting at the police who had gathered outside, and the gunfight continued for several minutes. "You are all a bunch of trash, no matter what uniforms you wear!" he called out. "All of you can just go fuck yourselves!"

"Drop your weapons!" the police kept ordering him. "Surrender!"

"Never!" he yelled back.

"For the last time!"

"Fuck you!"

Hennard was huddled as far back in the hallway as he could, but the police managed to shoot two more times and hit him in the abdomen. He had by then run out of ammunition for one of his guns and the pain from his wounds had rendered him immobile. He had not reached his kill point, and there was apparently still a lot of unspent rage inside of him. But he knew that he could not last much longer and he probably said to himself, at that moment, "They're not going to kill me! I'm going to kill myself before they have the pleasure. I'm in control here!" He wanted, for once in his life, to be the final orchestrater, to have his final hurrah, of everything including his own death. His life had been spent as a loner, but now, at the very end, he had come out of his shell and he had become more himself than he had ever been before. Killing people may have been the most intimate relationship he had ever had in his life. At last, at 12:52 pm, he muttered in a happy voice, "Good-bye, assholes!" Then he raised the Glock pistol to his head and shot himself in the temple. He sank down in the back of the hallway with a smile on his face.

He had shot and killed 23 people—10 with single shots to the head at point blank range—and he had wounded another 27. He did not shoot a 19-year-old dishwasher, Mark Matthews, who was found unharmed at 7:00 a.m. the following morning. The dishwasher had hidden inside the washer and slept on a conveyor belt inside an idled dishwasher in a corner of the restaurant's kitchen. A Luby's executive asked him later why he had stayed in the washer so long. "He said he never felt safe enough to get out of there."

GEORGE HENNARD'S LIFE

George Hennard was born on October 15, 1956, in Sayre, Pennsylvania to an American mother, Jeanne, and a Swiss father, George. Hennard's father was an orthopedic surgeon who was a career army doctor. From the time he was five, Hennard and his family—including his younger brother and sister Alan Robert and Desiree—were shuttled across the country as his father moved to various army hospitals. Both father and mother apparently suffered from O.C.D.; his O.C.D. took the form of workaholism, while hers was focused on the neatness of her house. According to acquaintances, Hennard's parents were both disgruntled people who were too caught up in their own lives to pay attention to George. What little interest they showed in him was negative attention that focused on his faults. As a result, Hennard turned out to be not that interested in other people and, like his parents, also focused on their faults.

Only a little is known about his early childhood. The bad things that happen to people in their early childhoods are often hidden behind closed doors. If a father loses his temper and slugs his children, that is never revealed to the public; if a severely disturbed mother squeezes her little boy's testicles and threatens to castrate him, that is never spoken about; if parents keep children locked in the basement and sexually abuse them, that is never acknowledged; if parents are so depressed that they lie in bed and let their baby cry all day, that is never even whispered about. When such parents are in public they hold their babies and smile lovingly, but behind closed doors quite the opposite may be happening.

The sparse information we have learned from those who knew the Hennard family suggests that Jeanne was an angry person who was a neglectful and abusive mother. According to acquaintances, she was particularly angry with men—angry with her father, her husband and also with men in general. Some angry women, in my clinical experience, use feminism to justify their anger with men, and she may have seen her son through a feminist lens and quoted slogans about men, such as how they harbor toxic masculinity. Her obsessive-compulsive disorder may have caused her to care more about things (the cleanliness of their house) than people, and she was described as a neatness tyrant. Hennard's relationship with her was reported by observers to be troubled, combative and sometimes physical. It is likely that from his earliest childhood she displaced all her anger with men on him. We cannot say for certain how cruel she was to him when he was a child, but from Hennard's debilitating anger with women and his complete inability to relate to them, I would conclude that his mother had been cruel.

She was a woman who was, first of all, angry with her tyrannical father, and then, as is so often the case, she had married a man much like her father. When it comes to attraction, we are often drawn to people who are unconsciously familiar (they remind us of a parent or sibling) and even though we may see negative signs, their familiarity makes it appear that they will be easy to relate to. Jeanne married a man she came to hate—a situation reminiscent to that of Seung-Hui Cho's mother—and that hatred branched out to her son. Some women are not natural homemakers or mothers, and in fact they often despise that role and view it as "domestic slavery." She was not a nurturing woman and she never showed any desire or joy about being a housewife or mother. When her son—who was probably not wanted and who was resented from birth on—turned out to be an angry boy whose anger was primarily directed at her, she did not know what to do about it. She did not understand how desperate he was for her love and approval, and it became a vicious cycle of her constantly putting him down and of his expressing his hatred for her and of her ramping up her hatred of him. It was a mutual hate society.

According to acquaintances, Jeanne's relationship with her son throughout his childhood and young adulthood was apparently an on-again, off-again nightmare. At times she would seem to be sweet and approving and he would almost begin to believe her, only find that she would later come down on him again and gaslight him by telling him he was a psychopath. Later, he would refer to women as vipers, and it seemed that his mother, in his eyes, was the original viper. However, there was never any recognition on her part that she had anything to do with how he turned out, and this may have further fueled his anger at her. A roommate later said Hennard often talked to him of his anger at his mother and about wanting to kill her.

Hennard was called "Jo," to distinguish him from his father, who was also named George. His father was a "my way or the highway" sort of dad. His career as an army surgeon was the most important thing in his life, and his wife and children were a distant second. He was apparently a self-centered man who moved from army post to army post without a thought about how this would affect his wife and especially how it would affect his children. His relationship with his son was distant. Hennard's father was never home and hardly ever spoke to him. If he did, it was to rebuke him for a bad grade in school or for some indiscretion. He would often spank him and later, when Hennard was older, they would sometimes come to blows.

Moving from town to town and from school to school throughout his childhood only served to exacerbate Hennard's antisocial personality. Each time he got settled in a new school and made friends, he would have to move. Eventually, he gave up completely on making friends or joining in any school activities or making good grades. Nobody seemed to care, so why should he care? His parents, who were always at odds with one another, paid little attention to their three children, and Hennard was left to try to figure things out on his own. He tried mightily, but he was not at all able to do so.

High school friends noticed his antisocial personality. "You never saw him with girls. He never hung around with anybody," said Paul Crowe, a neighbor at White Sands, New Mexico. "His parents never did care and were hardly ever around." Not only did Hennard not date a single girl during his high school years, he also had no friends. Nor did he engage in any extracurricular activities at school. He was completely uninvolved in high school society, nor did he care about school work. When he graduated in 1974, the only picture of him in the yearbook was his obligatory class picture.

Hennard joined the Navy and three years later, when he finished his tour of duty, signed up with the Merchant Marines, where he could be away from people, working mostly in the Gulf of Mexico until 1982. During his time in the Merchant Marines, he sailed on over 37 overseas voyages. As his sojourns multiplied, so did his troubles. He was a good sailor but did not get along with his superiors or coworkers, often getting into scrapes with them. However, he managed to work for the Merchant Marines for eight years. When he was arrested for marijuana possession in Texas in 1981, he was put on probation, and a year later he had his seaman's papers suspended after a reported racial argument with a shipmate in May 1982, in which he objected to the way "Blacks manipulate White people."

"He hated blacks, Hispanics, gays. He said women were snakes," recalls Jamie Dunlap, who shared an apartment with Hennard in Temple, Texas, for a year. "He always had derogatory remarks about women, especially after fights with his mother."

After his suspension from the Merchant Marines, he moved from one odd job to another in central Texas, installing furniture at offices in Austin, working for a cement company in Copperas Cove and doing handyman jobs all over. For six months, he played drums for an obscure rock band in Austin, then abandoned life there for Belton, where he lived in his family's large colonial home that had sat empty during his parents' acrimonious divorce in 1983.

His mother moved back into the 13-room mansion and then George joined her and was reported to have had a love-hate relationship with her. Matt Movsesian, a schoolmate who often visited his home, stated that Hennard and his younger brother typically avoided the living room for fear of dirtying it and incurring the wrath of their mother. "Their house used to be immaculate," Movsesian said. "They said the living room was 'Mom's little showcase.' Everything had to be just right."

During one summer in 1989, his behavior became increasingly bizarre. Jill Fritz, 23, and Jana Jernigan, 19—two sisters who lived a couple of blocks away from Hennard in Belton, whom he had apparently been admiring from afar—received a rambling, five-page letter from him, out of the blue. "You think the three of us can get together some day?" he asked, without ever having even talked to them. The deranged letter went on to express disdain for the sisters, calling them "spoiled rich brats," and then expressed a kind of desperate love for them and ended by pleading for their acceptance. "Please give me the satisfaction of someday laughing in the face of all those mostly white tremendously female vipers … who tried to destroy me and my family." The sisters did not answer this letter and crossed the street in order to avoid him if they saw him walking toward them.

In the years following his parents' divorce in 1983, he and his mother continued their roller-coaster relationship. He would live with her for a while, then have a blow-out fight and move to some friend's house or a cheap apartment. She was a woman who once had her own business selling antiques, but gave that up soon after the divorce. On one occasion, Dunlap reported that Hennard told him of a night when his anger turned physical. His mother slapped him and he responded by shoving her and storming from the house. Later, Hennard told Dunlap about the incident. "Within a matter of 15 minutes, he got real red-faced, and he yelled out 'That goddamned bitch! That worthless goddamned bitch!'" On other occasions, Dunlap said, Hennard would try to please his mother. He once put new tires on her car as a surprise, only to have his thoughtfulness rebuffed by the mother. "I didn't ask you to do that," she remarked.

"I liked the woman, but yeah, a lot of his problems were from the relationship they had together," Dunlap said. "He wanted more from her than she would give. When he talked about her, it was like he loved her and hated her." Hennard had the same tortured feelings toward other women. He would speak fondly of prostitutes he had been with during his 37 Merchant Marine voyages to distant parts of the world, but Dunlap and other acquaintances said they never knew Hennard to date a woman in the USA. "I think he really resented the fact that he desperately desired a relationship with a woman but couldn't have one. They were the unattainable objects. As time went by, it grew into an obsession and he read more into it."

According to Dunlap, his anger with women grew over the years, as his awkward attempts at courting them proved unsuccessful. Apparently, women were scared of him, but he did not recognize this fear; he saw their rejection as an attempt to destroy him.

His life after he lost his seaman's license settled into a routine. Neighbors described him as a workaholic like his father. He apparently did not sleep well at night, tossing and turning as he likely went through one nightmare after another. Every morning he would wake up before dawn and then drive to the same convenience store in Killeen where he bought his breakfast, which always included a newspaper and a pack of Old-Fashioned Dunkers Doughnuts. Then he would go back home to lift weights for a few hours. In the afternoon he would go out into the back yard to work on his car, the swimming pool or mow the lawn—usually shirtless, to show off his muscles. Every night, he drove to the Nomad Turnaround Grill in Belton and parked his prized blue Ford Ranger pickup in the parking lot and went inside to watch the big-screen TV as he ordered and ate the same dinner, consisting of a double cheeseburger with nachos, French fries and a Coke.

One night, on October 15, 1991 (his 35th birthday), while having his usual dinner at the Nomad Turnaround Grill, he exploded with rage as he watched the television coverage of the Clarence Thomas confirmation hearing. Anita Hill, a woman who had worked for Thomas, had accused him of sexual harassment, so the confirmation hearings turned into a sexual harassment hearing. "When an interview with Anita Hill came on, he just went off," said manager Bill Stringer. "He started screaming, 'You dumb bitch! You bastards opened the door for all the women!'" Some customers tried to argue with him, but he would have none of it. He shouted everybody down and soon everybody fell into silence and let him rant. When he became enraged, everybody knew not to interfere.

Jamie Dunlap was the only person who Hennard regarded as a friend. One evening, as Dunlap drove with him on the back roads of central Texas, Hennard's tears began to flow. He was rambling as usual about some women who had hurt him and his general distrust for them and for his mother, calling women "snakes after nothing but my money." The sobs came out and Hennard almost whispered, "I can't seem to make it with people. You're my only friend sometimes." To Dunlap, this was evidence of a deep hurt hidden beneath Hennard's often defiant appearance. This was the only time Dunlap recalled Hennard ever being anything but angry, and perhaps it was the only time he allowed himself to be vulnerable and real. Most of his life he liked to be alone near water. Water to him was nurturing and he spent his time in the Merchant Marines gazing at the ocean and while at home sitting alone near Lake Belton, not far from his home.

He had previously purchased two pistols—a Ruger P89 and a Glock 17—in Henderson, Texas. Later, in February, Federal park police in Nevada stopped and arrested an intoxicated Hennard for possession of two legally purchased but loaded guns at Lake Mead Recreational Area. Apparently, he had gone there to be near water. He was released on bond and failed to appear for a hearing the following month.

A week and a half before the Luby's massacre, Hennard abruptly strutted in and picked up his paycheck at the cement company in Copperas Cove where he was working at the time and announced that he was quitting. "I'm quitting, everybody, that's right, I'm quitting! What do you think of that?" He was elated. Coworkers recalled that he then began to ramble, wondering aloud what would happen if he killed someone. "He got to talking about some of the people in Belton and certain women that had given him problems," said 23-year-old coworker Bubba Hawkins. "And he kept saying, 'Watch and see, watch and see.'" It seemed to everybody present that he had gone mad, and in fact he had. He had made the decision, the night before, to end his life and to end the lives of as many others as he could.

The night before, Hennard had watched a documentary about James Huberty, detailing how that man had killed 21 people in California. He also watched *The Fisher King*, a 1991 movie in which a radio DJ inspired a man into killing several people at a restaurant in a spree shooting. Watching these two programs caused him to sit up and notice, and he could not take his eyes from the TV screen. At last, he saw a way out of his agony. He decided on the spot to quit his job the next day and go on his own mass killing spree.

The next day, as he announced that he was quitting his job, he probably remembered the movies he had seen the night before. "You will never see me again," he told his coworkers that last day. "He kept saying one of these days he's going to have to hurt someone and he really didn't want to do it, but he was going to have to," said Hawkins about Hennard's last hour. Hawkins said he was yelling for about 20 or 30 minutes, and the other employees gathered around him in awe, giving each other looks, not knowing what was happening or why he was saying what he was saying or acting the way he was acting. They had never seen him so deliriously out of his mind.

A few nights later, on the night before the blood bath at Luby's Cafeteria, he went to the Nomad Turnaround Grill and again, munched his hamburger and nachos, and once again watched the Clarence Thomas confirmation hearing. Again, he had an angry outburst as he stared at the people on the big-screen television set on the wall of the Grill. He began cursing Anita Hill, the woman who had accused Thomas of sexual harassment. "You dumb bitch!" he said. "What a dumb, manipulative bitch you are! What a dumb, lying bitch! I hope you die, you dumb bitch! I hope you get run over by a Mack truck! You are nothing but a man-hating bitch! That's all she is, a fucking goddam man-hating whore! Fuck her! Fuck her! Fuck her!" Lorraine Stringer, the co-manager of the Grill, later said that he just wouldn't stop. The people at the bar were booing him, but he just kept cursing away and not paying attention to the boos. "He cussed so much, my husband had to tell him we don't allow that here."

"It's a free country!" Hennard said to her husband.

"I understand. You can make comments, but just stop the swear words. People are offended."

"Right! Right! Nobody is ever allowed to be offended!"

"I don't want to have to ask you to leave, George."

He quieted down after that and watched the rest of the show without comment, but his eyes were angrily locked on the TV monitor. He may have been thinking that he would do it tomorrow. Tomorrow, he thought as he eyed the TV monitor. Tomorrow is the day! When the TV show ended, he got into his truck and roared the engine and squealed out of the parking lot.

He probably did not get much sleep that night. The next day he drove his blue truck through the window at Luby's Cafeteria.

CULTURAL FACTORS

George Hennard was an antisocial personality whose disturbance was primarily linked to a paranoid attitude toward women. This attitude was provoked in early childhood via his neglectful and abusive relationship with his mother and harsh, distant relationship with his father. but it was exacerbated by what was happening in American culture at the time. During the 1980s and 1990s, feminists had become very vocal. Week after week, women were accusing men of inappropriate behavior, harassment and rape. In the feminist book, *Women and Madness*, by Phyllis Chesler (reissued in 2005), the author attributes almost all of women's psychological ailments—including eating disorders, depression, alcoholism, addictions, sexual problems, postpartum depression, schizophrenia, and a host of others, to male oppression. These things were repeated in books, on television shows, and on social media on a daily basis, and Hennard could not help but be aware of it.

While many women felt uplifted by this trend, many men felt hurt and angered by it. It was a trend that made it seem that there was some kind of epidemic of sexual abuse and rape going on in the United States. For a man like Hennard, who was already angry with women because of a mother who constantly degraded him, hearing women on TV accusing men of all sorts of things, seeing men being fired from jobs, reading about them being cancelled from their positions in society, feminist militancy was probably a hard thing for him to swallow. In his rage, he could not see how feminism was helpful to women; he could only focus on what he saw as its seemingly relentless criticism of males, which may have brought up his mother's criticism of him.

Nor was Hennard the only man who was bothered by feminism. A sign of how much feminism was aggravating sensitive men was a new men's organization that got started at that time called, Men Going Their Own Way (MGTOW). This was a group of men who decided to have nothing to do with women. On the home page of its website, it said:

> MIGTOW—Men Going Their Own Way—is a statement of self-ownership, where the modern man preserves and protects his own sovereignty above all else. It is the manifestation of one word: "No." Ejecting silly preconceptions and cultural definitions of what a "man" is. Looking to no one else for social cues. Refusing to bow, serve, and kneel for the opportunity to be treated like a disposable utility. And, living according to his own best interests in a world which would rather he didn't.

There is no information about if Hennard knew of this organization, but had he known about it, he might have been one of the first to join.

He would likely have refused to "bow, serve, and kneel for the opportunity to be treated like a disposable utility."

In 1991, America was swept into a furor when a Black woman named Anita Hill accused a Black conservative named Clarence Thomas of sexual harassment just as he was in the process of being confirmed as a Supreme Court judge. Thomas had been nominated to the Supreme Court, and liberals were determined to prevent his joining that court, fearful that he might vote to overturn *Roe vs. Wade,* the Court's ruling that legalized abortion. Hill said in the October 1991 televised hearings, which went on for several weeks and had viewers glued to their television sets, that Thomas had sexually harassed her while he was her supervisor at the Department of Education and the EEOC. She said he had asked her out many times during her two years of employment as his assistant, and, after she had declined his requests, he had used work situations to discuss sexual subjects. "He spoke about…such matters as women having sex with animals and films showing group sex or rape scenes," she said, and added that on many occasions he had graphically described "his own sexual prowess" and "details of his anatomy." These hearings became a national pastime and the American public became entranced by them.

In the end, Clarence Thomas was narrowly confirmed, but his reputation as a judge and as a man had been permanently scarred. Many women felt liberated and inspired by these hearings and came to regard Anita Hill as a hero. Many men, on the other hand, saw her as an angry woman and felt psychologically castrated by the hearings. One of those men was Hennard.

It was the Clarence Thomas hearings that seemed to be the final thorn in his side. When he watched the hearing on television on the night before he went on his mass shooting spree, he proceeded to growl at the television set at the Nomad Turnaround Grill in what was perhaps his angriest rant. Customers at the Grill were shocked by his profanity-laced outbursts, which continued throughout the proceedings, and nobody was able to watch the show because of the constant barrage of invectives coming out of his mouth. Nothing had ever seemed to provoke him as much as these hearings.

Hennard may have viewed these proceedings as a parallel to what happened in his own family. He saw the Clarence Thomas confirmation hearing as a setup that enabled Anita Hill to displace her anger with men on a man who, ironically, had helped her with her career and had expressed an interest in her. Perhaps he saw Hill as a representative of his mother, viewing both women as angry with men and merciless. Perhaps he felt that if Anita Hill had been his mother, she would have accused him of sexual harassment or worse. He may have been doubly indignant when he saw these hearings because they showed a woman in a public spectacle taking down a man and being applauded for it. This was the opposite of what he deeply desired; at his lonely root, he wanted his mother and women who had done vicious things to him to apologize to him and care about him.

What was going on in American culture at that time was a bramble bush of abrasive events. It was a culture that was, to Hennard, a man-hating culture. He had not been born into a nurturing family, and the culture he was thrown into was not a nurturing culture.

Would he have gone on his killing spree the next day if he had not seen the hearings the night before? Probably he would have sooner or later, but not the next day. He had already made that decision after he watched the news about the Huberty incident and the documentary, *The Fisher King,* which led to his quitting his job.

The mass killings that were multiplying in American culture were an added motivational factor for Hennard, as they were for the other mass killers described in this book. While the anti-male culture fueled his anger at women, the mass murders excited him and provided him with a way out. All of these acrimonious factors of American culture had a heavy effect on him and served to bring about his final crash into unreality.

FINAL ANALYSIS

George Hennard was unfortunate enough to be born to parents who did not have the emotional capacity to raise a healthy child. Both of his parents apparently neglected and abused him from the beginning. His father was in medical school when he was born, and all his attention was directed at getting through that school. Afterwards, he become an army surgeon and took his family from army post to army post, evidently without any concern about how this was affecting his kids. He was apparently a strict, military man who spent little time at home and was unable to love his wife or young George. His interactions with his children were rare and he was probably not really there. He was not the type of father, let us say, who would spend hours grooming his son to be a doctor and help him to navigate through high school, college and medical school. Instead, he hardly spoke to the son and the son felt rejected by him. He was the type of man who—had his wife demanded that he spend more time with her and the kids—would probably have spent more time at work to spite her.

Jeanne Hennard was an angry, strong-willed woman who constantly clashed with her husband and her oldest son. Her reportedly anti-male attitude may have been one reason her husband stayed away from the house and was glued to his job. Both husband and wife seemed to have narcissistic personalities, in that they were both self-absorbed and unable to relate to their son or show any empathy for his unhappiness. She was a woman who put a great emphasis on appearances, and her son's blue collar, defiant style fell way beneath her standards. She suffered from obsessive-compulsive disorder and that disorder seemed to be her driving force. Matt Movsesian, a long-time acquaintance who often visited his home, reported that Hennard and his younger brother typically avoided the living room for fear of dirtying it and incurring the wrath of their mother. "Their house used to be immaculate," Movsesian explained. Her obsessive-compulsive monomania about the neatness of her house served to channel her aggression, but it was a wide channel. She apparently could never be supportive of her son. She would not fight for her son, but she would fight for the neatness of her house. Her O.C.D. would have compelled her to be in control, not in love.

She could not give her son what he needed—a nurturing mother who provided her son the hugs and kisses and dependability and support that would make him a healthy boy. Instead, the reports of observers described her as a neglectful and hostile mother who put down her son and left him to fend for himself and try to find nurture in a culture that had no nurture to give. I have found that such mothers tend to displace their generalized anger with men onto their sons. Their husbands are too strong and they cannot bring them down as they may wish to do, but their sons are weak and needy and they can easily bring them down a notch.

From childhood on, Hennard did not receive the kind of parenting that would make him feel loved, nurtured, confident and safe in the world, and he did not receive the kind of parenting that would make him confident with women. His narcissistic parents seemed ashamed of him and did not feel enhanced by this insecure, awkward, unruly boy and took no responsibility for the parenting deficiency that had caused him to be that way. From the reports about the frequent arguments between mother and son, it appears that if he went to her for support and comfort, she would attack him instead, and this would lead to quarrels that became physical.

In cases similar to Hennards involving angry mothers and sons, I have been told about typical conversations that occurred while they were drinking and watching television on an evening.

"How did it go with that girl down the street?" the mother asked.

"That bitch who lives on the corner. She turns up her nose every time she sees me."

"Of course, she does. With your attitude, you'll never get a woman."

"Well, if I have an attitude, you're the bitch who gave it to me!"

"Don't talk to me like that!"

"I'll talk to you however I want to!"

"Get out of my house!"

"Fuck you!"

The mother slaps her son. He shoves her, then runs out of the front door. Tears are in his eyes as he runs out slamming the door.

Perhaps she was the type of mother who compared her son unfavorably to one of his friends, who was more up to her standards. "Why can't you be more like your friend, Bill?" He was not at all like Bill; he had not been popular at school and had not make good grades. He got into scrapes and did not function in a way that made her proud. Her way of trying to love him and improve him was to shame him for his awkwardness. Shaming does not work, and it particularly does not work if you have never received love from the person who shames you.

In short, what Hennard most likely received from his mother was a scorn, not love. And so, he became a man who scorned his mother and scorned women. Indeed, Jeanne Hennard's treatment of her son may have been an instance of soul murder, Shengold's term for an extremely destructive style of parenting, which I mentioned in an earlier chapter. Soul murder happens when a parent neglects or abuses a child to such an extent that he is deprived of his own identity and ability to experience joy in life. From his childhood on, Hennard never seemed to have a moment of peace or joy or contentment. His one feeling was anger. Everything angered him, particularly women. He felt so bad about himself that, according to acquaintances, he never dated at all. His only sexual relationships were with whores he met during his ocean voyages. Like his mother, he became obsessive-compulsive. His life was a tight routine, a ritual of the same meals, the same restaurants, the same lifting of weights, the same work on his car or on his pool. Feeling powerless, he built up his muscles in order to feel some semblance of strength.

His antisocial personality caused him to want to avoid people, and joining the Navy and the Merchant Marines gave him the opportunity to do just that. In the Merchant Marines he could stay away from his mother, women, and people in general. He reportedly also had a love of water—of the ocean and of Lake Belton and was said to spend a lot of time staring at the ocean or sitting on the shore of Lake Belton. Water, in psychoanalysis, is symbolic of femininity and of the womb. In the womb, the fetus floats in a liquid solution. Hence, his fascination with the ocean and with bodies of water may have unconsciously harked back to the womb and represented a wish by him to return to the serenity of that mode of being.

His parents' divorce in 1983, brought him back with his mother and into the large house that she won in the divorce settlement. He hardly saw his father after that, and he kept moving in and out of the house, forever hoping that his mother would somehow change and love him. For some mothers, their son is the apple of their eye, but in Jeanne's case, her son was apparently the rotten apple of her eye. She apparently tormented him from the time he moved in until his shooting spree at Luby's Cafeteria in 1991, when he was 35 years old. Jamie Dunlap, an acquaintance, said that every time he had an argument with his mother, his hatred for women in general would rise, and that once, after a brutal argument, he spoke of wanting to kill his mother. He seemed to be drawn to his mother like a moth to a lightbulb. He kept going to his mother hoping for warmth, but instead he got scorched. He was compelled to repeat the same behavior over and over, a phenomenon that Freud referred to as a repetition compulsion.

His relationships with women were almost nonexistent. He attempted to court two sisters in his neighborhood, whom he had never met, by abruptly sending them a long, rambling letter in which he praised them and trashed them and then pleaded with them to go out with him in order to help him get revenge on the women who had spurned him. His relationship with his mother left him too confused, antisocial and gynophobic to relate to women in any way other than a scornful one.

Hennard was a man who was easily triggered, and throughout his life he seemed to be barely functioning in a stage 2 rage. He was a man who had never received two important things from his mother and father. From his mother, he had never felt loved, protected or safe and had hence never developed the buffer that healthy people have—the thick skin that allows them to tolerate the hundred and one pin-pricks of life. From his father, he never received the training on how to regulate his emotions and get ahead in life. Not feeling safe in the world, not having a buffer, and having no clue as to how to regulate his emotions and navigate life, he was deeply vulnerable. The only way he knew how to defend against this vulnerability was to use anger to intimidate everybody into leaving him alone. However, this anger had the side effect of giving him just what he wanted—in spades—and people would routinely distance themselves from him—especially women. This then became a self-fulfilling prophecy. The more he hated women for rejecting him, the more they rejected him.

In October of 1991, two events occurred which catapulted Hennard into stage 3 rage. The first happened on the evening before he quit his job in Copperas Cove, when he watched a documentary about James Huberty, detailing his mass killing episode in California, and then saw a movie about another mass killer. After watching these two shows, he apparently became inspired to execute his own mass killing. Yes indeed! he probably thought. This is what I have been looking for! The next day he quit his job at the cement factory and went on a tirade about women who had hurt him and people he was going to hurt. A witness described him as out of his mind, babbling almost incoherently for thirty minutes before rushing out the door. This was both a warning and a cry for help—one final cry before he went completely over the edge. This final warning is part of the pattern of all the mass killers studied in this book. He was telling these coworkers that he was going to kill people and, consciously or unconsciously, he was hoping that somebody would stop him and save him and the world. This followed the pattern, and just like in past instances of that pattern, no one wanted to really understand what he was saying. He seemed like someone so crazy that he could not be taken seriously.

Then, on the night before his mass shooting, he sat in his favorite diner and watched the Clarence Thomas confirmation hearings. Watching the hearings was like being given a dose of poison. He desperately needed a woman to see him, to understand the agony he had gone through all his life, to save him from his personal hell. His life was a futile search for a woman to nurture him the way his mother had not been able to do. Instead what he was witnessing on the big-screen TV was an angry woman putting down a man with a smile on her face. He became irate, launching into a rant of invectives. It must have felt to him like the very bottom had fallen out from under him.

These hearings, in which Anita Hill was blissfully scorning a man and, in Hennard's eyes, trying to destroy his integrity the way his mother had destroyed his, triggered stage 3 rage. Indeed, the hearings jabbed Hennard at the very core of his being. All of the formerly repressed and suppressed anger about hurtful incidents involving women—going all the way back to his childhood—was aroused by this event. The lifelong feelings of being unfairly treated by his mother, by women, by employers and by the world, exploded out of him. For the first time in his life, he let everything out in one swear word after another, perhaps hoping to display to everybody just how dangerous he was and just how much he needed to be restrained. In fact, the rage was in direct proportion to how powerless the hearings made him feel. "I'm not going to feel powerless ever again!" he seemed to be saying. This diatribe was like a final, solitary pep rally for the killing spree he planned on the following day.

Kennedy-Kollar and Charles, in a study entitled, "Hegemonic Masculinity and Mass Murderers in the United States," proposed an interesting theory about mass murderers that seems particularly fitting as a partial explanation of George Hennard. This theory suggests that mass killers come to feel that they are lacking the hegemonic masculinity that American males are "entitled to." Hegemonic masculinity is generally defined as comprised of strength, competitiveness, assertiveness, confidence, and independence. Hennard tried to be strong and assertive, but in all the wrong ways. He could gain muscle by lifting weights, but that would not give him real strength in terms of the maturity to deal with women or people effectively, and his attempts at assertiveness, such as writing a five-page letter to the two sisters in his neighborhood, only tended to backfire on him. While he strove for independence by staying away from people, the social isolation was not true independence but an awkward way to calm his extreme neediness and dependence.

George Hennard never had a chance. From the time he was born, his life turned upside down and he was tilted toward a helplessness and futile search for validation. He lived a lonely life of self-isolation in the Navy, the Merchant Marines, and in the psychological prison of his mind. He did not have a clue as to how to assert himself in a constructive way, so he lashed out at the world in whatever way he could. His parents did not know how to be loving human beings and they could not help him become one. Like the other men profiled in this book, he lived a life of pent-up rage and psychological self-annihilation. He craved understanding and care, but his anger at the world prevented him from getting the very thing he craved the most. His life was never his own life and his final act of rage was, sadly, merely a desperate, perverse last grab at respect.

SOURCES:

Luby's Shooting. In *Wikipedia*. Retrieved from: https://en.wikipedia.org/wiki/Luby%27s_shooting

George Jo Hennard. In *Murderpedia*. Retrieved from: https://murderpedia.org/male.H/h/hennard-george-jo.htm

George Hennard. In *Criminal Minds Wiki*. Retrieved from: https://criminal-minds.fandom.com/wiki/George_Hennard

George Hennard. *Real Life Villains Wiki*. Retrieved from: https://reallifevillains.miraheze.org/wiki/George_Hennard

George Jo Hennard, Jr. A Massacre at Luby's. *In Law and Justice – Other*. Retrieved from: https://indiantiger.org/george-jo-hennard-jr-a-mini-biography-of-a-mass-murderer/

Madigan, T. , Gonzalas, J. and Potter, K. (October 27, 1991). "Killer Was Like a Raging Volcano Ready to Explode." In *The New York Times*. Retrieved from: https://greensboro.com/killer-was-like-a-raging-volcano-ready-to-explode/article_cb9eace9-328a-5a7c-9bdd-a6f5b1edc59a.html

Shengold, L. (1991). Soul Murder: The Effects of Childhood Abuse and Deprivation. New York: Ballantine Books.

Terry, Don (October 18, 1991). "Portrait of Texas Killer: Impatient and Troubled. In *The New York Times*. Retrieved from: https://www.nytimes.com/1991/10/18/us/portrait-of-texas-killer-impatient-and-troubled.html

Burch, J. (Oct. 16, 2021). "Looking back: Luby's 1991 mass shooting 2nd worst in Texas history." In *25 ABC*. Retrieved from: https://www.kxxv.com/news/lubys-massacre-30-years-later/looking-back-lubys-1991-mass-shooting-2nd-worst-in-texas-history

Luby's Shooting. In *Encyclopedia Britannica*. Retrieved from: https://www.britannica.com/event/Lubys-shooting

George Hennard Tribute Page. In *Manifesto of Hidden Truth*. Retrieved from: http://forbiddentruth.mysite.com/George-Hennard.html

Kennedy-Kollar, D. and Charles, C. "Hegemonic Masculinity and Mass Murderers in the United States." In *The Southwest Journal of Criminal Justice* 8 (2). Retrieved from: https://www.academia.edu/1199492/ Hegemonic_Masculinity_and_Mass_Murderers_in_the_United_States

Dodd, L. (Oct. 17, 2021). "30 years later: Mass shooting trend lasts long after Luby's massacre." In *Killeen Daily Harold*. Retrieved from: https:// kdhnews.com/news/local/30-years-later-mass-shooting-trend-lasts-long-after-luby-s-massacre/article_26eb5c54-2ea3-11ec-9c3b-7fb53c36b2a3. html

Luby's Massacre. In *True Crime Tales*. Retrieved from: https://www. truecrimetalestx.com/lubys-massacre/

Chesler, P. (2005). *Women and Madness*. New York: Palgrave MacMillan.

CHAPTER 7

SALVADOR RAMOS

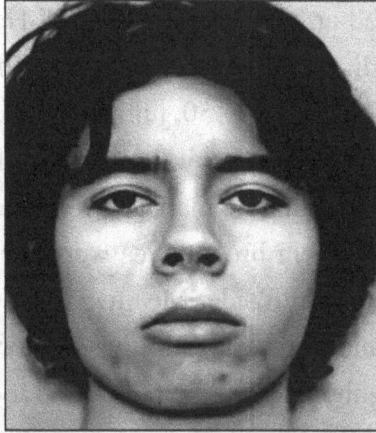

THE SHOOTING

On the morning of May 24, 2022, Salvador Ramos, an 18-year-old boy, had an argument with his 66-year-old grandmother over his phone bill. That morning, for some reason, he seemed to be in a rage.

"What the fuck! My phone doesn't work!" he probably yelled. "Did you pay my phone bill?"

"No, I didn't and I'm not going to!" she yelled back.

"¡Maldita vieja perra! Vete a la mierda!" he yelled in Spanish. "Go completely to hell, stupid old woman!"

"¡Tu vete al infiern!" she may have shot back. "You are a crazy, nasty boy and that's all you'll ever be! You have ruined our family! Get away from me! Your mother was right to throw you out! And I'm going to throw you out as well!"

"No, you're not going to throw me out! Nobody is ever going to throw me out again!"

They were in her home in Uvalde, Texas on a sunny day in late May and the wide-open Texas sun was shining on them through the window. Suddenly, he pulled a pistol out of his back pocket, smiled at his grandmother and shot her in the face. He looked at her and felt nothing as blood shot out of the hole under her left eye. "What are you doing?" she screamed at him. "You monster!" He went to her purse, took her out her credit card and her car keys, paid the phone bill, and ran out to her black 2008 Ford F150, jumped inside and tried to start it. He had never learned to drive and it took him a while to start it, and it was with some difficulty that he managed to maneuver it to the Robb Elementary School. His big brown eyes were focused on the road as the car swerved from side to side. Meanwhile his grandmother ran to a neighbor's house and said, "Salvador has gone crazy! Look what he did to me!" The neighbors called the police and took her to a hospital.

While he drove to the school, Ramos, using his Facebook account, was sending private messages to a fifteen-year-old girl from Germany whom he had been messaging online. The first message, which he had sent earlier, said he was going to shoot his grandmother; a second said that he had shot his grandmother; and a third, which he sent while almost skittering off the road, said he was going to shoot kids at an elementary school.

At about 11:27 a.m., he crashed the car into a ditch. He had driven the whole way to the school in second gear and eventually he veered off the road. Without hesitating for a moment, he scaled a fence to get to the elementary school. He was dressed for the occasion, clad in a black shirt and black pants and a tactical vest for carrying ammunition. The vest did not include ballistic protection or armor insert panels, as such vests often do. He wore a backpack which also had pockets to hold seven 30-round magazines. He carried an AR-15 style rifle in his right hand as he scaled the fence. Like the other mass killers studied in this book, he had probably suppressed his feelings to steel himself so that he was emotionally prepared for what he was going to do.

The shooting was similar to the other shootings detailed in this book, and it was also dissimilar. He proceeded to shoot a number of young students, which is similar, but he shot them all in the first ten minutes and then sat around for the remaining hour or so. In all, he shot nineteen students and two teachers, and wounded seventeen others, all without batting an eye or expressing any sympathy for those he killed.

He began by firing shots into the school windows from outside, which alerted those seated in the classroom on that side. Before the people in that room could warn anybody, he entered through an unlocked side entrance door. In a matter of seconds, he had slinked down the hall and entered two adjoining Classrooms, 111 and 112. Miah Cerillo, 11, was inside one of the classrooms, and she survived by smearing herself in her friend's blood and playing dead.

Her class had just finished watching the Disney film, *Lilo & Stich*, when their two teachers, Irma Garcia and Eva Mireles, got an alert about an active shooter in the building. Miah said that as Garcia attempted to lock the door to the classroom, Ramos shot the door's window, then backed Garcia into the corner and said, "Goodnight," as he shot and killed her.

The survivor described the scene in more detail. She said that Ramos said to the whole classroom, "You're all going to die!" and then opened fire on the other teacher, Mireles, and the students. Students were running here and there, diving behind their desks and trying to run for the door. According to Miah, Ramos played "sad music" on his phone during the massacre and had a sad expression while he did the shooting, as if he were conducting a funeral. When she was asked what kind of sad music he played, she replied, "It was 'I want people to die' sad music."

Arnulfo Reyes, a teacher in Classroom 111, who received multiple gunshot wounds, recalled that when he heard shooter's steps on the hallway, he instructed his students to "Get under the table and act like you're asleep." Ramos swung open the door, shot him, and fired around Classroom 111. Reyes said "I didn't hear talk for a while," but later on, he heard Ramos unleash a second round of gunfire at students, and Reyes said, "If he didn't get them the first time, he got them the second time." All 11 students in Classroom 111 died. Reyes pretended to be unconscious on the floor, but Ramos shot him again. He heard law enforcement approach his classroom three times from what sounded like the hallway, but they did not enter; during one of these occasions, he heard a student from the adjoining Classroom 112 saying, "Officer, we're in here. We're in here." As law enforcement had already left, Reyes said, "Ramos walked over there, and he shot again." Reyes later heard law enforcement out in the hallway telling Ramos to come out to talk, saying they did not want to hurt anyone. But the officers never entered the classrooms.

Ramos aimed his rifle and shot down one student after another—all of them 10- and 11-year-olds—with his sad, but determined face. He finished shooting everybody in the classroom and apparently decided they were all dead, but he did not go into other classrooms. When the shooting spree was over, he sat down on a chair in the classroom, with dead bodies all around him. He heard the sirens and the noise outside, but he sat in a chair with his rifle at his side, listening to the sad music, and did nothing more. Miah described it as an eerie scene. She glanced at him now and then as he sat in the chair waiting. It took about 74 minutes for the United States Border Patrol Tactical Unit to finally enter the room and confront Ramos.

The officers who had responded to the first calls wanted to get inside Classrooms 111 and 112, but they were unsure about the situation. One officer's daughter was inside. Another officer had gotten a call from his wife, a teacher, who told him she was bleeding to death. Two closed doors and a wall stood between them and an 18-year-old with an AR-15 who was sitting inside waiting for them. A Halligan bar—an ax-like forcible-entry tool used by firefighters to get through locked doors—was available. Ballistic shields were arriving on the scene, as was plenty of firepower. Four officers stood on each end of the hallway outside the classroom. Outside the school, officers were itching to move.

One of them was a special agent from the Texas Department of Public Safety, who had arrived around 20 minutes after the shooting started. He immediately asked, "Are there still kids in the classrooms?"

"I think so," a police officer replied.

"If there are, then we just need to go in," the agent said.

Another officer answered, "It is unknown at this time."

The agent snapped back angrily, "You all don't know if there are kids in there? If there are kids in there we need to go in there!"

"Whoever is in charge will determine that," came the reply.

The agent could not believe it. "I'm telling you there are kids in there and we need to go in there!"

Police Chief, Pedro Aredondo, the incident commander, finally took charge, and he wrongly assessed the shooting as a barricaded situation and called all police to "stay put." He had them cordon off the school grounds and wait outside for the right time to go in. At the same time, he ordered them to refuse to let anybody enter the school for over an hour, other than the handful of officers that were guarding the hallway at each end. As the police barred the door, there were violent conflicts between police and civilians. Anxious parents were shoving and shouting at the police and attempting to run past them and into the school to rescue their children.

"I'm going in to get my child! You can't stop me!" parents were screaming.

"Get away from that door!" the police shouted.

"Go ahead and shoot! You'll have to kill me to stop me!"

The police sometimes scuffled with parents and took them to the ground. The energy the police might have used to go into the school and rescue the children was spent wrestling with parents.

A report by the Texas House of Representatives Investigative Committee later blamed "systemic failures and egregious poor decision making" by many authorities on the confusion and delay in handling the shooting. The report said, "At Robb Elementary, law enforcement responders failed to adhere to their active shooter training, and they failed to prioritize saving the lives of innocent victims over their own safety... there was an unacceptably long period of time before officers breached the classroom, neutralized the attacker, and began rescue efforts."

Meanwhile, at a certain point, Ramos went into a closet and waited there for the police. He had apparently reached his kill point and had no desire to go into other classrooms and kill more children. While he waited in the closet, he most likely had time to reflect on everything. Perhaps he was imagining how the media would report his grand finale, and reveled about how upset everybody would be, especially the parents of the children he had killed. Perhaps he had a sense of satisfaction in passing the misery he had experienced all his life onto the parents and general public. "Now, at last, you all know how I have felt all my life," he may have said to himself in the dark closet. "Now, at last, you will feel the pain that I have felt. Good! I am glad! Go ahead and kill me. You can't hurt me anymore than I have already been hurt. Killing me will actually be doing me a favor."

After a hold-off of 70 minutes, off-duty Border Patrol officers finally took charge and got a janitor's master key to unlock the door (but found it was already open). They dashed into the classroom in their bulletproof vests and their rifles cocked and ready. Ramos heard them and, without a trace of fear on his face, kicked the door open and started shooting into the room. This was just what he had been waiting for, his final release from the pain of existence. The officers were all aiming their guns at him and they returned fire and killed him almost instantly with multiple shots to his head and body.

It was another mass shooting in America on top of another mass shooting on top of another. The mass shooting capital of the world had spoken again. The country was reeling again, and the world was shaking its head again. With each mass shooting, Americans hung their perplexed heads and the world shook its amazed head at the dysfunction that had taken over a once-great country. "What is going on in America?" people were asking. "Has America gone crazy?" Once upon a time almost everybody in the world looked up to America, but now the world could only roll its eyes.

THE FAMILY BACKGROUND AND LIFE OF SALVADOR RAMOS

Salvador Rolando Ramos' life was similar to other mass murderers, full of rejection and negation of who he was, and it was also dissimilar to other mass murderer in its details. Salvador Rolando Ramos was born on May 16, 2004, in Fargo, North Dakota. He was the son of Salvador Ramos, Sr., a construction worker, and Adriana Martinez, a waitress, and he had an older sister named Marisabelle, who was serving in the Navy at the time of the mass killing. He attended the same elementary school in which he later went on to kill a lot of children. He was not really a loner, like other mass killers, but a local boy who was known as a trouble-maker.

His parents moved to Uvalde, Texas when he was a young child. Not much is known about those early years, but there were many reports about his turbulent relationship with his parents, particular his mother. He was reported to have a stutter, which suggests that Ramos had some difficulty in learning to talk in early childhood. He also came from a family with a history of violent and criminal behavior. His parents separated soon after Salvador was born and were divorced sometime later, and he grew up in the home that his mother shared with his grandmother and grandfather, Rolando Reyes and Celia Gonzalez. His upbringing was rather chaotic.

Around the time of Salvador's birth in 2003, his mother Adriana Reyes was charged with attempting to write a bad check for $22.62 to a general store. Reyes had severe financial issues at the time of his birth, which probably did not put her in the best mood for taking care of a baby. She had a job at the Golden Dragon restaurant in Uvalde, however due to low pay she was living in an apartment with six other people, relying on public assistance and food stamps to take care of herself and her son. Reyes pleaded guilty to charges of fraud in 2005. She paid a fine of $250 and received probation with a mandatory 25 hours of community service. Two years later, she was charged with assault of a family member (the report does not say which family member). At that time, Reyes was found guilty and forced to undergo mandatory anger management counseling.

Salvador's father, Salvador Ramos Sr., was charged with resisting arrest in 2000. While court records do not reveal what instigated the situation, it is reported that Ramos Sr., after a brief tussle with officer Daniel Rodriguez, attempted to run away. He pleaded no contest and served 180 days in county jail and, in addition, had to apologize in writing to the Uvalde Police Department. In 2011, following a disagreement, Ramos Sr. struck a man named Jesus Perez with a beer bottle. Following this, he was subjected to drug and alcohol testing before facing a felony charge of assault with a deadly weapon.

Salvador was raised in a violent home by emotionally unstable parents, and he became a violent person. Classmates of his in elementary, middle and high schools and online mates noted that he had a stutter and a lisp and wore unusual clothing, which gave him an effeminate appearance and drew the attention of bullies.

"Hey, fag," they would taunt him. "I've got what you want! Come get it!"

He did not know how to deal with bullies and would tend to overreact by becoming incensed at them. "Fuck you, you fucking creeps! It takes one to know one!"

The bullies would laugh at him when he got angry at them.

He openly abused and killed animals such as cats and would livestream the abuse on Yubo. Others said that he would also livestream himself on Yubo, where he would threaten to kidnap and rape high school girls in his class. He also threatened to break into the elementary school he once attended and shoot the students. His threats were reported to Yubo, but Yobo did not delete his account. His antics were never reported to the police. Only his peers took notice of them, and they did not take them seriously. They thought that he was crazy but harmless.

Until a month before the shooting, Ramos worked at a local Wendy's, where he was reported to be an angry and abusive. According to the store's night manager, he was a cranky guy who went out of his way to keep to himself. One of his coworkers said he was rude to females, to whom he sent inappropriate text messages. He would try to intimidate coworkers by asking them, "Do you know who I am?"—hoping to convey to them that he was a dangerous person who was not to be toyed with. Ramos' coworkers referred to him by several nicknames, including "school shooter," because of his bizarre statements and because he had long hair and frequently wore black clothing. The administrators of Uvalde High School eventually kicked him out of school due to his many absences.

A year before the shooting, Ramos started posting pictures to his Instagram account of automatic rifles that were on his wish list. According to reports, a friend would often drive him around at night so that he could shoot at strangers with a BB gun or toss eggs at cars. He moved out of his mother's house two months before the shooting, after an argument broke out between them when she turned off the Wi-Fi. People close to Ramos' family said they frequently heard arguing in the house. Two months prior to the shooting, he posted a video of himself on Instagram aggressively arguing with his mother and referring to her as a «bitch.»

His mother was then living with a boyfriend named Juan Alvarez. Alvarez had been in a relationship with Ramos' mother for about a year and later, after the mass killing, he spoke of a tumultuous relationship between Ramos and his mother, which often included fights. Alvarez said Ramos would not talk to him. "He was kind of a weird one," he said. "He never talked to nobody." He said Ramos left their home to live with his grandparents two month prior to his killing spree.

Acquaintances of Ramos described his mother as a troubled drug user who would angrily shout at and hit her son. He railed at her because she refused to buy him clothes even when he complained that his clothes were attracting bullies to him. "Nobody bullies anybody because of their clothes!" she snorted. "All you do is complain every day and every night!" He had such violent arguments with his mother that police were called. After one argument, eight police cars pulled up in front of the house. According to Alvarez, Ramos also frequently complained about his grandmother, whom he later shot in the face. "Like mother, like grandmother," he said.

Two months prior to the shooting, Ramos posted a video of himself on Instagram in which he loudly proclaimed that he was quarreling with his mother and referred to her, as he often did, as a bitch. He had a girlfriend who lived in San Antonio, with whom he had a distant relationship. He could not drive, but on occasion he could hitch a ride when his mother or grandmother went to San Antonio, which was about 80 miles away, and spend an hour or two with her. Ten days before the killing spree, Ramos sent a private Instagram message to someone, perhaps this girlfriend, in which he indicated that he had decided on exactly when he would do the deed:

"Ten more days," he messaged.

The recipient responded, "Are you going to shoot up a school or something?"

"No, stop asking dumb questions. You'll see," he replied.

On September 2021, Ramos asked his older sister to buy him a gun, but she refused.

"No way," she quickly responded.

"I'm your brother. You should help me!"

"Definitely not!"

She knew all about his often-expressed plans to kill people and she wanted no part of it. The day after his 18th birthday, he legally purchased a Smith & Wesson semi-automatic rifle from a local gun store, and three days later he purchased another rifle. Investigators later found that his gun had a "hellfire" trigger device, which decreases the time required for the trigger to reset, ramping up the possible rate of fire. Ramos sent an Instagram message to an acquaintance he met through Yubo, which showed the receipt for another AR-15 style rifle purchased from a Georgia-based online retailer, Daniel Defense, eight days before the shooting. He also posted a picture of two rifles on his Instagram account three days before the shooting.

Yet, despite all of these written and stated warnings that he was buying rifles and was going to use them to kill people, nobody did anything about it. None of his contemporaries, who knew him and who nicknamed him "school shooter," ever tried to stop him, nor did they go to the police. While they recognized that he looked and acted like he was going to be a school shooter, they could not take the leap of thought to acknowledge to themselves or to anybody else that he was, indeed, a potential mass shooter. Perhaps, when you grow up with somebody, they have a familiarity that precludes objective evaluation. He was one of them, a member of a family, a local kid, and it may have been difficult for them to imagine that one of their own was a potential mass killer—even if he was sending messages all over the place about his plans to shoot up his former elementary school. Then again, maybe they just did not want to know about his dark plans because it was too horrible to know.

After the killing spree, the body of Salvador Ramos languished for nearly a month in the morgue as his family squabbled over who was responsible for taking care of his remains. Uvalde's two funeral homes refused to touch him and Ramos' body was eventually stored 150 miles away in a morgue in Lockhart, Texas. Eventually, Castle Ridge in Crystal City — at least 40 miles outside of Uvalde — handled Ramos' funeral arrangements. Ramos was later cremated even farther away, in a nondescript building on the edge of downtown San Antonio, more than 80 miles from Uvalde.

CULTURAL FACTORS

Salvador Ramos knew about all the mass killings in America, just as did the other mass shooters covered in this volume. It is one of the things nearly all mass killers have in common: their fascination with mass shootings. These mass shootings and the unrest in American culture had an effect on Ramos. In his particular case, he seemed to have become very much identified with these mass shootings and messaged about them, spoke about them and become known among his contemporaries as a mass-shooting aficionado. He was known to blab about his plans to kill people, but nobody took him seriously. Perhaps because he was short and his behavior was considered bizarre, he did not seem as if he could kill people. Like the famous comedian, Rodney Dangerfield, whose punchline was, "I can't get no respect," he could not seem to get respect, even when he threatened to blow everybody away.

Not only did the mass-murder atmosphere in America give him an identity, it also gave him a purpose and a direction. He was certain to have heard all about the school shootings that had preceded him, including the 1989 Cleveland Elementary School shooting of six, the 1991 University of Iowa shooting of six, the 1999 Columbine High School shooting of 15, the 2005 Red Lake High School shooting of seven, the 2007 Virginia Tech shooting of 33, the 2008 Northern Illinois University shooting of six, the 2012 Sandy Hook Elementary School shooting of 27, the 2014 Marysville Pilchuck High School shooting of 5, the 2015 Umpqua Community College shooting of 10, the 2018 Stoneman Douglas school shooting of 17, and the 2018 Santa Fe High School shooting of 10 —all of which had occurred within the previous 30 years. These shootings, along with all the other smaller violent events, were most likely an inspiration to him, each shooting like a rallying cry and an implicit permission for him to proceed with his own mass shooting plans. What happens in a culture stays in that culture and affects each person in that culture.

Like George Hennard, Ramos was angry at women. His mother and his grandmother seemed to have been his chief antagonists. Like Hennard, he was likely aware of, and provoked by, the anti-male sentiments that permeated American culture. For young men growing up in an era in which feminism appeared the be the main arbitrator of morality—a morality that was distinctly in favor of women—their needs for consideration and support must have seemed to be a hopeless fantasy. He was not only constantly put down and otherwise abused by his mother and grandmother, but also by the culture of America. I have treated many such men and become acquainted with how deeply it can affect them when they see women in movies, on television and in life degrading men. "When I see these idiot women who are all over TV these days putting down men, I just feel like I want to smash their faces in," one of my patients said.

In the end, Ramos may have felt as if the entire violent culture of America was against him, and that violence may have, in turn, stimulated his own violence.

FINAL ANALYSIS

There is not very much information about Salvador Ramos' early childhood, so I will have to deduce what it must have been like based on what is known about his family life later on and on my knowledge of similar situations. It was a family in which there was a lot of friction. Both the mother and the father had run-ins with the law. Adriana was charged with shoplifting, fraud and with assaulting a family member—the latter case resulting in her being ordered to have anger-management counseling. Salvador Sr. was charged with resisting arrest and later with hitting a man with a beer bottle. Parents who are angry and volatile do not make good parents; if they are so angry that they are out of control with others, then they will certainly also be out of control with their children, who are weak and defenseless.

Children can be conditioned to become violent, either wittingly or unwittingly. Napoleon Chagnon, the noted anthropologist, demonstrated in 1968 in his book about the Yanomami in the Amazon that a whole tribe can become violent. This tribe was the most war-like tribe in the Amazon at the time, whereas other tribes, that underwent a different type of conditioning, would not be warlike at all. Known as the "fierce people," the Yanomami trained their children from birth onward to be aggressive and militant. Brothers were applauded if they slapped their sisters and sisters were congratulated for kicking their brothers. They were also taught to sass their parents and to laugh when they killed domestic animals. By the time they came of age, they were ready to be killing machines. Ramos, raised in a violent family that, like the Yanomami, was conditioned to become violent.

Adriana, the mother, was known to suffer from substance abuse. Having a mother that was drugged out and had a violent temper was a double whammy for Ramos. Quick tempered, she may have had no patience for her baby son, and would most likely have been more prone to yell at him than to hug him. Drugged out, she may have also been neglectful. If she was this way when he was a needy infant and toddler, she may have traumatized him.

The fact that Adriana was ordered to have anger management counseling suggests how much her anger was out of control. Reports of family members and acquaintances corroborate that Salvador Jr.'s relationship with his mother was tempestuous. Adriana's boyfriend, Juan Alvarez, recalled several incidents in which the police were called, and one in which eight police cars showed up. That there were eight police cars indicates that police believed that some serious violence was occurring at the house. On occasion Ramos had spoken and messaged about wanting to kill his mother and he also expressed hatred for his grandmother. He ended up shooting his grandmother in the face the morning of the killing spree, a clear demonstration of the extent of his anger at her, and perhaps also of the fact that his anger at the whole family and at the world was at its peak.

Then there was the matter of his stutter, lisp and effeminate manner. Such things do not come out of thin air; they are produced by a certain kind of conditioning. A psychologist in the 1930s named Wendell Johnson, did a pioneering study of the cause of stuttering that has since been forgotten because his methods are viewed as unethical today and because his conclusions do not fit with today's accepted way of viewing stuttering. His study, sometimes referred to as the Monster Study, was an experiment performed on 22 orphan children in Davenport, Iowa in 1939. Johnson and a graduate student conducted the experiment at Iowa University. In this experiment, half of the children, aged five to fifteen, received positive speech therapy, in which the experimenter praised the fluency of their speech, and the other half of the children received negative speech therapy, in which the experimenters belittled the children each time they made a mistake. The first half of children, who received positive therapy, learned to speak well. However, many

217

of the children who received negative treatment began to stutter.

The experiments would go on and on.

"Repeat this sentence," the experimenter would say to the orphan.

The orphan would repeat it and the experimenter would respond harshly, even when the sentence was perfectly all right. "That's all wrong. You're not pronouncing your vowels. You're drawling. You're lisping. It should sound like this." The experimenter would demonstrate. "Try it again."

The orphan would be made to say the sentence over and over. After a while, the orphan would begin to stutter. "Wh, wh, wh, where can I now f, f, f, find a brown dah, dah, dah, dog?"

Each time they spoke they feared a punitive response and therefore learned to stutter as a defense mechanism to hold off the punishing response. Many of the normal speaking orphan children who received negative therapy in the experiment suffered negative psychological effects and had ongoing stuttering difficulties for the rest of their lives.

Of course, this and other similar experiments were totally unethical. One should never do experiments, no matter how valid they are, that are harmful to the subjects of the experiment. However, these and other experiments did shed light on the origins of stuttering: It is often the result of a punitive learning environment. In the case of Salvador Ramos, his stuttering might also have been an indication of what happened to him when he was learning to speak, before the age of three. His angry parents may have had no patience with him and bombarded him with negative feedback each time he made a mistake. In my therapy practice, I had a patient whose father would give him a lashing with a belt each time he made a mistake in learning the multiplication tables. He became a lifelong stutterer.

As for Ramos's lisp and effeminate manner, he might have gotten these through an identification with his mother. In psychoanalysis there is a phenomenon called "identification with the aggressor" and in psychology there is the Stockholm Syndrome. They are both about how children or adults who are terrorized by a parent or held hostage by their kidnappers, often grow to identify with their parents, captors and tormentors and remain loyal to them no matter what. In identifying with a mother who may have tyrannized him, Ramos may have in some way modelled himself after her, developing a lisp and an effeminate way of speaking in order to assuage her anger at him. The unconscious is a mind of its own, and things like lisps develop without any conscious effort and are out of the control of the conscious mind.

The signals that he had descended early in his life into madness were fairly obvious. Classmates reported how he openly abused and killed animals such as cats and would livestream the abuse on Yubo. Others said that he would sometimes livestream himself on Yubo threats to kidnap and rape girls, as well as threats to commit school shootings. All of these were signs of the buildup of rage inside of him, and indications of how extreme his pain had become. Blaring his cruelty on Yubo for anybody to see was a definite sign of a mental disturbance. When a boy is cruel to animals and has cruel urges toward women, which he openly streams online, that is both a sign of the cruelty that was done to him in early childhood and a cry for help.

Like other mass killers, he was reported to have been bullied, particular in middle school. Like others, he became an oddball whose antics stood out to others. But unlike others in this book, he fought back. By the time he reached high school, he was engaging in frequent fisticuffs and eventually even bought boxing gloves for himself and opponents to use when they got into fights in some playground or back ally.

He was in a rage and showing that through his Yubo videos, but no one could help him. Instead he was mocked at school and at home, and his life was probably a living hell. He seems to have been the whipping boy of the family, but he was also a spoiled boy who felt entitled, perhaps because he had been squashed and deprived. Coddling is not love; it is an attempt by parents to appease by compensating for not being loving. After the mass killing, his father said, "He should have killed me," a statement which may point to his guilt feelings. Ramos apparently had nowhere to turn for comfort, not his mother or father, not his grandfather or grandmother, not his sister, nor anybody in his extended family. Like other mass killers, he had a simmering rage and a need to be listened to, understood, respected and loved—all normal needs of humans. But he had never been taught how to fulfill these needs and never found a way to get them met.

A few months before his rampage, he asked his sister to buy him guns, and she said, "No way!" But she apparently did not know how serious he was about killing people. As soon as he turned 18, he bought two rifles and posted pictures of them, but these postings apparently did not raise much alarm. Ten days before the killing, he messaged someone, "Ten more days!" Someone got the message but did not know what to do.

On May 24, 2022, he shot his grandmother in the face over an argument about something that might seem frivolous, paying a cellphone bill. The subject of the argument didn't matter. He had already decided to kill her. On that day, he had reached stage 3 rage, and all this rage got directed at his grandmother, who by refusing to pay his phone bill became a proxy for the disdain heaped on him by his family. Any such incident at that moment would have been the last straw. He shot her in the face, but he might well have shot his mother or father in the face as well if they had been there. And then he headed for the school. Before and after the shooting he messaged a 15-year-old girl in Germany who he had recently been texting. This time he messaged someone in a distant land, so these messages were apparently not a cry for help, but just a way of symbolically holding someone's hand as he went through his killings.

It was just another day at an American school. It was just another school shooting on a sunny day in America. It was just another shooting by a kid storming into some classrooms of unsuspecting students and opening fire. It had happened many times before and it would probably happen many times again.

Why did he choose to do a school shooting? He himself had attended this school, and he had himself sat in the very classroom where he did his shooting. Did he have an abusive teacher in the fourth grade? Was this a class in which he was bullied? There was probably some conscious or unconscious reason why he went there, but we can only speculate about what it was. Like all mass killers, many of his reasons could only be known to himself—and maybe he himself did not know. He was simply a young man propelled by his excruciating pain, fueled by layers of rage and driven to act out what is probably the most extreme method that humans have devised for being heard.

After hundreds of mass shootings over many years, mass killings had by then become routine. You did not have to be a cop to recognize the signs of a mass killer. By that time, anybody could recognize the fellow student who had that look in the eyes, the fascination with guns, the boasts about killing. People saw the signs but were unfazed. Afterwards, people saw the headlines but were often too numb to react. At this point in America, nobody seemed to care as much anymore, or perhaps nobody wanted to care. At this point in America, nobody wanted to know. A telling factor with regard to Ramos was that nobody in the homes he shared with family members knew anything about the guns he had collected and was loading and reloading and cocking and aiming in his room. "We had no idea he was buying guns and keeping them in the house," his grandfather later said.

SOURCES

Robb Elementary School Shooting. In *Wikipedia*. Retrieved from: https:// en.wikipedia.org/wiki/Robb_Elementary_School_shooting

O'Neall, N. and Hernandez, L. (2022). "Texas school shooter Salvador Ramos' mom speaks out: 'Forgive me, forgive my son'." In *New York Post*. Retrieved from: https://nypost.com/2022/05/27/salvador-ramos-mom-asks-for-forgiveness/

Sollenberger, R. (2022). "Texas School Shooter's Dad, 'He should have just killed me.'." In *The Daily Beast*. Retrieved from: https://www.thedaily-beast.com/father-of-uvalde-shooter-salvador-ramos-says-he-shouldve-just-killed-me

Hampton, D.J. and Ali, S. S. (2022). "Texas shooter left home after a fight with mom over wifi, mother's boyfriend says." In *US News*. Retrieved from: https://www.nbcnews.com/news/us-news/texas-gunman-left-home-fight-mom-wi-fi-mothers-boyfriend-says-rcna30495

Exclusive! Revealed! In *Daily Mail*. Retrieved from: https://www.dailymail.co.uk/news/article-10864283/Sister-Texas-school-shooter-Salvador-Ramos-serving-Navy-came-home-comfort-grandma.html

Maitra, A. (2022). "Salvador Ramos' background explored as new details reveal criminal records of family members." In *SKpop*. Retrieved from: https://www.sportskeeda.com/pop-culture/news-salvador-ramos-background-explored-new-details-reveal-criminal-records-family-members#:~:text=As%20per%20Uvalde%20County%20Court%20records%20obtained%20by,misdemeanor%20in%201993.%20The%20family%20of%20Salvador%20Ramos

Fitz-Gibbon, J. (2022). "Salvador Ramos' grandmother released from hospital a month after school massacre." In *New York Post*. Retrieved from: https://nypost.com/2022/06/28/salvador-ramoss-grandmother-released-from-hospital/

List of Mass Shootings in the United States. In *Wikipedia*. Retrieved from: https://en.wikipedia.org/wiki/List_of_mass_shootings_in_the_United_States

List of School Shootings in the United States (2000-present). In *Wikipedia*. Retrieved from: https://en.wikipedia.org/wiki/List_of_school_shoot-ings_in_the_United_States_(2000%E2%80%93present)

List of School Shootings in the United States (before 2000). In *Wikipedia*. Retrieved from: https://en.wikipedia.org/wiki/List_of_school_shoot-ings_in_the_United_States_(before_2000)

Langford, T. (2022). "Uvalde School Shooting." Retrieved from: https://www.texastribune.org/2022/06/20/uvalde-police-shooting-response-records/

Monster Study. In *Wikipedia*. Retrieved from: https://en.wikipedia.org/wiki/Monster_Study

Chagnon, N. (1968). *Yanomani: The Fierce People*. New York: Harcourt Brace.

CHAPTER 8
PREVENTING MASS KILLINGS

Mass murders are not caused by any one factor, but by a multitude of factors. The accessibility of guns is not the cause of mass killings. Guns have always been accessible in America, but mass killings have been a recent phenomenon, occurring at the end of the 20th Century and the beginning of the 21st Century as our culture has deteriorated and dysfunctional families and dysfunctional cultural values have grown.

Mass killings happen because of emotions that become overheated. One can compare them to the eruption of volcanoes. The breeding ground of volcanos is festering rocks. Deep within the Earth, the rocks that form the base of a mountain become hot. Pressure and radiogenic heating make it very hot deep in the Earth and over time, they become so hot that some rocks melt completely and they become a thick flowing substance called magma. Since the magma is lighter than the solid rock around it, magma rises and collects in magma chambers. Eventually, some of the magma pushes through vents and fissures and explodes to the surface (1).

Dysfunctional families and dysfunctional cultures also fester. Conflicts and strife build up over the years in families and in collected families—that is, in culture. Emotions become hot and strife builds until it leads to emotional explosions. We might say that cultural violence in the form of mass killings are emotional eruptions and are a signal that culture has reached the boiling point. Mass killings are one of the outcomes of that cultural boiling point; the ultimate outcome of culture at the boiling point is war, and mass killings are a kind of war—a war against society. The source of mass killings is the urge to kill. Guns are simply a means to kill, but one of many. Guns can be banned, but the urge to kill will still be there and will find another avenue of release or another way to get guns.

The urge to kill has its roots in the rise of anger that happens in dysfunctional families and cultures. It develops gradually. A few years after the end of World War II, America's children started revolting against their parents and told their parents how to parent them; hence parents were no longer parents. During the Vietnam War, Americas students revolted against their schools and told their schools how to school them; hence teachers were no longer teachers. From the Vietnam War on, many young people revolted against their government and particularly police, and hence police could no longer be police. Then various extreme political and religious groups formed movements that protested in unpeaceful ways, and hence American society was no longer peaceful. This, in turn, provoked strife in our families and our culture and cultivated a collective unrest and anger.

The strife in our families and in our culture has been further inflamed by the psychiatric establishment. The psychiatric establishment has implied for years that parents have little or nothing to do with how their children turn out, especially if they turn out badly. "Don't blame parents," goes a popular slogan. According to the psychiatric establishment, children turn out depressed because they have a chemical imbalance, not because their mother let them cry in their cradle for hours while she lay in bed wondering whether to kill herself; children turned out to be anxious because they were born that way, not because their father slapped them silly and never let them have a moment of peace; children became criminals because of their genetic makeup, not because they grew up watching their parents abuse and lie to each other and abuse and lie to them. The psychiatric establishment has made chemistry, genetics and biology responsible for dysfunctional behavior, protecting parents from any liability and thereby implying that behavioral disorders cannot be cured, only controlled by medicine.

In fact, the theory of a chemical imbalance has recently been refuted and debunked. The theory started in the 1980s but was never more than a theoretical speculation that became repeated over and over again until it seemed like a proven fact. Jim Folk, in an article written in 2021 at the British Anxiety Center, wrote:

> The chemical imbalance theory as a cause for anxiety and depressive disorders never was true. In fact, no experiment has ever shown that anyone has an 'imbalance' of any neurotrans-mitters or any other brain chemicals. The entire theory was hypothetical. Over the last ten years, independent research has continually shown the chemical imbalance theory to be false. Furthermore, independent research has shown medications used to 'correct' the imbalance were largely ineffective with many fairing no better than placebo (2).

Dysfunctional families are created by dysfunctional parents who, in turn, raise dysfunctional children. One of the features of a dysfunctional family is dishonesty. Either the parents or the children will insist on their version of reality and they will censor any other way of viewing things. If a parent squashes his children's attempts to criticize his parenting by saying, "Don't tell us we are bad parents!"—this is a sign of family dysfunction. Dysfunctional cultures are an outgrowth as well as a source of dysfunctional families. If a government does not allow freedom of speech—does not allow people to say the government is wrong, it is a dysfunctional government. If a government or the people in a government insist on their version of reality and censor any other way of viewing life, it is a dysfunctional government. When dysfunctional leaders are in charge of a society, then that society is in fact being led by its most disturbed element.

In order for a family to function well, it must have unified values that create an atmosphere of calm and hope. In order for a culture or a government to function well, it also must have unified values and hope. Since 1960, mass killings have multiplied in America. There was one mass killing every five years for about twenty-five years. Then there were two mass killing a year, then three, then four. In 2021, there were 32 mass killing in one year—mass killings defined as the killing of four or more people consecutively (3). These killings are rising exponentially as the strife ramps up in our culture and our families and culture become more dysfunctional.

To prevent mass killings, we need to do whatever it takes, including the things that might be hardest to do. The causes of mass killings must be addressed and if addressing those causes is offensive to people, that will be the price we will have to pay to solve one of our most pressing problems. Some people regard families and parenting as almost sacred. These people think that we should not look at parenting to find out what is going wrong, because that means we are blaming parents. Parenting, to them, is a private matter. However, if we are to examine all the possible sources of mass killings, we should exclude nothing from consideration. We must use the algorithm method.

Similarly, some people do not want us to study culture. In particular, they don't want us to study their political and religious movements— movements that have become prominent in American culture and in the world for the last hundred years and have shaped who we have become, and religions that demand that members obediently follow a divine, unquestionable path. These movements and religions have done some good for their participants and those participants do not want critics to be snooping around. So, while participants make many claims about the benefits of these movements and religions, they are defensive about opening their doors to examiners. People involved with these movements seem to hold them as beyond reproach—similarly to the way some people hold parenting beyond reproach. In fact, it may well be that the same people who would forbid us from looking objectively at families are the ones who would forbid us from looking at political and religious movements. But in order to solve the problem of mass killings, we must look at both.

Mass killings are a complicated phenomenon and are linked to a multitude of causes, as I have previously noted. Hence, to prevent mass killings will require a deep understanding of families and cultures and the broad-scale revision of both.

HEALING OUR FAMILIES

In order to heal dysfunctional families, we must get to the source of the dysfunction and revise the way our children are parented. There has been a decline of family values and a dramatic rise of social problems, as pointed out in the first chapter. Peace and unity have disappeared, replaced by societal conflict and strife. Not only do we have a rise in mass killings; we also have a rise in crime and addiction and a decline in the cohesion of families, with more than one-third of families now single-parent families. Restoring families to a place where they can once again produce healthy children will be one of the most difficult things America has ever done, more difficult than solving global warming or colonizing Mars. Indeed, we would not have to colonize Mars if we were not destroying our own planet. We need to straighten our own backyards before we look for other yards to move into. Curing families will have to happen in steps.

Step One: Awareness. The first step is to recognize the importance of good parenting and to understand that how children turn out depends on how they are parented. In all of the case histories in this book, the mass killers suffered childhood traumas. It is almost always the case that the earliest trauma—whether it is emotional, physical or sexual abuse—has the deepest effect on development. Most everything that happens in childhood affects the personality development of the individual, but especially the earliest stuff. Raising a healthy child is perhaps the most important job anyone can have and the principles of being a good parent must be based on science, not on sentiment. It is a complicated job that requires a parent to be healthy enough and aware enough to understand children's feelings and to know how to deal with them. Healthy parents raise healthy children by giving them the love and respect they need and by setting the boundaries they require in order to become adequately socialized.

Step Two: Registration and Monitoring. Scientific principles of parenting must be set up. Society needs to monitor and regulate parenting to ensure that the parenting in our culture is heathy parenting. We regulate food, medicine, and boats (all riders on boats are required to wear safety vests), but not parenting. Being a parent is not a human right. It is a responsibility that must be carefully planned. All those who want to be parents should be required to register with a government agency and be evaluated to see if they have attained a baseline of mental health. In this way, abusive or neglectful parents would be filtered out. Couples who are not firmly bonded would be filtered out. Individuals who have a severe personality disorder and those that suffer from major depression, schizophrenia or other severe disturbances would also be filtered out. Those who give birth to a child without registering with the government agency would be subject to a fine and required to give up the child. Children would not be sent to a foster home or an orphanage, but to a special child-rearing center where they would be raised by professional parents who have been trained in the principles of raising healthy children.

Step Three. Child Care Centers. Child care centers should be established to replace America's failing foster-parent and adoption system. All children by couples who have accidental births or by couples of unwanted children or by parents who do not properly register to have children, would be sent to child care centers. These centers would be group homes run by professional parents. Child care professionals will be carefully selected and required to go through lengthy training in which they undergo their own psychotherapy, first of all, and then learn the principles of raising a healthy child. The principles will not be based on the political sentiments of the left nor on the religious sentiments of the right, but on scientifically proven policies that produce healthy children. They will raise children who learn to understand themselves, regulate their emotions, solve problems, develop the capacity to love and have empathy, and understand how to respect their own feelings and the feelings of others. Such children will be able to adjust to circumstances, resolve conflicts, and perform the hundred-and-one tasks that are required to function well in the world.

Step Four: Parent Training. All parents should be required to undergo parent training. In parent training they would learn, first of all, to understand themselves. Parents who do not understand themselves and are not in touch with their feelings, cannot raise a healthy child. Parents must understand the importance of establishing a peaceful family environment, for that is the kind of environment in which a healthy child grows. Parents must understand a child's stages of development so as to know what to expect in each stage and how to deal with it. They should be taught how to handle crises that might occur in each stage. For example, in the toddler stage, from two to four, children want to establish self-mastery, which is good, but their attempt at establishing self-mastery can sometimes go too far so that the child may want to be the boss of not only everything it does but also of the whole household. It is important for parents at this stage to be supportive of the self-mastery, but to also set boundaries if the child goes too far. The complexity of parenting is such that even the healthiest parent needs to be thoroughly trained to deal with a multitude of situations.

Step Five: Two-Parent Families. Research has shown that healthy parenting will most likely be attained if a child has both a father and a mother. The trend of single-parenting must be reversed. I understand that there will be great resistance to this notion, but this has been well researched, although the research has been dismissed or hidden by people who do not agree with the research. There seems to be an instinctual need by children to have both a mother and a father, which provides the organic balance they require. This is not to say that all fathers are good fathers or all mothers are good mothers or two-parent families are always better than single-parent families. But the combination of a father and mother has been shown to provide the best results more often than not.

Research on outcomes of homosexual or transgender parenting show that such parenting is not as successful as often as heterosexual parenting. In such families—as I have discovered in my research—children are generally indoctrinated to believe that same-sex parents or transgender parents are just as good as heterosexual parents, and they are not allowed to doubt this. Not being able to talk honestly with parents about important matters may have a deleterious effect on a child's personality development. Homosexual or transgender parents may cry foul at this suggestion, but for them—as I have found in my research—protecting what they believe is their human right to have children and their assumption that they know as much as they need to know about it, is more important than learning the age-old scientific principles of how to raise healthy children—which may go against what they think they know.

The importance of good parenting cannot be over-emphasized. It is one of the most complex jobs one can have, and one that is perhaps least appreciated, since it is not a salaried position that pays $10 million. In a previous book, I defined what a mother and a father does:

What does a mother do?

A mother takes her newborn into her arms and says, "You are mine,"
And the baby feels as if it belongs to the human tribe.

A mother smiles at her baby with love
And makes the baby feel like a lovable human being.

A mother respects the baby's needs for food, sleep, hugs and play
And makes the baby feel like a respected person every day.

A mother cares about her baby's cries
And makes the baby feel safe in the world.
And makes the baby feel alive in the lonely cosmos.

A mother lovingly shows her children what works and what doesn't work
And guides them on how to get along in life.

A mother lets her children fall down and pick themselves up,
So that they develop confidence in themselves.

A mother treats all her children fairly,
So that one child does not feel more important
And another child does not feel less important.

A mother smiles at her girl and boy children with the same smile
So that her girls do not feel they are better than her boys,
And her boys do not feel more important than her girls.

A mother knows her feelings and her children's feelings
And teaches her children how to handle their feelings and the feelings of others.

A mother knows herself and contains her cravings and temper
So that her children live in harmony.

What does a father do?

A father plucks up the newborn with a cheerful grin
And holds the baby up to the sky,
Letting the baby feel his strength and his protection in the world.

A father gazes at the baby with a loving smile
And makes the baby feel welcome in the world of men.

A father holds his child high and tosses it into the air
And swings it around and around in the sun
To instill in the child the joy of trust and love of freedom.

A father is aware of the child's need to laugh, cry, go away and
come back
And thereby makes the child feel alive in the world.

A father sometimes says yes and sometimes says no,
And the child learns to understand his dad's edges and the edges
of others.

A father is in touch with his feelings and in control of his temper,
And his children lovingly learn to know his authority and the
authority of others.

A father treats all his children fairly,
So that one child does not feel more important
And another child does not feel less important.

A father smiles at his boy and girl children with the same smile,
And his boy children do feel more special than his girl children
And his girl children do not feel worthier than his boy children.

A father knows his feelings and his children's feelings
And helps them to understand their own feelings and the feelings
of others.

A father is happy in the world,
And his children feel his harmony (4).

This definition of the jobs of mother and father is a heterosexual model, but that model can be adapted to alternate models. For the last hundred years or so, political and religious groups have created sentiment and pseudo research that appears to show that fundamentally religious or gay or transgender parenting is just as good as heterosexual parenting or better, or that one parent is as good as two parents or that the most important thing for children to learn is about homosexual and transgender rights. There has been a lot of research that purports to prove the validity of same-sex or transgender parenting, but the research that is used in that research has not been properly validated. Researchers in biased studies often interview children of transgender parents and ask them if they are happy or if they think their parents are good parents. Transgender parents, out of unconscious guilt feelings, may oversell themselves to their children in order to convince them that they are happy and that their family is a happy family. Any statements to the contrary will often be considered unacceptable, if not treasonous. This attitude will affect any research done.

An example of such a study was published in the journal, *Parents, Science and Practice* (5). Authors recruited participants in the study through the social media. Transgender parents, their children and their teachers, were administered a range of standardized interview and questionnaire assessments of parent–child relationship quality, quality of parenting, psychological adjustment, and gender-related minority stress. The conclusion: Parents and children in transgender parent families had good quality relationships and children showed good psychological adjustment. A study that relies on the testimony of observers is not a scientific study, because parents, children and teachers may all be biased. A truly empirical study uses a method of study that does not rely just on the testimony of the participants. Research has shown that mistaken eyewitness testimony in court cases accounts for about half of all wrongful convictions (6).

However, all married couples, regardless of sexual orientation or gender identity, who are able to produce healthy children could apply to be parents under the revised guidelines and would have to go through the same evaluation and training process.

HEALING CULTURE

A healthy culture is, first of all, a culture that is at peace. A peaceful cultural environment, just like a peaceful family environment, provides an atmosphere that is conducive to healthy functioning and to a contented, productive and cooperative society with the highest quality of life. A dysfunctional culture is one in which there is strife, unrest and a low quality of life. Therefore, in order to heal our culture, we must do whatever it takes to restore it to a state of peace. Peace means that our culture is no longer divided, but is a unified whole. Peace means that there are no longer political forces that are agitating the culture and bringing about strife and unrest. Peace means that our society is fair for everybody and no individual or group is favored over others. When potential mass killers grow up in a culture that is divided into parties and factions, in which some are favored over others, they cannot help but be affected by it.

We had peace in our culture in the past, but after World War II America began to prosper and lose its grip on society. A generation of children were raised to feel that they were entitled to share that prosperity. Another generation came and another. Human rights were more important than human responsibilities, and our culture began to get out of control and to deteriorate until the United States began to unravel and factionalize, becoming another version of the Wild West. Restoring peace and harmony to American culture will require a return to the values that made it great. Like restoring functionalism to families, making our culture functional again will call for a huge effort that will need to address its glaring issues. It will have to reign in the factors that caused it to get out of control and restore an attitude of unity and cooperation. To do this, many groups that have gotten out of control will have to be brought back under control and will have to give up some of their most cherished beliefs.

Banning Violent Protests. Before the 1960s, individuals and groups in American culture were encouraged to engage in peaceful protests. Keeping protests peaceful helped to maintain a peaceful atmosphere in America. Martin Luther King, in the 1950s and 1960s, was known for his peaceful protests on behalf of racial equality for Blacks, and he set an example for such protests. But starting in the 1970s, protests started becoming unpeaceful. Students protesting about the Vietnam War took over campus buildings, confronted police by calling them names like "pigs," and threw bottles of piss and bags of shit at police when law officers were called on to control riots. The Kent State shootings in 1970, also known as the Kent State massacre, happened at the height of the Vietnam War protests. During this event, police killed four and wounded nine other unarmed Kent State University students whose rioting had gotten out of hand. (7).

The dominant liberal press took the side of the students, and this became a prototype which led to more and more rioters provoking police by resisting arrest, sometimes using violence, and portraying police as brutal "pigs." This became an ongoing ritual. Then Blacks began to riot whenever they perceived police being brutal to a Black man. Such rioting was depicted by the liberal press as an act of vindication by an oppressed group, thus the media rewarded rioters for their violence and the violent method of protesting proliferated. Then a new twist in the ritual occurred when the first video was taken of police brutality. This trend began with Rodney King, a Black ex-con man who was beaten by Los Angeles Police Department officers after he led them on a 110-mile-an-hour, eight-mile chase through Los Angeles in the early-morning hours of March 3, 1991, during which he was driving while intoxicated and ran many people and cars off the road. An uninvolved individual, George Holliday, filmed police beating King from his nearby balcony and sent the footage of the beating (but not of King's militant resistance to police) to local news station, KTLA. King mocked a police order to lie down. When the first officer told him to lie down, he slapped his hip and shook his rear at the officer. Cops repeatedly hit him with batons and wrestled him to the ground, and he kept standing up again. He was a tall, muscular Black man and the White police officers panicked and used more force than necessary. The video footage showed an unarmed King on the ground being beaten by three cops. The footage was picked up by news media around the world and caused a public furor. When a jury acquitted the three officers, a mob of Blacks rioted in Los Angeles, resulting in 54 deaths and hundreds of millions of dollars in property damage (8).

Afterwards, White police "brutality" against Blacks was videotaped again and again, selectively showing only police action, not the resistance of the Blacks, which led to more riots. A typical example of this happened on August 9, 2014, when Michael Brown, an 18-year-old Black man, was shot by Darren Wilson, a White police officer. This incident provoked riots by Blacks in three separate waves during August of 2014, November of 2014, and again a year later in August in 2015 on the anniversary of the killing. Widespread rioting, vandalism, looting, arson, and gunfire occurred and many people and police officers were injured. Before any facts were in, Officer Wilson was assumed to be guilty of police bias and brutality. Michael Brown's friend and accomplice testified that Brown had raised his hands and walked toward Wilson and said, "Hands up! Don't shoot!" The slogan, "Hands up, don't shoot," went viral, and people assumed that Wilson shot Brown while he was surrendering. This led to more riots. However, after an FBI investigation Wilson was exonerated. Brown actually never held up his hands and said, "Don't shoot." In fact, he was rushing at Officer Wilson.

The investigation found that Brown had stolen things from a convenience store, which prompted the store to call police. Wilson spotted Brown and pulled his police car to the side of the street, siren blaring. He called Brown over, and Brown reached through the window and attempted to take Wilson's gun. A struggle ensued and the gun went off twice. Then Brown walked away from the car and Wilson yelled for him to stop. Brown then turned and charged at Wilson. Wilson was obliged to shoot him. However, radical liberals created a false narrative that caused Blacks to riot and the riots had the effect of swaying public opinion. As a result, the government of Ferguson, Mississippi and the police force became the focus of heavy criticism. Wilson, the police chief and three others were forced to resign and two Blacks were later elected to the town council before all the facts were in (9).

In 2013, when Black Lives Matter was organized, it began to direct followers to film more and more instances of police "brutality." Soon the slogan, "Defund the police!" was heard around the world. After an increasing number of instances in which cameras captured "police brutality," it seemed as if there was an epidemic of it. This resulted in police departments being defunded all over America, and prompted a heightened wave of crime (10). As Black riots became the standard, other groups began to copy that standard.

The reactionary right also stirred the pot of political conflict by engaging in their own riots. On January 6, 2021, followers of then-President Donald Trump stormed the Capital Building in Washington, DC, attempting to overthrow the election of Joe Biden (11). Trump claimed in a one-hour speech preceding the riot that the election was stolen by Democrats. A mob of his supporters forced their way into the Capitol Building, seeking to keep Trump in power by preventing a joint session of Congress from counting the electoral college votes to formalize the victory. Five people died during the riot and many people were injured, including 138 police officers. Trump was known to make provocative remarks during his rallies, such as the one he made about his opponent, Hillary Clinton, during his election campaign in 2016 at a North Carolina gathering. "If she gets to pick her judges – nothing you can do, folks. Although, the Second Amendment, people. Maybe there is. I don't know" (12). This, of course, is not the way a good President should speak—making an indirect suggestion that people should use their second-amendment rights (gun ownership) to shoot Hillary Clinton, her Supreme Court picks, or both.

Violent protest must be absolutely and completely banned and groups who protest violently must be fined, jailed, and otherwise punished in such a way that they will no long think about committing such an act. Such acts must not be portrayed as acts of liberation, but rather as acts of destruction to American culture. Violence in our culture can only stir up violent tendencies in potential mass murderers.

Regulation of Political or Religious Groups. Political and religious groups need to be regulated. All political groups, whether civil or church-related, should be required to register with the government and held to rules, such as the rule of peaceful protests. There should also be rules with regard to the use of skewed statistics, misleading pronouncements and slogans that lead to societal division, favoritism and violence. Any movement that violates these rules should be fined and, in severe cases, disbanded, just as companies who violate antitrust statutes must be fined and broken up.

In families, children cannot be allowed to control their parents, and in culture, groups cannot be allowed to control their governments. Parents must be firmly but lovingly in control of their children and governments must be firmly but lovingly in control of citizens.

Political movements (such as the Black rights movement) and religious groups (such as reactionary Christians and Muslims) are more interested in advancing their political or religious agenda than in peace. Hence radical Muslims have used religious doctrine to justify violent behavior toward non-Muslims. Radical Blacks have manipulated public sentiment against White police. Reactionary Whites have formed militia groups. Radical liberals form the militant Antifa. All groups, left or right, create propaganda that perpetuates half-truths or lies. Laws must be passed to regulate all groups and prevent them from getting out of control.

Restoring Political Unity. A divided house cannot stand. For years the United States was divided between those who call themselves liberals and those who call themselves conservatives—or, between Democrats and Republicans. This division widened over the years. In the 1950s, Republicans and Democrats respectfully differed with one another on how to deal with the various issues of government. "We are all under the same big tent," they would say. Respecting differences was a way of dealing with differences and a way of maintaining unity and peace. But over the years Democrats and Republicans came to no longer respect each other's different ways of approaching how to govern. Instead, they began to see each other as enemies whose views were dangerous and had to be dismissed and even outlawed, and their communications with one another were filled with name-calling, mockery, accusations and cancellations.

One Democratic candidate for President, Hillary Clinton, referred to all conservatives as "deplorables." In doing this, she dismissed about 70 million people, making no distinctions whatsoever, but putting them all in the same category (13). Ann Coulter, a noted conservative writer, spoke out after a conservative activist blew up a federal building, saying, ""'My only regret with Timothy McVeigh is he did not go to the New York Times Building" (14). In saying that she galvanized more hatred and fueled the flames of conflict.

The source of divisiveness is groupthink and doublespeak, terms first found in George Orwell's novel, *1984* (15). Groupthink refers to people who are unable to think independently of their group. Doublespeak refers to telling lies that are made to seem to be the truth. As Democrats became more radical their goal was not peace and prosperity, but rather control over American government, values and culture. As Republicans became more reactionary, their goal became gaining power and ideological influence over America. Communication between them was warlike. It is the same thing that happens to divided families. Parents who are in conflict continually scapegoat each other and engage in right-wrong, warlike arguments. Their goal is to win the argument, not to resolve it. Divided liberals and conservatives (Democrats and Republicans) were intent on winning the ideological war, not in resolving differences and achieving unity.

Restoring unity to American culture, may require a great leader who is truly neutral in outlook and able to see both sides of the argument. This leader would need to be skilled in constructive communication and be able to relate to both conservatives and liberals and establish trust with them. Such a leader would be, basically, a cultural psychotherapist. A cultural psychotherapist might establish regular town meetings, which would be like extended therapy groups, inviting people from all walks of life to speak honestly without fear. There would be rules of conduct prohibiting people at the meetings from raising their voices or talking over people. People would be required to listen to others respectfully, even if they strongly disagreed with them, and wait for their turns to respond. Courtesy and respect would be the guiding principles of such meetings. By encouraging all sides to honestly express themselves, the town meetings would represent a way of truly opening up a dialog between the divided sides.

The leader would also encourage and model a new kind of political philosophy—a centrist philosophy—that would embrace the best of both the Democratic and Republican parties. In the end, this might lead to the establishment of a third party, a Centrist Party. The first line of a famous poem by William Butler Yeats goes, "Things fall apart, the center cannot hold." Yeats was fully aware of how important it is for a culture to have a strong center. In order to restore political unity, America would need to reestablish that strong center. When the violence in our culture stops and peace is restored, that will go a long way toward preventing mass killings.

IMMEDIATE REMEDIES

A few remedies that might be applied immediately—a behavioral solution—might be useful. Knowing that mass killers are copycats, the media should be wary of how they report on a mass killing. If possible, reporters should not become fascinated with a mass killer and make this killer into an antihero. The more publicity the mass killer gets, and the more he is elevated into a kind of mythical figure, the more other mass killers will be inspired and want to copy him. In short, mass killings should be reported on as though they are not that important, and, in fact, as some routine incident that is not of particular newsworthiness.

Perhaps laws can be passed prohibiting the media from publicizing a mass murder. Or laws could prohibit the media from using the mass killer's name, thereby preventing him from being famous. The less publicity a mass killer is given, the less he will become an inspiration that invites copycats.

Banning all guns might reduce the amount of mass killings. Certainly, those with the urge to become mass killers will probably find a way to kill, either by getting illegal guns or by using bows and arrows, but banning guns entirely to non-hunters will be helpful.

Strengthening our justice system and our police is another way of approaching this problem. Better training of police in handling shooter situations might help, and more funds and support for police and for faster, more smoothly organized courts would also help.

CONCLUSION

Mass killers are the products of dysfunctional families and cultures. Making our families and our culture functional will be a tall order. In studying the six stages of civilizations (16), I have found that once civilizations have reached the sixth stage—the decadent stage—they are like snow balls rolling down a hill; they cannot be stopped. By the end of the 20th Century, America had reached the decadent stage of development—and it had reached it more quickly than almost any other civilization in history. In the decadent stage, a society falls out of control, loses its moral fiber and becomes divided. Once in that stage, it regresses back to a primitive mentality of seeking instant gratification and rationalizing rather than thinking in a logical way. The decadent society descends into a state of turmoil in which sane people are no longer listened to and the worst people become leaders.

I have written this study of mass killers along with a theory of what is wrong in our families and in our culture and with a rather complicated prescription for what needs to be done. I am not optimistic that such a complex and arduous revision of our values and our approach to dealing with mass killings in America will be carried out. Yet, I offer it with the idea that maybe, just maybe, someone will find a way to do some of these things and thereby do some small bit to at least slow down the trend of mass killings.

REFERENCES:

1. Power of Plate Tectonics. In *Ology*. Retrieved from: https://www.amnh. org/explore/ology/earth/power-of-plate-tectonics/volcanoes

2. Folk, J. (2021). Chemical Imbalance Theory False. In. *AnxietyCentre. com*. Retrieved from: https://www.anxietycentre.com/articles/chemical-imbalance/

3. List of Mass Killings in the United States in 2021. In *Wikipedia*. Retrieved from: https://en.wikipedia.org/wiki/List_of_mass_shootings_in_the_United_States_in_2021

4. Schoenewolf, G. (2022). *The Way to Be*. Bushkill, PA: Living Center Press.

5. Imrie, S., Zedeh, S., Wylie, K. and Golombok, S., "Children with Trans Parents: Parent–Child Relationship Quality and Psychological Well-being." 2020 Aug 4. doi: 10.1080/15295192.2020.1792194

6. How Reliable are Eye Witnesses? In *Constitutional Rights Foundation*. Retrieved from: https://www.crf-usa.org/bill-of-rights-in-action/bria-13-3-c-how-reliable-are-eyewitnesses

7. Kent State Shootings. In *Wikipedia*. Retrieved from: https://en.wikipedia.org/wiki/Kent_State_shootings

8. Rodney King. In Wikipedia. Retrieved from: https://en.wikipedia.org/wiki/Rodney_King

9. Shooting of Michael Brown. In *Wikipedia*. Retrieved from: https://en.wikipedia.org/wiki/Shooting_of_Michael_Brown

10. Maimon, D. (2022). "Surging Crime Rate Ends 'Defund Police' Movement." In *Yated Ne'eman*. Retrieved from: https://yated.com/surging-crime-wave-ends-defund-police-movement/

11. January 6 United States Capital Attack. In *Wikipedia*. Retrieved from: https://en.wikipedia.org/wiki/January_6_United_States_Capitol_attack

12. Kurtzman, D. (2019). "Craziest Republican Quotes of the 21st Century." In *Liveabout dotcom*. Retrieved from: https://www.liveabout.com/craziest-right-wing-quotes-ever-4080634

13. Reilly, K. (Sept. 10, 2015). "Read Hillary Clinton's 'Basket of Deplorables" Remarks about Donald Trump Supporters." In *Time*. Retrieved from: https://time.com/4486502/hillary-clinton-basket-of-deplorables-transcript/

14. Coulter, A. On Blowing Up the New York Times. In *LiveAboutDotCom*. Retrieved from: https://www.liveabout.com/craziest-right-wing-quotes-ever-4080634

15. Orwell, G. (1961). *1984*. New York: Signet Classic Library.

16. Schoenewolf, G. (2022). "The Eight Stages of Civilizations." In *Forbidden Psychology: A Book for Dark Minds*. Bushkill, PA: Living Center Press.